DAWN LANGMAN undertook a mainstream speech and acting training in Australia, followed by seven years of performing and teaching at secondary and tertiary levels. Her quest for an integrated approach that includes the spiritual dimension led her to train with Maisie Jones at the London School of Speech Formation in the method developed by Rudolf and Marie Steiner. She then taught for ten years at Emerson College in Sussex. Following this, Dawn trained in Michael Chekhov's acting technique with Ted Pugh and Fern Sloan of the Actors Ensemble in New York. Returning to Australia, she founded the School of the Living Word, where for eight years she continued to research the integration of Speech Formation with Chekhov's technique. She currently teaches this methodology at the Drama Centre, Flinders University, South Australia. Dawn is the author of *The Art of Acting, The Art of Speech* (both 2014) and *Tongues of Flame, The Actor of the Future Vol. 1* (2019).

By the same author:

The Art of Acting, Body – Soul – Spirit – Word, A Practical and Spiritual Guide

The Art of Speech, Body – Soul – Spirit – Word, A Practical and Spiritual Guide

Tongues of Flame, A Meta-Historical Approach to Drama, The Actor of the Future Vol. 1

WORD MADE FLESH

The Actor of the Future, Vol. 2

DAWN LANGMAN

Original artwork by Raphaela Mazzone

TEMPLE LODGE

Temple Lodge Publishing,
Hillside House, The Square
Forest Row, RH18 5ES

www.templelodge.com

Published by Temple Lodge 2019

A catalogue record for this book is available from the British Library

ISBN 978 1 912230 36 5

Cover by Morgan Creative
Typeset by DP Photosetting, Neath, West Glamorgan
Printed and bound by 4Edge Ltd., Essex

Dedicated to the Community of the Logos

Creative Speech transforms the human larynx into a grail cup

Eurythmy integrates the human ether body with the life that sustains the universe

Contents

Acknowledgements

Thanks to Tanya Coburn for her invaluable layer of editing and her support in the battle with phonetic symbols. To Clare Strahan my editor for coming back on board, for her belief in my work and her faithful commitment over many years to bring it to the world. To Raphaela Mazzone, whose patience and commitment to embody the spirit of my work in images have helped my vision manifest. To Diane Tatum, who allowed Raphaela to take countless photos of her eurythmic manifestations of the beings of stars and planets, consonants and vowels: for the conversations that helped refine our insights as the photos were transformed into drawings and for her unequivocal support and positive feedback for this volume.

Thanks to Sophia Walsh whose workshops in Dornach inspired my research over the years to find a way to work with these gestures that would allow the exploration of the cosmic dimensions of human character. To Margot Horne whose lifetime study of the stars and planets has guided me and given me the confidence to present my research. To Jean Lynch, my inspired Celtic eurythmy teacher in the London School of Speech Formation, whose workshops exploring zodiac and planets so many years ago still nourish my creative springs.

To my dear friends and colleagues, Dr Diane Caracciolo, Dr Jane Gilmer, and Penelope Snowden-Lait for their faithful encouragement, support and invaluable feedback through the many stages needed to bring this volume to completion.

To my dear friend and poet Lindsay Dearlove for refining my attempts at poetry.

And to the genius of Rudolf Steiner whose spiritual scientific path of research and clear conceptual framework is the ground of all my explorations.

Prologue

When the laws we call *technique* are detached from the living apprehension of the spirit which is their source they are reduced to *rules* devoid of warmth and wisdom. If we rebel against their tyranny and rely exclusively on talent, we may be flung back and forth between self-doubt and grandiosity. The central purpose of *The Art of Acting* and *The Art of Speech* was to lay the foundation for an art and craft of acting rooted in the spiritual conception of the human being arising out of Rudolf Steiner's work: one that would nurture the actor's sensibilities rather than exploiting them.

This exploitation easily occurs when the expectations placed on actors do not take into account the need for processes that nurture healthily the vulnerable layers of their psyche, which often have their source in the 'sacred wounds' of their biographies.[*] These are then mined by the 'industry' for the depths of emotional insight and intensity they yield; these depths can be the actor's greatest gift but at the same time threaten their healthy functioning as human beings. Steiner's insights show us how to integrate our journey to become an actor of the future with our evolution as a healthy human being. Through them technique becomes a living spring from which inspiration and expressive capability never cease to flow and nourish our artistic core.

The path explored in those two books leads to an integrated voice and body instrument: a spirit-permeated psycho-physical presence that radiates into and transforms the surrounding space. In volumes 2, 3 and 4 of *The Actor of the Future* we apply these integrated methods to the indications Steiner gave to actors, particularly in the *Speech and Drama* course. It is a path of practice that assumes the reader is familiar with *The Art of Acting* and *The Art of Speech* as well as the context provided for it by the meta-historical approach to drama explored in Volume 1 of this present work.

---

[*] For an exploration of artistic sensibility see *The Art of Acting*, pages 18–40 'Understanding the nature of the actor and the artist'.

Introduction

The great mainstream actors who have inspired me through the years demonstrate a fusion of the ordinary everyday experience we share, with intimations that expand my consciousness to sense what lies beyond.

> Again,
>   again
> your force of life
> sweeps away my flimsy mental scaffolding:
> frail matchstick constructs
> of the abstract mind.
> Through you, I see how fearlessly
> Love takes on every shape:
> most like itSelf
> when it appears to disappear
> and goes about its business
> in the other.

A great artist permeates the soul's subjective world with the majesty of universal laws. These in turn are humanised and warmed by the artist's soul. The brilliance of our greatest actors has often been achieved without them having any conscious knowledge of these laws and certainly without the processes recorded in these books. Nor are such explorations likely to be relevant to seeking a career in our present film and theatre industry which excels already in its power to entertain and to explore the unconscious depths of human nature as they manifest in everyday behaviour. These present capabilities are partly the result of the last century of research which yielded ways to excavate the subconscious depths that drive our characters and interactions and reveal the power of the past to shape the present.[*] The rest is veiled behind the karmic mystery of talent.

It will not suffice, however, for actors in the future to rely on that talent or the innately worse or better aspects of themselves to portray human beings of the future; either the depths of evil still to be exposed or the evolving consciousness required to transform them. Therefore, volumes 2, 3 and 4 of *The Actor of the Future* set out a path of practice that invites us to cultivate these future faculties. They present a methodology for actors who seek to reveal not just the subtext that informs the endless

---

[*] *The Actor of the Future 1*, Chapter 5.

repetitions of our everyday existence but the *supertext* that also works within our souls and has the power to transform them. This series is for those who would explore such a vision of the future human being.

The Great Work

As discussed in *The Actor of the Future 1*, Malcolm in *Macbeth* and Cordelia and Edgar, in *King Lear* are examples of human beings who learn to master their emotions; who evolve to be *the lords and owners of their faces*.[1] Each wins a crown that signifies their sovereignty not only in the outer world but in the inner kingdom of the soul. This is a level of development that all human beings can aspire to in our present stage of evolution.

Yet this ability to order our emotions is only the first stage of our soul's transformation on its journey to become the *spirit-self*.[*] To progress on this path we must understand that our soul is not just some vague conglomerate of feelings, passions and emotions; nor is it an accidental by-product of cellular secretions and electrical impulses in brain and nervous system. Rather, the inner life that we must gradually raise to consciousness and penetrate is the activity within us of higher spiritual beings. We cannot perceive them with our five material senses but we can develop organs of cognition that will expand our consciousness into the macrocosmic picture of the soul described by St John in his Revelation.

> The Woman clothed with the Sun and with the moon under her feet
> and upon her head a crown of twelve stars.

Steiner adopted the traditional esoteric term *astral body* to refer to that aspect of our constitution that is the bearer of our soul or inner life. The name suggests a body made of stars. But these are not the swirling balls of gas or other elements that scientists perceive inhabiting an otherwise empty space. In the same way that the human being we meet is so much more than the outer form that we perceive, what scientists observe as the heavenly bodies we call the stars and planets are only that aspect of the life of the divine creator beings that has condensed into material 'outer' form.

In Chapters 5 to 8 we explore how the sounds of human language that allow our inner life to be articulate are echoes of the macrocosmic word by which we have been spoken into being and our human constitutions woven as a vessel for that word. This approach provides the actor with methods of character creation that arise from a

---

[*] *The Actor of the Future 1*, Chapter 5.

vaster understanding of the human soul than is recognised in present mainstream culture: methods that develop the very organs of cognition that will grant the first intimations of these beings that I call our High Work Masters.[2]

Through the *sound-experience* explored in Chapters 1–4, first we learn to pay attention to the soul sensations that arise in everyday experience. Then we learn to recognise each nuance as a consonant or vowel. As we practice, we develop organs of perception that enable us to sense those soul sensations are the work of higher beings who bestow an aspect of their consciousness on us. We feel them drawing near, and working through us, transforming us into a conscious channel for their consciousness – co-creators with them of the transformed substance of our astral bodies. We learn that the name of each sensation is a vowel or consonant that sounds forth from a Being and that our capacity to sense it is the same as our capacity to speak it. The actor of the future will evolve by learning how to play the scales of Their activity.

Our soul, or inwardness, is an aspect of our being which material science views as an accidental by-product of nerve and cellular activity. Some would even posit that the 'soul' does not exist because we cannot measure it in the same way that we measure matter. Yet the work embarked on in this series will develop organs of perception able to discern that what material science calls the nothingness of empty space is a vast immensity of inwardness that spans our solar system and its zodiac. Then we will understand that St John's imagination of the woman clothed with the sun, with the moon under her feet and crowned with a circle of twelve stars is a picture of the macrocosmic soul.

As described in *The Actor of the Future 1*, the work of the divine human Self to transform the astral body from within will culminate in our ability to freely align our microcosmic souls with the macrocosmic beings who first bestowed them on us, thus becoming co-creators with them. This future stage of evolution is not attainable within the present planetary cycle called the *Earth* but will be the main task of our planet's next incarnation called *New Jupiter*.* However, the final flowering of spirit-self will never come about unless we first plant seeds and nurture them. *Sound-experience* is one such seed.

In the present film and theatre context our first attempts at an art of acting that aspires to such realities must inevitably seem foolish. In this regard, I share some words written in 1954 by the playwright, Christopher Fry. He gave them to me, pencilled in his own hand, when I was privileged to meet him at his home in Chichester in 1989. He told me how he had once kept a donkey in his garden. Its

---

* Epilogue in *The Actor of the Future 1*.

agonised attempts to birth its voice gave him courage when his own creative voice was blocked. This is what he wrote in sympathy. I call it Donkey Meditation.

> What the donkey means to convey . . . is the quite simple modulating vowel sequence: Ee-aw. His approach to it is one of fear, and that I can perfectly understand. He stokes himself up towards it in a series of fearful rusty gasps, as though the first Liverpool to Manchester train was remembering how it killed Mr Huskisson MP in 1830. Then, taking courage, his vocal cords seem to labour and push back an enormous iron gate, to let through one supposes, the message seething in his heart. With a croaking groan the gate closes again; the donkey sobs terribly once or twice, and again the gate is forced back on its grinding hinges; and this way happens several times . . . until you think the donkey must break his heart; and then communication is made, not, indeed, exactly as conceived: the Ee-aw of his vision is denied him; what he accomplishes in fact is Aw-ee, but we are fortunate if in our own way we can ever come so near to our vision as he does in this rather Miltonic inversion.

Those who start out on this path to the actor of the future, like Shakespeare's Bottom, must have seen *a most rare vision*. And, like Bottom, those who first attempt to speak of it may well appear like asses. In Peter Schaffer's *Amadeus*, Mozart tries expressing to his peers his *most rare vision*: the spiritual intention in his music. When their reactions tell him not only that they do not understand but also disapprove of this intimate exposure of his being, he retreats into the role of joker. He apologises that after all he is a jackass and offers them his hooves to shake. Likewise, Apuleius in *The Golden Ass* tells of the time he spent transformed into an ass as preparation for the goddess Isis to initiate him into her mysteries.

We are currently more skilled in exploring and expressing the descent into darkness than the ascent into the light, yet we cannot separate the future evolution of the actor's art from the future evolution of the human being and the dramas that will reflect and prefigure it. Humanity will not remain forever trapped in the dark chambers of the underworld, sentenced to endless repetitions of the past, or distractions from their harsh reality. We are evolving into new dimensions of ourselves that the dramas of the future must increasingly reflect if they are to maintain relevance. If our art is to minister to those who suffer, like Berowne in *Love's Labour's Lost*, we must transform the glib and clever words that cross our lips too easily. For if we are to tell not only *why we are here and why we suffer*[3] but also show the way of our redemption, our speech must be born, like the donkey's, out of such a labour.

Rudolf Steiner's *Speech and Drama* Lectures

In 1924, during the last months of his life and in response to requests from people in a range of professions, Rudolf Steiner delivered cycles of lectures on a wide variety of subjects. Among them was the *Speech and Drama* course requested by actors seeking inspiration to renew their art. Due to public interest, these 19 lecture/demonstrations were adapted for a broader audience. I am one of many currently devoted to their exploration.[4]

Along with material published in English as *Creative Speech*[5], the course suggests many innovative ways to work with text and character. I question, however, whether these innovations can be fully implemented without some pre-existing faculties and skill. In lecture 13, for example, Steiner suggests how a character can be created out of specific consonants or vowels. To the reader with no consciousness of consonants and vowels beyond the everyday experience of language and no facility in working with them through the practice of Speech Formation and Eurythmy, the examples given in the lecture may seem arbitrary or prescriptive. Applied naïvely, they result in a one-dimensional approach to character and provide no clues as to how we might discover for ourselves such connections between the sounds of speech and different characters.

When applied within the context of our integrated methodology, Steiner's indications open pathways into the evolving consciousness of human beings that was explored in *The Actor of the Future 1*. The integration of Steiner's Speech Formation with Chekhov's psycho-physical technique develops organs of perception that both enable the investigation and become the instrument of its expression. Steiner's insights expand our understanding of the human being beyond what the abstract intellect can grasp, yet if we approach them without a responsive instrument or think we can bypass the necessity to access the richly textured layers of psychology that best current acting practice demonstrates, the results will be simplistic.

It was not Steiner's task to provide a systematic methodology. He planted seeds which valued colleagues past and present have cultivated in their many different ways within the very different contexts of their work. That theatre born of these experiments is not yet sufficiently mature to reach the wider world does not make me doubt its potential and validity.[*] Immersion in this content over many years simply confirms how impossible it is to plumb its depths and master it within a single life. There are indications in the *Speech and Drama* course I have not been able to investigate that no

---

[*] Refer to Chapter 5, 'The Century of Research' in *The Actor of the Future 1*.

doubt have been taken up by others. Volumes 2,3 and 4 of *The Actor of the Future* simply share my research on the path to find holistic methods for my students and myself, processes that penetrate the spaces in between the isolated stars of Steiner's indications and that let us make our own discoveries.

Chapter 1

Building the bridge between gesture, voice and speech

In lecture 2 of the *Speech and Drama* course, Steiner identifies six archetypes informing our responses to the world and how these are revealed in corresponding tendencies of speech and gesture.[6] For many years, the lack of a precise way to differentiate between our ordinary gestures and their artistic transformation has confused many who have tried to work with Steiner's observations. Chekhov's full-bodied process for arriving at an archetypal gesture provides a systematic method for exploring the powerful dynamics activated when the six archetypes identified by Steiner are condensed into a gestural continuum that moves through many levels.[*]

For only when we penetrate our ordinary naturalistic gestures, go inside them (as it were) and expand them into full-bodied gestures are we able to investigate their inner structure and dynamics and expose or reveal the spiritual archetypes informing them.

Before we begin our exploration I remind readers of the term *body-of-sensation* or *sensation-body*. I use this to name the intense sensations generated when we move full-bodily or create a full-bodied archetypal gesture, as Chekhov's psycho-physical approach demands.[7] Because these sensations permeate our whole instrument, they constitute a super-sensible body which we learn to sustain, to integrate with other layers of our work and then apply to a specific task. As we progress further in the work described in this volume and the ones that follow, this *body-of-sensation* will grow ever richer in complexity and substance: an evolving organ of perception able to discern ever finer states of consciousness and being and channel their activity.

To remind ourselves of the process described on page 90 of *The Art of Acting* and some of the fundamental elements of gesture we begin this next level of our work by exploring what happens when we clench our fist.

Exploration 1 – Gesture

1. Stand alert and available.
2. As you slowly clench your fist, pay attention to the sequence of sensations that arise. To sustain a gesture is not the same as holding on to it. Holding on to a

---

[*] *The Art of Acting*, Chapter 1 for a detailed exploration of this process of reducing outer movement from level 10 to 1 in relation to *qualities of movement* and page 207–211 in relation to *gesture*.

gesture means maintaining its outer form when the life no longer flows through it. The outer form then becomes an empty shell which blocks the further flow of energy.

3. To sustain a gesture you must learn how to renew it; in this case you must unclench your fist. Do so and let your hand expand to its limit. Once again pay attention to the journey of sensation this arouses.

4. Observe that the sensation of expanding or contracting can be sustained beyond the hand's ability to physically go further.

5. Observe how the impulse to transform from one into the other arises prior to the hand responding.

6. Continue to contract and expand your hand, each time gathering more of your body into its movement until your whole body is contracting and expanding. This full-bodied movement we refer to as level 10 on a scale of 1-10. Pay attention to the alternating body-of-sensations aroused when your whole instrument is permeated in this way.

7. Reduce the outer movement until once again it is only your fist that is contracting and expanding (level 1 or 2).

8. See if you can do this and sustain the level of sensation in your whole instrument, that was generated when you moved at level 10.

Even though your outer gesture is to clench your fist your whole body-of-sensation permeates that gesture and radiates into the space around you. This means that even your naturalistic gesture is embedded in the whole space that you inhabit and is a focus of power and intention.

By magnifying the initial gesture in this way you can explore the archetypal process that condenses into clenching or unclenching your fist. Your ordinary gesture now becomes a vessel for this greater archetype: expanding and contracting.

Once we apply this process to the six archetypes identified by Steiner we discover that each encapsulates a stage of initiation in the archetypal drama of the human soul on its journey to maturity.

Chekhov's method for transforming naturalistic into full-bodied gesture ensures that the gestures explored can permeate the actor's instrument in such a way that they support the corresponding quality of speech without unnecessary tension in the throat. Likewise, his method for transforming full-bodied into naturalistic gesture ensures that even our most ordinary gestures can be permeated with a depth of substance that, in turn, can penetrate the space around the actor, affect the other actors in its field, and radiate into the audience.

Chekhov's technique, therefore, allows us to explore the intimate connections between gesture, voice and speech that Steiner made and support their integration. The process reveals the basic elements of which our responses to the world in speech and gesture are composed and will allow us later to organise them in a 'periodic table'.

These are the archetypes or fundamental tendencies identified by Steiner in the myriad gestures we observe around us in the world:

1. *Pointing*
2a *Holding on to ourselves*
2b *Stuck[8] intensification of 2a*
3. *Rolling forward of arms and hands*
4. *Flinging out a limb*
5. *Reaching to touch*
6. *Stepping back on to our own ground*

Steiner connects each archetype with the distinctive *quality* of voice and speech produced when the muscular tensions inherent in that gesture penetrate our whole instrument including mouth and vocal organs. He calls this range of archetypes *revelations of speech*.

Exploration 2 Gesture/speech

To make these expressive possibilities more conscious, let us search for these archetypal tendencies in the ordinary gestures that surround us.

1. Make specific times for observation. Draw and/or describe the gestures you observe.
2. Explore each one in turn. Feel your way inside it. Expand it into a level 10 full-bodied gesture, then reduce it again in the way described in exploration 1. See if this process enables you to find the inner impulse that gives rise to it.
3. Still alternating between level 10-1, try putting into words what it expresses.
4. Identify and group any gestures with the same tendencies.
5. Identify gestures that reveal more than one of these 6/7 tendencies.

Exploration 3 – Gesture/speech – partner or group

1. Demonstrate to your class or partner the gestures you observed. Identify those with a common tendency. How would you name that tendency? What intentions or objectives does that tendency express?
2. Compare your observations to the gestural tendencies identified by Steiner.
3. Can you find a gesture that does not display any of these 6/7 tendencies? If so, describe its features. Have you observed any gestures that combine two or more of these tendencies?

Exploration 4 – Gesture – partner or group

First we will explore the condition that gives birth to gesture.

1. Starting at a distance, approach each other slowly until you merge. Use your ensemble skills to move as one body, one mind.[*] Observe how you have no need of gesture when you share one consciousness, one body.
2. On a drumbeat or hand clap, separate as far from each other as you can.
3. At that distance, use your arms and hands to explore Steiner's seven tendencies, as well as any others you observed.[†]
4. Keep the dialogue of gesture going while you move closer once again until you merge. Observe how gesture disappears when there is no separation.
5. Repeat the process. This time try to articulate in words what each gesture means. What does it communicate? By doing this you begin to identify the intention or objective embodied in that gesture.
6. In the light of your observations consider whether gesture expresses either the need to separate, stay separate or re-connect.
7. Share your discoveries.

To investigate further we need an organ of perception fine enough to sense the subtle field we generate between ourselves and others.

Exploration 5 – Gesture – boundaries – partner work

1. Start as far from your partner as the space allows. Approach each other slowly. Pay attention to the subtle thresholds or boundaries you cross as you draw closer.

---

[*] *The Art of Acting*, pages 261–2.
[†] See step 3 of Gesture/Speech exploration 1.

Sense at each boundary or threshold how you can 'grant' or 'refuse' permission' to each other to proceed.

2. Repeat several times until you are attuned to the field of thresholds that arise between you.

3. This time when you sense the inmost threshold of each other's space, behind which lies your partner's intimate self (its position may be different for each one) express the subtext by putting words to the sensation. For example: *do I trust?* or *I trust* or *I don't know if I trust you enough to let you cross this last threshold that separates us from each other* or *do I feel safe or threatened or unsafe, invaded?*

4. Step back from this boundary. Approach it again. Explore what makes it possible to step across. Find words to match the sensations.

5. Do this several times. Are you aware that your sense of yourself is not entirely contained within your skin but extends into a subtle field around you? Pay attention to the shift in sensation as you approach and cross each boundary within your partner's field and as your partner crosses into yours.

Although these first explorations are with a human being perhaps you can discern how your choices to connect or separate are made not only in relation to an object or aspect of the world outside yourself, but also in your inner world: to something you remember, think about, or feel.

Exploration 6 — Gesture/speech

1. Repeat the steps of exploration 4 but at each boundary or threshold explore the choice provided by each archetypal gesture. Find words to express the objectives implicit in the sensations they arouse.

2. Compare your own observations with the following.

- *I want to point something out to you, to others or myself: draw attention to it.*
- *I want to gather the outer world inside myself so I can process it.*
- *I want to find a way out of this situation or problem but the harder I try the more blocked or stuck I feel.*
- *I want to find out more about you/it so I sensitively feel my way around you/it.*
- *I want to fling you/it out of my space.*
- *I want to connect with you/it or join with you/it.*
- *I want to make or maintain a boundary between myself and you/it.*

Based on your discoveries, consider Steiner's observation that the instinctive antipathies and sympathies we feel as we make our way around the world reveal our destiny. If gesture signals our intention to connect or separate, then it is the means by which we navigate our lives.

When experimenting with these archetypal choices always work with the whole range of movement from level 10-1. It is a mistake to think that everyday life does not include occasions when our gestures are intensified to level 10.

Nevertheless full-bodied archetypal gesture differs from the largely naturalistic gestures of our everyday experience. Our capacity to move with ease between the levels untangles the confusion that has sometimes surrounded the artistic application of these gestures to our work.[9]

If you begin with more naturalistic gestures (level 1) expand towards the full-bodied gestures that express their archetypes (level 10). If you begin with full-bodied gestures practice reducing them to everyday dimensions while sustaining the sensation of the full-bodied gesture. You should be able to move easily in both directions. When your whole instrument is permeated with the intense sensations that are generated by a full-bodied gesture, identify the objective it expresses and put it into words; *I want to . . . (name objective).*[*] Let the gesture generate the words. Observe and describe the instinctive quality of voice and speech the gesture generates.

Mastery of these seven gestures allows us to respond and make transitions in any order and in any context. I have so far presented the gestures in the order Steiner gave. As we focus on each one in turn, I present them in the order of my exploration. I have named each gesture as a *choice*. By this I mean that at each boundary or threshold we encounter between ourselves and the world we make a choice to respond in one of the six/seven archetypal ways or some combination of them. To avoid confusion for those familiar with Steiner's numbering, this table places his next to my own.

Choice 1 Connect in sympathy	Revelation 5 — Reaching to touch
Choice 2 Clearing space/antipathy	Revelation 4 — Flinging out a limb
Choice 3 Establish and maintain my boundary	Revelation 6 — Stepping back on our own ground
Choice 4 Project my own will into the other	Revelation 1 — Pointing

Contd.

---

[*] *The Art of Acting*, Chapter 4, for the relationship between gesture and objective.

Choice 5 Sense our way around resistances, sift our perceptions and thoughts, to search, to question, to feel forward in the face of hindrances	Revelation 3 — Rolling forward of arms and hands
Choice 6 Enclose the world within myself, in order to digest, consider it	Revelation 2 Holding on to ourselves
Choice 7 Paralysis of the limbs — intensification of choice 6	Revelation 2b — 'Stuck' — intensification of 2a

The seven full-bodied archetypal gestures generate strong pathways of sensation that reveal the sounds whose qualities and gestures most support the achievement of that nuance in our speech. Once those pathways are established we can use them to precisely sculpt and form our speech throughout a text. Only the full-bodied gesture can act as an organising principle with power to radiate its tensions and dynamics into the organs and muscles responsible for speech, supporting the appropriate vocal quality. Once our ability to match our vocal nuances precisely with our full-bodied gestures is achieved we can begin the process of reducing outer gesture to its subtlest level without compromising vocal expressivity.

Therefore it is essential that we move flexibly between the full-bodied gesture that encapsulates each archetype and the particular expressions of that archetype in everyday experience.

If we are not satisfied with the mere reproduction of everyday appearances, a study of gesture that occurs naturally in life must pass through this potentially self-conscious phase of working with these archetypal choices, until we master the technique. Then we can recreate each aspect of behaviour, illuminate it with our consciousness, and use it flexibly and freely.

Mastery implies we can reduce the outer gesture (10–1) without reducing our expression of the range of soul-life in the subtlest nuances of voice and speech.

Exploration of the archetypal gestures/revelations of speech

Exploration 7 – Gesture/speech – Seven Choices

In addition to exploring each choice in relation to a partner, try it in relation to objects such as a letter or a plant.[*] To clarify the difference between naturalistic and full-bodied gesture each choice is illustrated with the everyday example of relating to a plant as well as with its full-bodied archetype.

Choice 1: to connect in sympathy

Stage 1: reaching to touch with the soft parts of the hands, palms and fingertips forward

This response indicates that in some degree we desire to close the gap, heal the separation and unite with another. We accept or invite the other into our space and/or accept the invitation into theirs. We express this choice by reaching out to touch or stroke the other with the soft parts of our hand, our palm or fingertips. The gesture can be delicate and subtle at one end of the spectrum or at the other, bodies may touch or merge in an embrace. By reaching to touch, we discover whether and to what degree we are willing to cross each other's boundaries and let our own be crossed.

1. Identify the objectives this gesture reveals and put them into words, observing your quality of voice, for example: *I want to move closer/get nearer to you; touch you, caress you, unite or merge with you.*

Stage 2: voice and speech quality: gentle

Our soul reveals this intention in a voice that is gentle and caressing. Like the soft surface of our palms and fingers we stroke the other with our voice. This vocal quality can sound weak or sentimental unless we permeate the vowel with the consonant's activity, supported by the full-bodied gesture, which also supports the projection of our voice into space.

1. Vocally, gentleness and warmth can be achieved by consciously permeating voice and words with the consonantal qualities of /l/ and /m/, the long vowels /ɑː/(star), /ɔː/(awe) and/uː/(shoe), and the diphthong /aɪ/(life). Use the gesture to support the stroking of the other with these words:

    Love illumining all! Love aligning all!

---

[*] See illustrations.

Choice 1: to connect in sympathy

Figure 1 Full-bodied archetypal gesture: connecting in sympathy

Figure 2 Naturalistic gesture: connecting in sympathy

2. Apply this gesture with its words in different contexts and dimensions, for example, reaching to touch and stroke:

- something small and delicate like a wild flower or kitten or a wounded bird
- something of the same dimensions as yourself, like another human being
- something larger than yourself, like a beautiful mountain or a peaceful ocean or a sunset.

Choice 2: clearing space/antipathy

Stage 1: gesture of flinging out a limb

Partner work

1. Stand at a distance from your partner.
2. A, invade B's space by running into it.
3. B find the strength to physically fling A away from you and clear your space.
4. Reverse roles.
5. Work on your own. Translate the tensions and dynamics of that physical encounter into a full-bodied sequence of gestures that express your intention to eject what violates your space. Fling him/her/it clear of your boundary.
6. Identify your objective and put it into words, for example: *I want to fling you/it/him out of my space* or *I want to get rid of you* or *I want to wipe you/it off the face of the earth.*
7. Speak your objective so that the words are born out of the gesture. Observe your vocal quality.

Choice 2, stage 2: voice and speech quality: hard

We instinctively achieve a harsher voice by pushing from our throat. However, the resulting tension damages our larynx, obscures our clarity of speech and causes us to lose control of our artistic expression.

As artists we must be able to produce the necessary hardness without damaging our throats. As well, we must be able to express ejection of something from our space through the whole range of volume, from soft and delicate to very loud.[*]

A longer passage may require us to sustain an aggressive voice. By stressing every word with equal power, we will lose the flow of language and numb the listener's

---

[*] *The Art of Speech* pages 150–164 for the exploration of volume and projection.

Choice 2: clearing space/antipathy

Figure 3 Full-bodied archetypal gesture: clearing my space

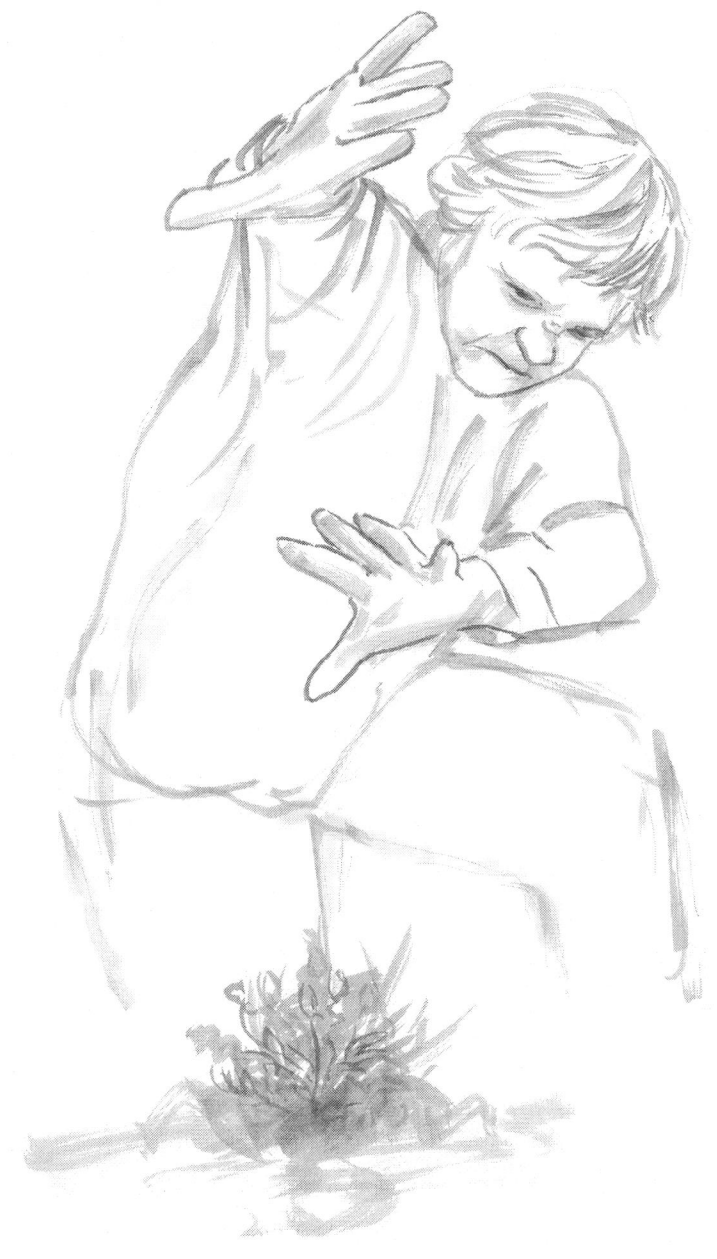

Figure 4 Naturalistic gesture: clearing my space

capacity to hear what we are saying. Therefore we must decide which word or words must bear the main gesture and its emphasis.

/k/ can teach our voice to sharply cut through space. The placement of the vowel /ɛ/ (men) and its application to the English diphthong /eɪ/(date) provide the hard-edged vocal definition needed to express this gesture. The placement for the short vowel /æ/ (man) also sharpens our voice to a cutting edge.

If these vowels are released from the throat with ample breath, launched by the explosive power of /k/ and driven by the dynamic of the full-bodied gesture, the voice will be hard edged without strain and communicate rejection or antipathy without wounding either speaker's throat or listener's ear.[*]

1. Try achieving this with the following sequence of words. Release the first word 'Caitiff!' on one large gesture that clears the space and makes a pathway for the syllables that follow. These can then be released in a succession of rapid-fire small gestures that follow in its wake.

    Caitiff! Axe cracking neck to dead!

The next word sequence also provides the opportunity to sculpt the English dipthong /eɪ/(hate) with the clarity of edge provided by the shorter vowels.

2. Gather the overall dynamic into a sequence of four cutting gestures and release each word, one gesture at a time.

    Hate slams the gate. Hate shuts the gate.

The illustration (figure 3) shows how the gesture's intention and dynamic is released from a contraction. In the same way the word or words which carry the central thrust of our antipathy must be prepared in that contraction and released along with the dynamic of the central gesture. The words preceding them will then be sucked into the vortex that prepares for the release, and those that follow will be flung out in its wake.

Choice 2, stage 2 exercise

This exercise is based on the reversal of the old magic spell: 'A-bra-ka-da-bra' (pronounced with long vowel /ɑ:/(star) becomes 'Ka-da-ra-bra-ba').

1. Use the /k/ to transform the open vowel /ɑ:/(star) into the hard-edged blade of the short vowel /ʌ/(cup). Gather the whole line into a contraction. Prepare the soft palate at the back to tense and release the *ka* into the space, free of the throat.

---

[*] This process has been explored in detail in the section on volume and projection in *The Art of Speech*, Chapter 3.

Coordinate the release of the first syllable with the main gesture, letting the other syllables follow in its wake:

ka-da-ra-bra-ba

Next we release the main gesture with the final syllable, *ba*. The consonants of the preceding syllables are now used to build the tension of contraction and prepare for the full release of the gesture at the end.

2. To prepare for the /b/ to hit the space firmly integrated with the vowel, pause before releasing it, sustain the tension, breathe in the final syllable and release it on a full breath.

ka-da-ra-bra-ba

3. In the final version, gather the preceding syllables into a contraction. Use the consonants to build the tension in the breath and voice. Pause a moment to breathe in what must be released, then release the main gesture with the second to last syllable, on a full breath, powered by the *br* and sweeping both last syllables in its wake.

ka-da-ra-bra-ba

4. Apply this to a short sentence, for example:

Get out of my life! Get out of my sight!

Each time shift the word that bears the main stress in the line.

Get out of my sight.
Get out of my sight.
Get out of my sight.

Thus, by integrating the breath and sounds of the stressed word with the release of the main gesture within the overall dynamic of the sentence, we gain control of our artistic intention. This protects our throat as we produce the necessary hardness in our voice.

Choice 3: establish and maintain my boundary

Stage 1: gesture of stepping back on my own ground and marking the boundary of my space with flat palms, extended vertically or slanting.

1. Your partner approaches 'your' space. You sense potential threat. Choose to establish and maintain your boundary and thus prevent its violation. Step back to

Choice 3: establish and maintain my boundary

Figure 5 Full-bodied archetypal gesture: establishing/maintaining a boundary

Figure 6 Naturalistic gesture: establishing/maintaining a boundary

re-establish 'your' space. Hold the other at a distance by marking your boundary with your hands; placing one or both at a vertical or slanting angle with fingers and palms stretched flat. Project your intention through the gesture

2. Identify your objective and express it in your own words. For example: *I want to stop you from coming any closer* or *I want to make my position clear* or *I want to protect my space* or *I want to assert myself.*

3. Experiment with establishing your boundary at different distances and in response to differing degrees of challenge.

Choice 3, stage 2: voice and speech quality: abrupt

1. Continue to explore this choice, observing it in life, and improvising various examples.

2. Identify the voice and speech qualities that characterise this choice.

3. Observe that your voice is firm and each syllable is edged with a staccato-like abruptness. A succession of abrupt edges interrupts the smooth flow of language. Here are some examples that demonstrate a sequence of such boundaries. Each stroke indicates an interruption to the flow:

   Don't/talk/to me/like/that!

   Articulate clearly with a strong dynamic of intention and use the ends of words as barriers that arrest the flow.

   You can go if you like/but I'm/staying/here.

Although only *like* ends with a hard edged plosive, /k/, this sentence requires us to consciously form the /m/ with a harder edge and the vowels with the staccato quality of the short vowel /ɛ/(m<u>e</u>n). Sounds that naturally support this gesture are the consonants /n/, /k/, /t/, /d/, the vowel /ɛ/ and diphthong /eɪ/(d<u>a</u>te).

4. With your partner, improvise some of the contexts that provoke each other to step back on your own ground and maintain your boundary. For example: pressure your partner to smoke a cigarette, take drugs, come with you, resume a relationship that had been broken off, etc. Integrate your full-bodied gestures with the following words. Once you can establish and maintain your boundary in relation to your partner, practice the three B lines by yourself, increasing in intensity.

   A: (*approaches*). Come on!
   B: No!
   A: (*tries again with increased intensity*). Please!
   B: No knocking/can crack/me!

A: (tries again with increased intensity). But...
B: No knocking/can make/me/crack!

5. The qualites of /n/ and /k/ support and are supported by the gesture. Always begin the gesture at level 10. Then reduce it from level 10–1 as you build the skill and confidence to communicate the gesture vocally.
6. Swap roles.

Choice 4: to project my own will into the other: *effective*

Stage 1: gesture of pointing

We perceive the other only because he/she/it appears separate from us. Pointing indicates that our attention is drawn to the existence of someone or something 'outside' ourselves, or to some specific attribute of its existence. As with all the archetypes, this manifests in our internal landscape as much as in the outer world. We point things out to ourselves within our minds as well as point to things outside ourselves. We point things out to others. Pointing reveals the *will* involved in our perception. We cannot perceive anything if we are passive; to pay attention, our will must actively engage with the world. Quantum experiments indicate that what we perceive is an effect of our perception. We could say that the act of perception is in itself *effective*.

Choice 4, stage 1: Partner work

1. A choose something at a distance and, without using words, point it out to B.
2. B identify what A is pointing to.
3. A observe the will required if your gesture is to be effective or, in other words, successfully communicate what you perceive.

This simple exercise engages many layers of perception. First we point to the thing itself, whether it is an idea or image in our mind or a concrete other. In doing so, we have an effect on it. But we can only be effective if we project our will out beyond our boundary, across the space that separates us, sending a part of ourselves into the object of attention. *Here I am and there it is*. It is as though, by pointing, we spear it with our will.

We point to have an *effect*, perhaps on an individual or on a group or crowd, and draw them into our perception. We will them to see what we see. In a certain sense our objective is to dominate the other, make them an extension of our will, turn the 'not me' into 'me' so that my will may be done through another.

Choice 4: to project my own will into the other: *effective*

Figure 7 Full-bodied archetypal gesture: pointing

Figure 8 Naturalistic gesture: pointing

Introducing the voice

1. Improvise situations in which you point something out to yourself within your mind, point to things outside yourself, point things out to others.
2. Identify the objectives expressed in a pointing gesture.
3. Put them into words, observing your quality of voice. For example: *I want to point this out to myself/to you, draw your attention to . . . I want you to see what I see. I want you to do what I want . . . I want to make you do what I want.*

Choice 4, stage 2: voice and speech quality: incisive

As you point to different objects play with ordinary words and phrases such as *Look! Look there! See! Over there! Look at that! Go there! Come back!* Our voice is incisive when we point to something.

1. Identify which consonants and vowels are naturally incisive and use them to support and exercise this vocal quality. For example, the plosives: /t /, /d/, /n/, / k/, /g/, /b/, /p/. The vowels /ɪ/(s<u>i</u>p) and /i:/(m<u>e</u>) formed with the tongue at the front of the mouth and the lips stretched tightly along the line of teeth, support the incisive vocal quality.
2. Integrate these plosives with a full-bodied pointing gesture. Project each consonant so that it lands on an object of attention at different distances.

   These consonants provide the definition that helps us shape our words incisively.

3. Try the following sequence of syllables that brings vowels and consonants together to achieve incisive speech:

   > tricked deep dingle
   > deep biting narrow copper
   > dark too dark.[*]

The sharply defined consonants and the vowels, especially /ɪ/ and /i:/ of lines 1 and 2 prepare our placements and our tempo, so that we can shape the longer, broader vowels in line 3 with the incisiveness of the early ones.

4. Layer the opening lines of this sonnet by Hopkins with pointing gestures and incisive speech integrated with your heart centre.[†]

   Look! Look up at the stars! See all the little fire folk /Sitting in the air.

---

[*] *The Art of Speech*, Chapter 3, page 42.
[†] *The Art of Acting*, Chapter 3 and *The Art of Speech*, Chapter 3.

5. In this next line, layer the gesture and incisive voice with the will centre:

> Get the men to dig deep trenches! Try tricking them!
>
> (DL).

Also in the last line of *Hamlet*:

> Go, bid the soldiers shoot.

Hamlet's soliloquy provides numerous examples of pointing to things within his own mind. For example:

> For who would bear
> The oppressor's wrong, the proud man's contumely,
> The pangs of despised love, the law's delay,
> The insolence of office and the spurns
> That patient merit of the unworthy takes
> When he himself might his quietus make
> With a bare bodkin?

Choice 5: to sense our way around resistances, sift our perceptions and thoughts, to search, to question

Stage 1: gesture of arms and hands rolling forward, palms upward

If what is separate from myself eludes or resists my understanding, I can feel my way towards it with a searching gesture. In the face of hindrances I sense that I cannot approach directly but need to move around the evidence as if enquiring from all sides. Archetypically, we observe the arms and hands roll forward, palms and fingers facing upwards. Like delicate antennae they roll and curl, sifting and sensing their way towards their object. My objectives might be: *I want to find out more about you – sense my way into you. I want to understand what's going on, why this is happening.*

Choice 5, stage 2: voice and speech quality: tentative, trembling, vibrating

The soul that reveals itself in this gesture is still somewhere in the pole of sympathy, seeking to reunite in some way with the separated other but without any certainty of outcome. The consonant that most supports this gesture vocally is the rolled r which keeps us airborne, unable to 'land', and permeates the voice with its trembling, vibrating quality. Its energy permeates our arms, lifting them away from the ribcage, to float and drift or fly in the airy realm. Spreading all the way into our palms and fingers, the rolled r revolves the sensing under-surfaces of arms and hands, turning them

Choice 5: to sense our way around resistances, sift our perceptions and thoughts, to search, to question

Figure 9 Full-bodied gesture: sifting our perceptions

Figure 10 Naturalistic gesture: sifting our perceptions

outward, exposing them to search delicately like a b<u>r</u>eath of b<u>r</u>eeze or, like a hu<u>rr</u>icane, to bear the brunt as it passionately stirs and questions.

1. Prepare with full-bodied *flying* and integrate the rolled r.
2. Reduce the outer movement to a minimum. Sustain the sensation while you integrate a series of gestures with these phrases, playing with the whole range of intensities; from tentative transparency at the more delicate pole of questioning to urgency and desperation at the other pole:

> Restlessly reasoning, revolving round and round this riddle of reality, I wonder/question is it real, this trembling truth? Is it reasonable? Is it wrong? Is it right? Is it really real?

Once the rolled r has prepared our instrument with the activity required to permeate our speech with its trembling, vibrating quality, we need to practice sustaining this when we apply it to our less active English r, formed closer to the lips.

We express the searching, questioning gesture in our voice with an upward inflection. This is not something we can simply add or 'stick on' to the last word of a line. The upward inflection must arise from the source of the question, be borne aloft and carried by the gesture. Like a fragrance from within, it must permeate each word within the whole. *How? Why? When? Where? Who? Which? What?* In the English language notice how many of our question words begin with the insubstantial breath sound /ʍ/(w<u>h</u>en). Composed of /w/ — often the sound that marks the barrier for stammerers, who struggle at that threshold to release what lives inside them — combined with /h/, the not yet precisely differentiated in- or out-breath. The feeling-forward gesture in combination with the /ʍ/ can achieve in these single words the delicate nuance of tentative transparency. On the other hand, these fire sounds, when combined, can fan the breath into extreme intensity. Yet however passionate our questioning, our speech must never land with statement-certainty but must communicate not-knowingness.

Choice 6: to enclose the world within myself, in order to digest, consider it

Stage 1: gesture of holding on to oneself

I perceive the world outside myself, separate from me. I reach out to the world to gather information. I enfold and seal it deep within myself so I can process it, digest it with my thinking.

Since I have enclosed the world inside me, I no longer sense its support outside of me. Needing some resistance, something solid to support me, I hold on to my own

Choice 6: to enclose the world within myself, in order to digest, consider it

Figure 11 Full-bodied gestures: holding on to self

Figure 12 Naturalistic gesture: holding on to self

body, to myself. I clench my fists or wrap my arms around myself, or press a finger into the side or tip of my nose. I can use any part of my body to press against another, create resistance with itself and thus experience the firmness of my own existence. My objectives might be: *I want to digest this information/understand you/this. I want to take you/this in.*

Choice 6, stage 2: voice and speech quality: full toned, deliberate

This gesture reveals a paradox. On the one hand, when I take the world inside myself, the world and I are one again. On the other hand, when I create this closed circuit with myself, I cut myself off from the world. When I express my deliberations vocally, my voice is full of substance and dense with my thinking's effort to penetrate the world's resistance to its understanding.

Pressing into the resistance of my own body results in a *moulding* quality of movement that integrates with the enclosing gesture and condensing quality of /b/. This provides the driving force to condense what has not yet been understood into the firm contours that clarity demands.

The long vowels such as /ɔ:/(<u>awe</u>) and /u:/(sh<u>oe</u>) and all the diphthongs also generate the depth and warmth of inner substance in the voice.

1. Integrate the full-bodied gesture with the following words:

   By beaten bowers bide brave

2. The repeated /b/ in Hamlet's famous words integrated with full-bodied wrestling with ourselves — holding on to our own body — supports the deliberate quality of speech which can then be sustained through the second clause:

   To be or not to be, that is the question

3. As do the repetitions of /b/ in the well known adage:

   But I believe that beauty is in the eye of the beholder

This gesture should not be fixed or static. Holding on to oneself is the final stage of a process that begins with reaching out into the world to gather information. The gesture must be constantly renewed, part of a continuum that moves between the world outside and the world within. This keeps it alive, providing the dynamic that drives through the density of voice toward the conclusion of the thought or sentence.

Choice 7: intensification of choice 6

Figure 13 Full-bodied gesture: paralysis

Figure 14 Naturalistic gesture: paralysis

Choice 7: intensification of choice 6

Stage 1: gesture of paralysis of the limbs

I return to the world outside me to take it in but it resists, pushes me back to the world inside me once again. I try to go inside myself again but now it too resists, pushing me back towards the world outside again. I try again ... and again. *I don't know what to do. I don't know what to think. I don't know what to say. I'm stuck.* Each dynamic blocks the other, finally locking in a gesture expressing that my soul feels blocked or trapped; I can't move out or in, incapable of making a decision. My limbs feel paralysed. The dynamics in gesture 6 of the body in resistance with itself intensify to the extreme.

Choice 7, stage 2: voice and speech quality: slow and laboured.

My voice feels trapped. I don't know what to say. It's almost impossible to speak. To achieve the expression of this gesture vocally, I use each end consonant to make a barrier that stops the flow of words even as I try to push them through.

> Can't! Can't move! Don't know what to do! Don't know what to say! Can't work it out! Stuck!

Here then is our equivalent of the chemist's Periodic Table. It orders the basic elements that compose our life of gesture. This is not an arbitrary choice of metaphor since chemistry identifies the basic elements, the building blocks of matter and the principles that order their propensities to combine and separate: the forces of antipathy and sympathy, attraction and repulsion.

The Alchemical Periodic Table

Relationship of soul to the world	Gesture	Voice and speech quality
Choice 1: to connect/ sympathy	I reach to touch, soft palms and pads of fingers forward	Gentle
Choice 2: to clear my space/ antipathy	I fling out a limb	Hard
Choice 3: to create and/or maintain my boundary	I step back on my own ground and mark my boundary with flat palms extended vertically or slanted	Abrupt

Contd

Choice 4: to project my own will into, have an effect on the other	I point	Incisive
Choice 5: to feel my way forward in the face of hindrances, to sift my perceptions, to search, to question	I roll my arms and hands forward with my palms upwards	Tentative, trembling, vibrating, not reaching a conclusion
Choice 6: to enclose the world within myself in order to digest and process it	I hold on to myself	Full toned, deliberate
Choice 7: intenstification of choice 6; to be unable to take action in the outer or the inner world	I cannot move, my limbs are paralysed	Slow and laboured

Exploration 8 – Gesture/speech – combinations

Since life is never one dimensional, the complexity of everyday behaviour reveals these seven gestures in many combinations. Once we have mastered each one with its accompanying quality of speech, we can expand our flexibility and expressive range by combining them. Here are a few examples:

- Flinging out your arms and hands with fists clenched.
- Reaching to touch while feeling forward searchingly.
- Maintaining your boundary with fists clenched.
- Holding on to yourself and pointing, for example, with a pointing finger pressed into the nose, cheek, chin or forehead.
- Flinging out a pointing hand or finger.
- Maintaining your boundary and flinging out a limb.
- Reaching to touch with your right hand while you maintain a boundary with your left, as in Figure 15.

Combinations exercise

As your mastery increases the combinations will become increasingly intuitive.

1. Prepare each component gesture first, with its accompanying speech exercise.

Figure 15 The figure reaches out to touch with the right hand while maintaining a boundary with the left

2. Alternate each gesture. We know that only the full-bodied penetration of our instrument generates the depth of sensation that supports the voice/speech quality without the need to push from the throat. It is important therefore that the shift from one gesture to another achieves the thorough transformation of our body-of-sensation before we speak.

3. Increase the tempo between alternating gestures until your instrument is permeated with a fusion of both gestures. Do not compromise the thoroughness of transformations.

Exploration 9 – Gesture/speech – layering

Although gesture is a function of our will, due to the intimate connection of our soul and body – our psycho-physical constitution – it cannot help but generate or be generated by emotion. However, gesture, in itself, is not emotion. For example, it's easy to confuse the gesture of flinging out a limb with anger or hatred and yet it is perfectly possible to clear one's space sadly or playfully or tenderly. If we confuse gesture with emotion our application of these gestures will be limited and one dimensional. Layering these archetypal gestures with our other tools expands the range of their contribution to our craft, and creates ever richer pathways of sensation. Here are some suggestions, beginning with Chekhov's tool of *qualities and sensations*.[*]

1. Layer the gesture of *flinging out a limb* with the following qualities and sensations: sadly, compassionately, angrily, scornfully, threateningly, playfully, laughingly.

2. Layer the gesture of *reaching out to touch* with a quality of threateningly, cynically, manipulatively, as well as the more obvious, compassionately, tenderly.

3. Layer the gesture of *feeling forward in the face of hindrances* with the quality of searchingly, bitterly, angrily, desperately, curiously, hopefully, despairingly.

4. Experiment with your own layerings of gestures and qualities.

5. Integrate these experiments with the work with vowels described in Chapter 2 that follows.[†]

6. Layer the archetypal speech gestures with other Chekhov tools: *qualities of movement, tempo and dynamic, expanding and contracting, centres,*[‡] *PGs and comic and tragic styles.*[§]

---

[*] *The Art of Acting*, Chapter 3.

[†] See also *The Art of Acting*, Chapter 3 and *The Art of Speech*, Chapter 1.

[‡] *The Art of Acting*, Chapters 1, 2 and 3.

[§] *The Actor of the Future 3*, Chapter 5.

Just as the great works of language arise from the finite range of consonants and vowels, so from this finite range of gestures spring infinite nuance and complexity[*]. This manifests at the most unconscious level of our daily interaction as well as the highly conscious full-bodied explorations of artistic practice. Figures 16–19 demonstrate some of the ways in which these archetypal gestures reveal themselves in everyday communication.

Exploration 10 – Gesture/speech – layering the archetypal gestures with objectives

1. Make a list of objectives. For example: *I want to dominate, I want to find out what's going on, I want to protect you, I want to hide the truth, I want to expose the truth, I want to understand you.*
2. Choose one and create a PG (Psychological Gesture) that embodies it.
3. Sustain the body-of-sensation that each PG generates.
4. Layer it in turn with each of the archetypal gestures and their speech qualities.
5. Try this with the other objectives on your list.

Partner work

6. Each choose an objective.
7. Prepare your PGs and while sustaining your body-of-sensation, engage with each other.
8. Use the archetypal speech gestures to explore the range of interaction that develops in the field of dynamics generated by the interweaving of your two objectives.

Applying the archetypal gestures to a text

Mastering the full-bodied archetypal gestures provides a pathway that supports our qualities of voice and speech. The first level of application to a text consists of practicing until we can achieve the integration of our choice of gesture with its speech quality. In lecture 9 of the *Speech and Drama* course, Steiner suggested that we train the integration of our speech and gesture by moving the gestures that we hear while someone speaks a text.

---

[*] *The Art of Acting*, Chapter 4.

Figure 16 Left: maintains a boundary, Right: combines pointing and holding on to self

Figure 17 Left: combines pointing and holding on to self, Right: arms and hands rolling forward

Figure 18 *Left: establishes a boundary, Right: combines pointing, holding on to self, and stepping back to maintain a boundary*

This process requires a delineation of the boundaries around its function. It must be understood that the speaker's way is not the 'right' or only way to speak the text. Although it is the fruit of the speaker's own artistic inspiration, it would violate the artistic freedom of a student or a colleague to insist that the speaker's rendering is anything other than one valid choice within a range of possibilities. It is not art if the choices made by one artistic individuality are merely copied by another. When it is understood, however, that this process is a potent tool for integrating speech and gesture, and ultimately builds the student's confidence to manifest their own artistic choices, it can be freely undertaken. In more advanced stages of the exercise the artistic choices of the speaker can be worked through together and agreed with by the one who moves.

The goal, however, is to reach such flexibility of integrated body/voice response that we are not sentenced to repeat the same journey through the gestures like a formula; rather, we are free to make fresh choices in each moment of rehearsal or performance and trust we have an instrument capable of manifesting them.

Exploration 11 – Gesture/Speech – working with a speaker

1. A choose a speech (or poem or story) that you have previously penetrated with a set of gestures based on your artistic choices.
2. B become familiar with the text and agree to A's choices for the purpose of the exercise.
3. A speak the text so that the gestures are revealed clearly in your voice/speech qualities. B listen with your whole instrument and express what you hear with full-bodied gestures.
4. Repeat this several times.
5. When B can move smoothly through the gestural journey of the speech, speak the text allowing the words to arise out of the movement. Do this until A is satisfied you have achieved a perfect integration of your gestures with their voice/speech qualities.

Exploration 12 – Gesture/Speech – applications to text

1. Work through a text until you can move full-bodily through its gestural transformations. Do not leave one syllable to chance but ensure each one is penetrated with a conscious choice. When you can sustain the appropriate voice/speech qualities, reduce the outer gesture from level 10–1.

2. Working through a text like this you may sense that one or two specific gestures dominate a speech or poem, scene or character. Practice sustaining a predominant gesture while you layer it with the moment-by-moment transformations of more transient gestures.

Now we are ready to explore how the body-of-sensation aroused by working with objective and PG anchors the six/seven speech gestures in the core objectives of a character and acts as a lens through which the seven speech gestures can reveal the character's journey through the text.

Exploration 13 – application to character and text – layering the seven archetypal gestures with PGs

Take Hamlet's soliloquy, 'O what a rogue and peasant slave am I' from Act 2, Scene 2.

1. Identify at least two conflicting states in Hamlet's soul just prior to the speech; for example: *I want to kill my uncle* but *I don't know whether I can trust what the ghost said or what anybody says. I want to find a way to trust my own experience.*
2. Embody each state in a separate PG.
3. Sustain the body-of-sensation aroused by PG1 and layer it with the speech gestures to reveal Hamlet's journey through the text.
4. Do the same with PG2. In this way the seven gestures are always anchored in at least one core objective of the character.
5. When you feel confident to integrate the speech gestures with one objective at a time, allow your body-of-sensation to suggest how Hamlet alternates between the two objectives while you use the speech gestures to explore the text.
6. When you are confident with alternating the objectives full bodily, experiment with merging them. Feel how they can weave in and out of each other. Sometimes one objective might be stronger, sometimes the other, or sometimes they might equally compete in Hamlet's soul. Always, however, they enable us to anchor the speech gestures in the character.

The degree to which gesture manifests outwardly when we perform depends on the ensemble's/director's style. Full-bodied archetypal gestures would be appropriate, for instance, when performing a classical Greek tragedy in a style resembling the original.* For a naturalistic style, the gestures must adjust accordingly. A play by Anton

---

* Refer to *The Actor of the Future 3*, Chapter 3: 'Tragic and Comic Styles'.

Chekhov may require more subtle outer gestures. Some may even be in opposition to the inner gestures if these arise from a subtext that contradicts the text. Our modern aversion to exaggeration makes us fearful that anything not underplayed might be unnatural. In life, however, human beings in extremes of circumstances or emotion often express themselves with great intensity in voice and gesture.

The goal of our work is to expand our range of expression as an integrated instrument. We practice until we can successfully communicate what we intend. Training our instrument requires commitment to a choice until we can actually *do* what we imagine. Before we reach this goal our artistic instincts may experience frustration. We delude ourselves, however, if we believe we have creative freedom before the full range of expressive possibility has been achieved.

To ensure a healthy balance between spontaneity and rigour, we might devote part of our practice and rehearsal time responding to whatever impulses arise without concern for our ability to perfectly execute our choices. This freedom must be followed by times when we recognise: *Oh yes, this is what I wanted to express but didn't actually manage.* That motivates us to return to the discipline of committing to a choice until we have the skill to manifest it.

The archetypal gestures and the Greek gymnastics

We now examine how the ancient Greek gymnastics relate to the seven archetypal gestures.[*] In lecture 2 of *Speech and Drama* Steiner claimed:

> [The Greek gymnastic exercises] are founded upon the connection of man with the cosmos. Starting from this relationship he has to the cosmos, man is in these exercises, perpetually forming, as it were, another relationship, a relationship to gesture; and in gesture the force, the dynamic of the human being is present ... in the fundamental mime movements of the stage we have faint reflections of the five exercises of the Greek gymnastics. If therefore we set out to study these reflections of the five exercises of the Greek gymnastics, we shall be on the right path for discovering how gesture can come to the help of the word in dramatic art; for there is, in fact, no justifiable gesture for the stage that is not a kind of shadow picture of some one of these five exercises of the Greek gymnastics.

Practicing the seven archetypal speech revelations transforms our body/soul gestalt into an organ of perception with which we can investigate this claim.

---

[*] *The Art of Acting*, pages 124–134.

Running

Running is the first Greek Gymnastic exercise. It awakens the activity I need, to establish my presence when I stand or walk on stage. As I explore the dynamics of *stepping back on my own ground* (choice 3), my body-of-sensation recognises that to stand and move on stage my feet must ever and again make and maintain a boundary between themselves and earth: not allowing me to merge with it but firmly keeping it at bay so I can experience that I stand on the stage of earth.

Leaping

In order to *leap* or jump, my feet must first unite with the earth in *sympathy* (choice 1), merge with it, just enough to gain a grip. Then, because I have allowed it to invade my space I must use my feet and my whole body to *fling the earth away from me* (choice 2).

Wrestling

To *wrestle* with another, I must sense the subtle interplay of three of the archetypes. By *reaching to touch* (choice 1) I get to know the qualities of my assailant and to work with them. By *creating a boundary* (choice 3) I sense how to assert myself and finally to *fling my partner from my space* (choice 2).

Discus

To *fling* (choice 2) the discus on its path away from me, first I must wrap myself around it in a series of contracting and expanding spirals. This sequence of sensations reminds me how I reach to touch the world in *sympathy* (choice 1), then fold it inside me, *holding on to myself* (choice 6) in order to deliberate, digest. Then I uncurl in a series of expanding spirals, *feeling my way forward* (choice 4); testing for the moment of release, I flick my wrist, reversing the momentum and suddenly, my hand *flings* (choice 2) the discus far away from me and follows as it spirals out into a *feeling forward in the face of hindrances, a question* (choice 4). Where will it land? I do not know but I release it to the cosmos and now my hand follows in its wake and *reaches out to touch* (choice 1) and trace its path, even as the muscles of my face respond and emulate its gesture.

Javelin

When I *throw the javelin*, I sense how it becomes an extension of my arm through which I can project my will into the world by *pointing* (choice 5).

The origin of the six archetypes in the ancient mysteries

Steiner tells us in Lecture 2 of *Speech and Drama*:

> ... These are the six revelations of speech which were known in the Greek mysteries as the six shades or variations in the forming of speech, and were in those times the basis of all instruction in speech. Besides these there are no others...

As discussed in *The Actor of the Future 1*, in ancient times those who sought to regain perception of supersensible reality did so through initiation in the Mysteries. Theatre historians regard the rituals performed at Abydos in Egypt and Eleusis in Greece as the seeds of Western theatre. Despite the lack of outer evidence, fragments of accounts report that the culmination of both rites was a ritual, temple drama in which priests channelled the specific deities they served.

My body-of-sensation stirs when I imagine gestures that could communicate the death and resurrection of Osiris at the temple of Abydos and, in a much later time, *The Triumph of Horus* at Dendera; and at Eleusis, the grief of Demeter and rescue of Persephone.

Figure 20 Bacchus/John the Baptist

Mediaeval and Renaiassance paintings often indicate the invisible realm behind the veil of physical perception, with a *pointing* gesture. In a ritual context, I imagine Isis pointing to the evil one, Set, exhorting her son Horus to destroy him; Horus aiming his harpoon and then releasing it to pierce the ritual cake, shaped like a hippopotamus to represent the enemy.[*] Or the narcissus pointed out by Eros to Persephone with the exhortation not to pluck the flower, lest she be expelled from the gods' dwelling on Olympus.[10]

The ritualised full-bodied questioning gesture forms a chalice into which the gods can pour their substance. Imagine Isis searching through the world for the body of Osiris. Likewise Demeter, in grief at Persephone's abduction and disappearance down to Hades, searches through the world, first for her daughter and then for the saviour of her daughter, asking everyone she meets — *feeling forward in the face of hindrances.*

Egyptian art is full of images that *reach to touch*. Isis reaching to touch each part of the broken body of her lord Osiris, as she lovingly recovers the pieces and restores life to his form with her magic spells. And when the soul purified at last on her journey after death has reached Osiris' sacred dwelling place, worthy now to meet Him face to face, she reaches out to touch the God — beholding in His countenance her own divinity. Desire for experience and sympathy towards the world causes Persephone to *reach to touch* the flower: no longer satisfied to dwell in paradisal harmony, eternally at one but without experience of self. By *stepping back on her own ground* she establishes a boundary, a step of necessary disobedience on the way towards a firm identity. Later, in Hades, she reaches for the draught of forgetfulness and the pomegranate seeds that Pluto offers her, perhaps also *feeling forward tentatively* as she hesitates to make the final move.

Figure 21 Pectoral with Scarab

Set/Seth also *steps back on his own ground* to rebel against Osiris, plotting to destroy him. Horus too must establish and maintain his boundary when he is exhorted to 'stand firm'[11] and confront the evil Set. The objective embodied

---

[*] *The Actor of the Future 1*, 'The Triumph of Horus', pages 164–165

in this gesture is beautifully expressed in *The Egyptian Book of the Dead*. On her journey after death when the soul merges once again with the universe, she prays not to lose the sense of self so dearly won through life on earth: *May I remember my name in the house where the days and years are numbered.*

The gesture of *flinging out a limb* is seen in the Egyptian bas-reliefs depicting Set dismembering the body of Osiris, and Horus flinging his harpoon into the effigy of Set to avenge his father's death.

Egyptian art is full of human figures who *hold on to themselves*: their fists are clenched, arms pressed tightly to their sides or diagonally across their hearts. Not *I think* but *the gods think through me* as their eyes behold infinity; the mind of the priest or Pharoah channelling divine intelligence.

Figure 22 Left: Tuthmosis III, 1458–1425 BCE, Right: Queen Hatshepsut, 1508–1458 BCE

In Greek myth, Odysseus and Theseus lower their sight, retreating inwards as they contract from the eternal wisdom into selfhood that wrestles for its own solutions, starting on the path that ultimately leads to Rodin's *Thinker*.

Figure 23 Auguste Rodin's, The Thinker

The divine serpent bites its own tail. The macrocosmic wisdom, to be conscious of itself, must create resistance with some part of itself, engage with it, hold on to it, create a closed circuit, inside which it digests itself and knows itself to be the all.

Figure 24 The Ouroboros serpent

This next image, from the Indian tradition, reveals the ONE infinite, eternal con-sciousness that upholds and informs all transitory states of matter.

Everyday perception beholds a static figure but our 'sensitive membrane' resonates with the archetypes we have learned to recognise and reveals to us the mystery of stillness. Like our still yet spinning planet, the stillness of the god depicted here results from the most intense activity: a perfect balance of dynamics out of which arise the stable systems that support our life and consciousness for their appointed times.

Figure 25 The Seated Buddha with many arms

Giving and receiving,[*] evolved to their highest level of expression, are revealed to be the same: both forms of our *feeling forward* archetype. As consciousness surveys itself, the thumbs and fingers touch and *hold on to each other* in myriad delicate ways, each a minute ouroboros, while down below, folding the whole as yet unmanifest creation in their gesture and not yet ready to release their will and step onto the path of outer action, the legs are *holding on to each other* and complete the circuit. We can also sense this image is a kind of macrocosmic form of the seventh choice; a stasis not experi-

---

[*] Explored in pages 137–8 of *The Art of Acting*.

enced as being paralysed or '*stuck*' because it transcends the reactions of the separated ego. Such intimations of a chaster will, prepare us for the exploration of Eurythmy gestures in chapters 5–8.

When we appreciate the sacred origins of gesture, new substance pours into our actions on the stage imbuing them with the cosmic dimension of our presence in the universe. Rooted in this ground, even the smallest gestures connect us to our soul's greater journey as, Persephone-like, we cast ourselves out of paradisal oneness and create a boundary between the self and all forms of otherness in order to establish our identity. Thus, we make our way through Hades, preparing to return with the bridegroom to the universal consciousness. This, as we have said, is the eternal archetype concealed in every drama.[*] For even at the macrocomic level, our cosmos came into being with a gesture, a Big Bang, a flinging away of Self from itSelf into a multitude of galaxies, whose momentum continues to fling them into ever further distances of separation.[†]

Figure 26　The dancing god, Shiva, brings about creation through the six gestures

---

[*] *The Actor of the Future 1*, Chapter 1.
[†] *The Art of Acting*, Context, Chapter 3 and Epilogue.

There are many depictions of the God Shiva dancing the creation inside the ouroboros. Figure 26 is based on these. Here we see him, legs unfolded, stepping and stamping, imprinting the divine will into earthly matter. His gestures reveal the six degrees of separation and connectedness by which the soul, in recurring interacting cycles of ever greater combinations and complexity, accomplishes her journey.

In Chapters 3 and 4 we explore the Eurythmy gestures that embody the objectives of the creator beings who serve the evolution of the human being. Through their macrocosmic gestures we begin to sense the divine counterparts of these archetypal gestures that embody our soul's journey on the earth. The levels of sensation they engender will be our first intimations of the chaste and more profound and complex sensibilities that Beings at quite other levels of existence pour into the ego's separation drama on the earth so that it can make the journey back to wholeness fully conscious of itself. We shall explore how the consonants and vowels open a pathway to the macrocosmic soul and spirit of our universe that creates us in its likeness.

Chapter 2

Sound Experience (1)
Expanding the horizon of the Vowels

Before embarking on these next levels of investigation and artistic application of the vowels it is important to remember that due to the discrepancy between spelling and pronunciation in the English language*, I have identified the vowel we are considering by citing it's phonetic symbol along with an example.† However, even this attempt will not address all the ambiguities arising from the many variations of accent and pronunciation in the varieties of English spoken in the world.

I have solved this problem for myself by anchoring my research into vowels in the pure placements in the mouth, not as a basis for moral judgements of correct or incorrect pronunciation, but as a compass of experience against which all the variations can be valued for the revelations they provide of the ever changing and evolving spectrum of humanity's experience.

So, for example, I have found it gives a clearer edge to the English diphthong /eɪ/ (d<u>a</u>te) if it is sounded with the pure placement of the /ɛ/(m<u>e</u>n). This leads to a deeper experience in English of how the aspect of the soul encompassed in the pure vowel /ɛ/ (m<u>e</u>n), as identified by Steiner, can be used artistically. Likewise, I have found that to sound the English diphthong /oʊ/(n<u>o</u>) with the placement of the /ɔː/(<u>awe</u>) leads to a deeper experience in English of how the aspect of the soul encompassed in the pure vowel /ɔː/(<u>awe</u>), as identified by Steiner, can be used artistically.

In this sense all of us who are explorers on this path will have a different journey as we follow the map provided by Steiner's insights and the first generations who explored them. The important thing is that we continue to explore and that any discrepancies that might appear between what any of us have discovered can be considered not necessarily as right or wrong but as a valid part of research into something greater than us all. It is in this spirit that I share my discoveries.

The path from Imagination to Inspiration and to Intuition

The work with consonants and vowels undertaken in *The Art of Speech* can be applied to ever more advanced levels of artistic exploration. In these next chapters we cultivate

---

*Explored in detail in *The Art of Speech* pages 17–19 and in Chapter 1, pages 41–69.

† See Appendix B.

the organ of perception that allows us to investigate Steiner's insights into the relationship of consonants and vowels to the macrocosmic beings referred to as the zodiac and planets, and the infinite dimensions they open to the actor's art. In doing so we progress from Imagination to Inspiration and to Intuition. The use of capitals distinguishes the everyday meaning of these terms from Steiner's use of them to denote the stages of spiritual cognition.

In the last chapter we developed our capacity to explore the continuum within a gesture, to expand its tiniest expressions into ever larger forms that enable us to recognise the greater archetypes condensed into their tiny counterparts. We learned in *The Art of Speech* to experience each vowel and consonant as a micro-gesture in the mouth. So too, we can expand into full-bodied gestures, the muscular tensions that cause our larynx and our tongue, our teeth and lips and palate to condense into the micro-gestures that create the sounds. We know that gesture expresses the intention of a being. So now as we learn to move within a sound's continuum from micro-gesture in the mouth to full-bodied gesture, our sensing instrument attunes itself more finely to the nuance of intention embodied in each sound.

Each vowel and consonant becomes a portal through which we can progress to ever higher levels of cognition. Through Imagination we awaken to the living process and dynamic of each sound. Then, as we attune ourselves to stand and move and speak within this process and dynamic, through Inspiration we begin to sense a Presence, greater than our everyday perception of ourselves, who senses through us. And finally through Intuition[*] we become a vessel for the will of that Presence. We are in the realm of Beings who express a great creative gesture in the universe through that specific consonant or vowel. We can explore how the sounds of speech are shaped, not only out of human understanding and experience but out of macrocosmic gestures and intentions that imprint their signature at every level of creation including human character. It is Eurythmy's task to cultivate a sense for these.

First, however, we cultivate Imagination of the vowels.

Ensouling the vowel — sound-experience work

Unless we bridge the gap between experience and language an audience will feel disconnected when an actor speaks. This disconnection was first passionately chronicled by Antonin Artaud. Since then the increasing inability of words to 'communicate' has subsequently led to a theatre that relies on visual effects.[†] Yet, that these

---

[*] *The Art of Speech*, Terms of Reference.
[†] *The Art of Speech*, Introduction.

on their own do not communicate is demonstrated by the fact that they must be enhanced by visual effects and the ever louder decibels of sound or music that are found necessary to elicit an intense response. We may be partly satisfied by this but some aspect of our being is not content to simply 'have experience'. It longs through words to seek and understand the meaning of experience. Have words evolved for just this purpose, only to be made obsolete? Or can our consciousness of words evolve beyond the present intellectual paradigm into a new dimension of reality? One goal of speech formation is to bridge the gap between the sounds of speech and our experience.[*]

Expanding the horizon of our work with vowels

Through the explorations on pages 49–59 of *The Art of Speech* we have learned to sense how vowels reveal the gesture of our soul towards the world.[†] Now we must cultivate these first sensations further until our inner life can be experienced *as* vowel. This involves consciously reversing the deadening process language went through in our childhood. In infancy our inner life declared itself in vowels pulsating with intensity. But our early years in school replaced these living vowels with vacuous chanting as we learned the 'letters' and intoned these abstract symbols that had lost their connection to experience.

The Art of Speech teaches how to tread the pathway back to that original intensity, experience the body-of-sensation that each vowel generates when it penetrates our instrument. The larynx and other organs specifically connected with our speech learn to resonate precisely with each nuance of our inner life, striving to perfect the instantaneous translation from vowel to precise sensation and back again to vowel.[12] These first explorations cultivate a closer integration of our soul life with the spectrum of the vowels.

Vowel exploration 1

1. In as many moments of the day as you are able, become still.
2. Pay attention to sensation/s in your soul.
3. Try matching vowels to each sensation until you find the one that most closely corresponds.

---

[*] *Art of Speech*, Chapter 1.

[†] *The Art of Speech*, Chapter 1.

Vowel exploration 2

It is possible to colour any vowel with any sensation or emotion. Indeed it is one of our artistic goals to be capable of this. But your goal in this exploration is to find the vowel which most exactly corresponds to each nuance of response.

1. Make use of an event or environment such as a beautiful garden, a neighbourhood slum, a shopping mall, the ocean in a storm or a peaceful sunset. For five minutes attune your body/soul/spirit to the sensations that arise as you immerse yourself in the environment and atmosphere.
2. Search for the vowel sensations that most closely correspond to sensations aroused by the experience .

Vowel exploration 3

Once again, choose an environment rich with sensation, but this time, work in reverse.

1. Choose a specific vowel and let its nuance of expression determine your response to the environment. Express this response in movement and gesture.
2. Only speak the vowel when you are totally inside the experience it offers of the scene around you.

Vowel exploration 4

1. Back inside your practice space, recreate these journeys of sensation in full-bodied movement.
2. Speak the vowel when it arises organically, integrated with your movement.

A study of Eurythmy strengthens your growing sensitivity to the nuance of each vowel and its capacity to permeate your psycho-physical/body-soul gestalt.

Vowel exploration 5

1. Listen with your whole instrument while someone able to ensoul the vowels sounds each one in turn.
2. Allow each sound to penetrate your instrument from the tips of your fingers right into your feet.

3. Let your body-of-sensation evolve into a full-bodied gesture for each one.
4. Inhabit the full-bodied gesture while you speak the vowel.
5. Reduce the outer gesture while you speak the vowel.
6. Refine the gesture further into a thoroughly penetrated naturalistic expression of the precise nuance of experience embodied in that vowel.
7. Alternate between naturalistic and full-bodied gestures.
8. Explore the relationship between the gesture arrived at by your own investigation and the eurythmy gesture indicated for that vowel in Chapter 5.

The next three explorations require working with a neutral mask. This discourages the tendency to express responses only in your face and encourages the full-bodied gesture engaging feet, legs, hips and torso, shoulders, arms, neck and head. Your whole body now becomes your countenance.

Vowel exploration 6 – partner work

A is performer. B is audience.

1. A, wear a neutral mask.
2. In your imaginary stage-wings, choose a vowel and permeate yourself with its quality.
3. Sustaining that quality silently, enter and move around your imaginary stage. Perform simple actions: sit, stand, approach an object, pick it up, put it down, etc.
4. B try to identify A's vowel quality.
5. B, when you think you know, demonstrate the full-bodied gesture while you speak the vowel.
6. Change roles. B choose a different vowel while A observes.

Vowel exploration 7

1. Repeat steps 1–2 from *Vowel exploration 6*.
2. Enter your imaginary stage and silently perform a simple action permeated with your chosen vowel, such as entering a room or garden, reading a letter or noticing a flower.
3. Demonstrate it to the group or class who must identify it before you speak. When they have succeeded you may speak.

Vowel exploration 8 – partner work

1. A, direct B in a sequence of actions, each one permeated with a vowel. Do not give the next instruction until you are satisfied B has achieved what you ask. For example: *move over to that chair in a quality of* /ɜ/(h<u>er</u>d). *Now speak the vowel gently and as intimately as your breath. Now sit and as you do, change into a quality of* /ɑ:/ (st<u>a</u>r). *Speak the vowel. You glance at the table and see a book. As you do so change to* / i:/(m<u>e</u>). *Speak the vowel. Begin reading and change to* /u:/(sh<u>oe</u>). *Speak the vowel.*[*]

Vowel exploration 9

Speak only when your instrument is thoroughly attuned.

1. Permeate your instrument with each vowel quality in turn, sustaining it and letting it determine your interaction with a neutral object like a small beanbag/juggling ball. Do this with other objects; a piece of fruit, a book, letter, key, etc.

As you become more sensitised you may observe that a vowel attracts emotions. This is illustrated in the images that follow. However, a vowel is a gesture. Gesture expresses *will*. And although that gesture may arouse an emotion or be the consequence of an emotion it is not that emotion. A single gesture can awaken different emotions. For example, the first image shows the soul in the /ɑ:/(st<u>a</u>r) gesture; the will to be open – the emotion might be awe or wonder. However, someone in that the same open gesture might equally be feeling peace, joy, anticipation or the deep acceptance of some painful recognition. Later we shall learn how to layer vowel gestures with particular emotions. For the moment, observe the sensations and emotions that arise when you step across a threshold, each time permeated by a different vowel/soul gesture.

---

[*] See Appendix B.

Set 1 – stepping across a threshold

Figure 27 /a:/(st_ar)

*Figure 28 /æ/(m*a*n)*

Figure 29 /ɛ/(men) /eɪ/(date)

Figure 30 /iː/(me)

Figure 31 Pure vowel /ɔː/(awe), English diphthong /oʊ/(no)

Figure 32 /ɜ/(he̱rd) German ö – Left: serious, Right: comic

Figure 33 /juˑ/(imb<u>ue</u>) /uɪ/ (<u>sweet</u>) German ü – Left: serious, Right: comic

*Figure 34 /ʊ/(sh*o*e)*

Figure 35 /aɪ/(life)

Figure 36 /ɔɪ/ (joy)

Figure 37 /aʊ/(<u>out</u>)

Set 2 – responding to a piece of fruit

In this set, the figure is responding to a piece of fruit. Once again, although an emotion may arise, do not confuse this with the gesture. For example, in Figure 44, the gesture for /ju/(imb<u>ue</u>) /uɪ/ (s<u>wee</u>t) German ü, the tension in the fingers and the whole instrument suggests the will to penetrate with fine discernment. In this case, the emotion is wary or suspicious. However, that same gesture might attract a quality of curiosity or wonder or delight. What is important is to focus on the way in which the same action (responding to a piece of fruit) can be permeated by a different soul/ vowel gesture.

Figure 38/a:/(st<u>a</u>r)

Figure 39 /æ/(m<u>a</u>n)

Figure 40 /e/(men) /eɪ/(date)

Figure 41 /iː/(me)

Figure 42 pure vowel :/ɔː/(awe), English diphthong: /oʊ/(n͟o)

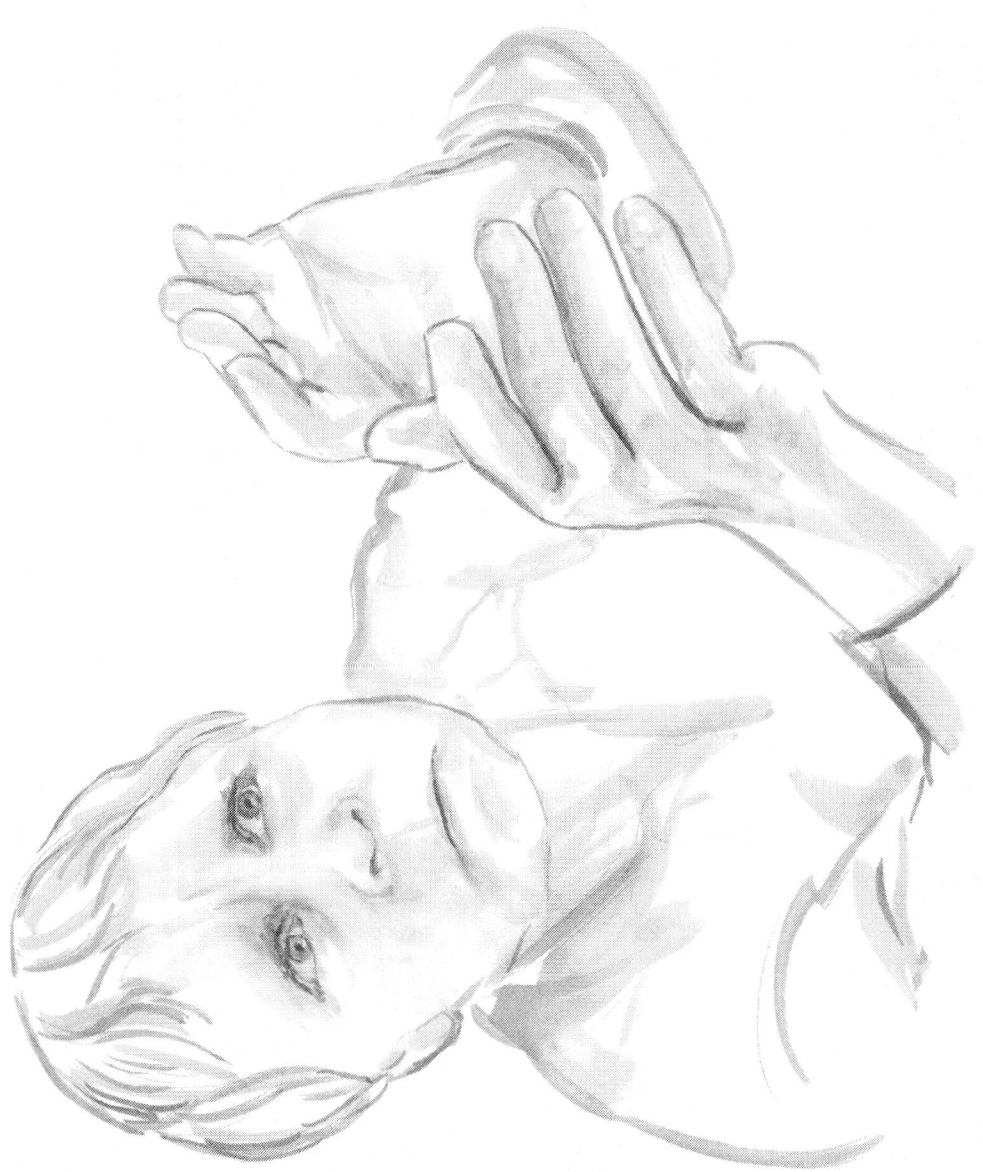

Figure 43 /ʒ/(h<u>er</u>d) German ö

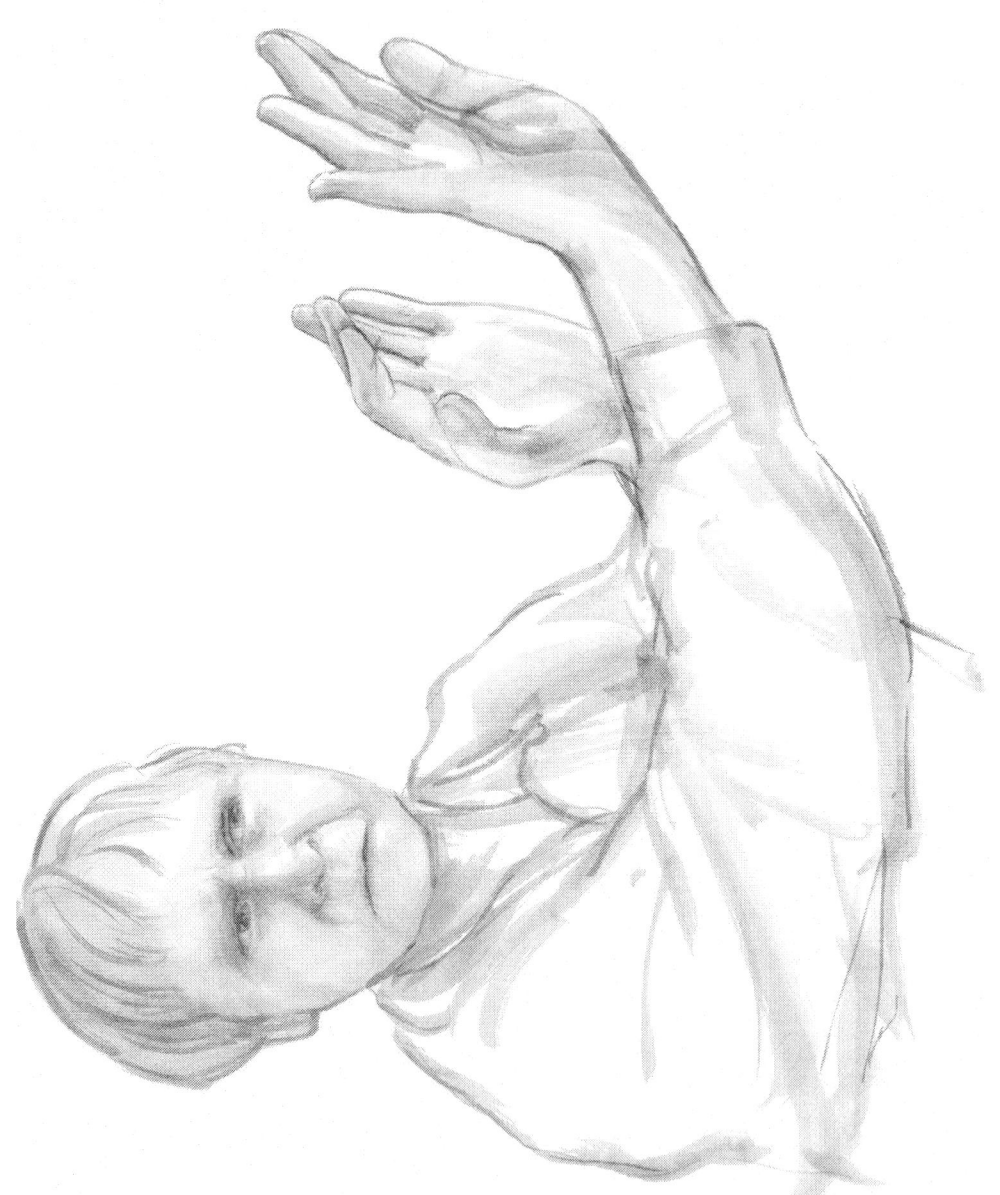

Figure 44 /ju/(imbue) /uɪ/ (sweet) German ü

Figure 45 /u:/ *(sh<u>oe</u>)*

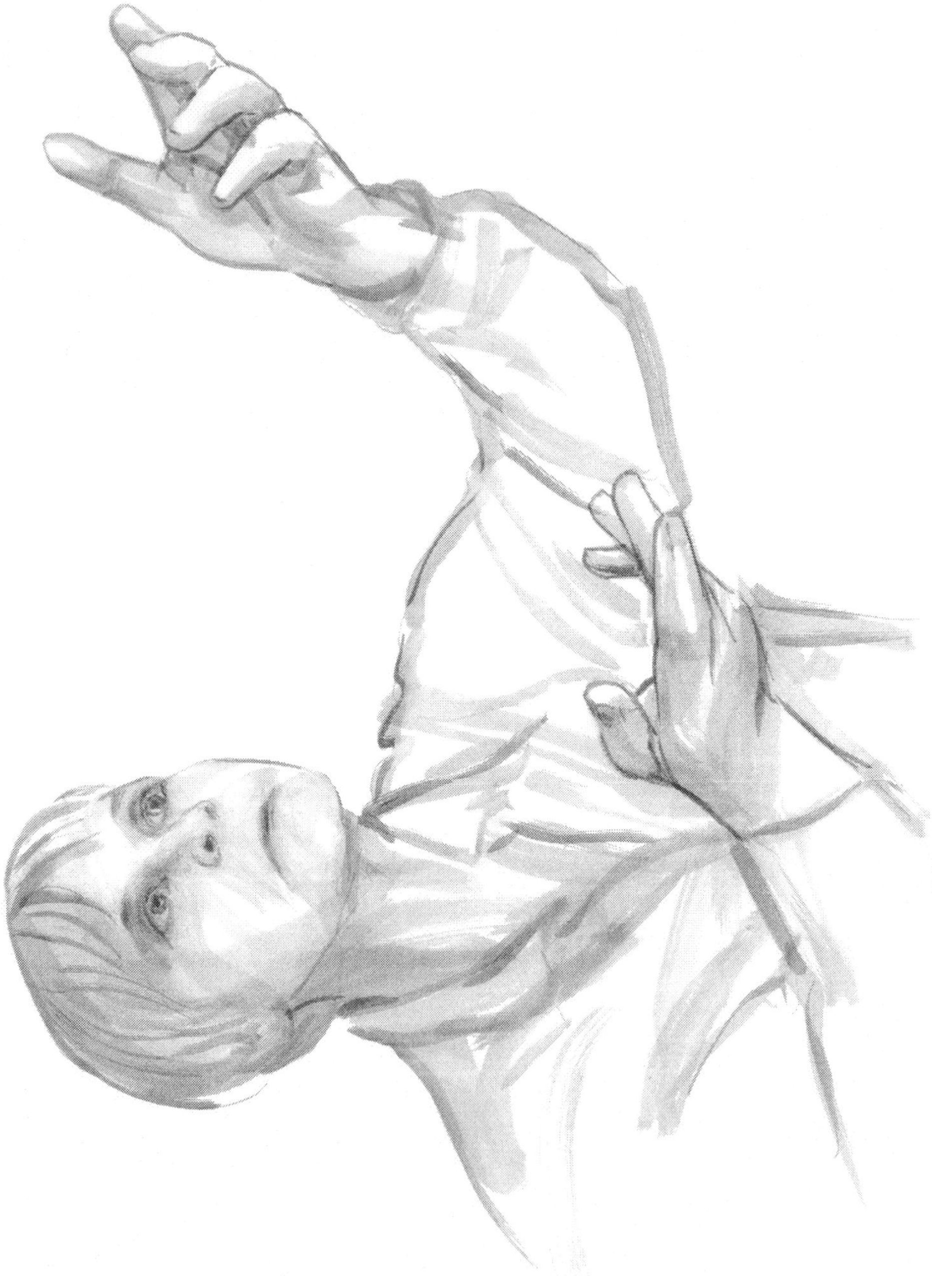

Figure 46 /aɪ/(life)

Figure 47 /ɔɪ/(j*o*y)

Figure 48 /aʊ/(<u>out</u>)

Figure 49 Dipthongs

Figure 50 Circle of the vowels

Try these sets of sequences yourself. Create your own based on other simple actions permeated with each vowel or choice of vowel transformations. For example: reading a letter, searching for a key, or a ring, finding an old photograph.

Having made the distinction between vowel gesture and emotion, we are ready to consciously explore their interaction by integrating vowel work with Chekhov's tool of *quality and sensation.*[*]

Vowel exploration 10

1. Revisit the work with *quality and sensation* as described in *The Art of Acting*, Chapter 3.
2. When you have warmed up your quality of choice, e.g. sadly, tentatively, confidently, fearfully, etc., experiment until you find the vowel/s that have the most affinity with that sensation.
3. Speak them, allowing them to radiate through your full-bodied instrument.

Vowel exploration 11

As mentioned earlier, specific vowels may suggest particular emotions but should not be exclusively identified *with* those emotions. The vowel is a *gesture* of the soul. To learn to distinguish soul-gestures from emotions,

1. attune yourself to a specific vowel.
2. when your whole instrument is permeated with its gesture, layer your gesture with specific qualities in turn. For example: the vowel /ɔː/(awe) in qualities of sadly, shyly, hopefully, angrily, joyfully, compassionately, etc. This should begin to clarify the difference between the vowel gesture and the emotion or feeling that can permeate that vowel.

On the basis of these explorations we approach the indications Steiner gave regarding how to work with a specific vowel in connection with a feeling or emotion.[13] In the way he indicates specific movements/gestures in relation to specific sounds, we recognise how profoundly Steiner understood the intimate relationship between the soul and body that Chekhov labels *psycho-physical*. A systematic methodology for actors based on this is the aim of the deeply grounded process developed in The *Art of*

---

[*] *The Art of Acting*, Chapter 3.

Acting and *The Art of Speech*. It allows us to approach his indications as opportunities for research and discovery.

Vowel exploration 12 – vowel moods from Shakespeare

We have learned to permeate especially created speech exercises with their corresponding vowel qualities[*] and are now ready to experiment with text that has *not* been especially designed for our purpose. These cameos from Shakespeare's plays allow us to practice permeating a dramatic moment with a vowel gesture, crystallised into a few lines of text. It will help to focus on the task in hand if our character development is simple. A Chekhov tool or two such as *centre, archetype, atmosphere* or *PG* and *objective* will suffice to establish the basis of the mood or interaction, for example: the choice of an archetype such as 'king' or 'miser' or 'lover': or an atmosphere of a moonlit night or a seashore after a terrifying storm: or a quality such as 'bitterly' for Shylock and 'sincerely' for Portia.[†] Of course, you need to have a basic understanding of the character and given circumstances. All the characters can be attempted by everyone, regardless of gender. The following vowel suggestions are not definitive. Let your own artistic instinct suggest other choices and examples. Your goal is to make a choice and then achieve it.

1. *The Tempest*, Act I, Scene 1
Vowel mood /a:/(st<u>a</u>r)

Situation: The young prince Ferdinand is washed up on the shore of Prospero's island, believing his father and companions have been drowned in the tempest that wrecked their ship. He hears Ariel's enchanted music.

> *Ferdinand*: Where should this music be? I' the air or the earth?
> It sounds no more; and sure it waits upon
> Some God o' the island.

2. *King Lear*, Act IV, Scene 2
Vowel mood /ju/(imbue) /uɪ/ (sw<u>ee</u>t) German ü for Lear, /ɔ:/(awe) for Cordelia

Situation: Lear, driven mad by the betrayal of his two daughters, Goneril and Regan, has been rescued from their cruel pursuit by his third and youngest daughter, Cordelia. He wakes up in her tent and after some confusion recognises her and expresses his remorse for how he treated her.

---

[*] *The Art of Speech*, Chapter 1.
[†] *The Art of Acting*: Archetypes, page 230; Atmosphere, page 179 and Quality, page 176.

Lear: If you have poison for me I will drink it.
              I know you do not love me. Your two sisters
              Have, as I do remember, done me wrong.
              You have some cause. They have not.

Cordelia: No cause! No cause!

3. *Twelfth Night*, Act 1, Scene 5
Vowel mood /iː/(m<u>e</u>) for Viola, /aʊ/(<u>out</u>) for Olivia

Situation: Viola, a young woman shipwrecked and washed up on the shores of Illyria, has disguised herself as a youth and found employment with the duke, Orsino. She has been sent to woo Olivia on his behalf. Olivia has learned to defend herself from unsolicited attentions with a mask of ice-cold arrogance. Her defence is pierced by the young messenger.

Viola: I see you what you are, you are too proud.
          But if you were the devil you are fair ...
          My lord and master loves you: O such love
          Could be but recompensed, though you were crowned
          The nonpareil of beauty!

Olivia: How does he love me?

4. *Twelfth Night*, Act 1, Scene 5
Vowel mood /aʊ/(<u>out</u>) into /ɜ/(h<u>er</u>d) German ö for Olivia

Situation: Olivia, wealthy, beautiful and longing for true love, has held herself aloof from the attentions of the many suitors who pursue her. She is shocked and bewildered to find herself attracted to the young messenger who has delivered the latest suit from Duke Orsino and whose sincerity has pierced her mask.

Olivia: How now!
          Even so quickly may one catch the plague?
          Methinks I feel the youth's perfections
          With an invisible and subtle stealth
          To creep in at mine eyes.

5. *Hamlet*, Act 1, Scene 1
Vowel mood /uː/(sh<u>oe</u>) for all four characters.

Situation: On the castle battlements at midnight, the soldiers wait with Hamlet's friend, Horatio, to see if the ghost of Hamlet's father will appear again.

(The older Hamlet's ghost and Horatio are present but silent.)
Marcellus: Peace, break thee off. Look where it comes again.
Bernardo: In the same figure like the king that's dead.
Marcellus: Thou art a scholar; speak to it Horatio.
Bernardo: Looks it not like the king? Mark it, Horatio.

6. *The Merchant of Venice*, Act IV, Scene 1
Vowel mood /i:/(me) for Portia, /ɛ/(men) /eɪ/(date) for Shylock

Situation: The beautiful Portia has disguised herself as a lawyer in order to plead in court for the life of Antonio, friend of her beloved, Bassanio. Since there is no point of law that can prevent the moneylender Shylock from taking his revenge by cutting a pound of flesh from Antonio's body, she appeals to Shylock's mercy.

> *Portia*: Then must the Jew be merciful.
> *Shylock*: On what compulsion must I? Tell me that.

7. *The Merchant of* Venice, Act 5, Scene 1.
Vowel mood /aɪ/(life). Both characters can begin in this but Jessica can change to /ɜ/ (herd)

Situation: In the drenched-in-moonlight orchard of Portia's home in Belmont, the two lovers celebrate their elopement.

> *Lorenzo*: The moon shines bright. In such a night as this,
>   When the sweet wind did gently kiss the trees
>   And they did make no noise, in such a night
>   Troilus, methinks, mounted the Trojan walls
>   And sighed his soul toward the Grecian tents,
>   Where Cressid lay that night.
>
> *Jessica*:   In such a night
>   Did Thisbe fearfully o'ertrip the dew
>   And saw the lion's shadow on herself
>   And ran dismayed away.

8. *The Merchant of Venice*, Act III, Scene 2
Vowel mood /ju:/(imbue) /uɪ/ (sweet) nearest to German ü for Bassanio, /ɛə/(dare) nearest to German ä for Portia, changing to /ɔɪ/(joy)

Situation: Bassanio and Portia have declared their love but cannot marry unless he chooses the right casket. He has rejected the gold and silver ones and now approaches the lead. Both know that their future happiness depends on this choice.

Bassanio: But thou, thou meagre lead,
　　　　　　Which rather threatenest than provest aught,
　　　　　　Thy paleness moves me more than eloquence;
　　　　　　And here choose I: joy be the consequence!

Portia:　 How all the other passions fleet to air,
　　　　　　As doubtful thoughts, and rash embraced despair,
　　　　　　And shouldering fear, and green eyed jealousy!
　　　　　　O love,
　　　　　　Be moderate; allay thy ecstasy:
　　　　　　In measure reign thy joy; scant this excess.
　　　　　　I feel too much thy blessing; make it less,
　　　　　　For fear I surfeit.

Vowel exploration 13 – Layering the vowels with character

We will use Hamlet to explore how the archetypal gesture of each vowel is modified when it is layered with the choices that create a character.

1. Use *visualisation and incorporation* to arrive at a short sequence of actions that embody these three moments:
   a. In Wittenberg Hamlet is informed by letter of his father's death, his mother's subsequent marriage to his uncle and his uncle's coronation.
   b. Back in Elsinore, observing them together, Hamlet understands not only is his mother married to his uncle but loves him passionately.
   c. Hamlet finds the letter from Ophelia informing him that she must have no further contact with him.
2. Polish your sequences and use them to explore his objectives at this point. Arrive at a PG to express the one you choose, for example: *I want to expose the lies. I want to tear off the masks. I want to know the truth. I want to know if I can trust you. I want to kill Claudius. I want to force my mother to look at herself,* etc.
3. Use your PG to dive into Hamlet's intensities and while sustaining those intensities, explore each vowel gesture.
4. Layer each one in turn until each vowel is permeated with the PG, and the PG permeated with the vowel.
5. When your whole instrument is ready to support your speech, speak the vowel.
6. Play with the following words and phrases based on or from the text, allowing each word to call forth a response in Hamlet's soul. Feel free to add others to the list. Explore how the range of vowels, layered with the character's PG, allows you to

taste each word until you are able to express precisely through your voice, the range of nuances in Hamlet's soul.

/aː/(f<u>a</u>r) *Father! Mother! Uncle! Laugh!*

/æ/(th<u>a</u>t) *a rat! a man! a plan! stand! mad!*

/ɛ/(m<u>e</u>n) and /eɪ/ (formed with placement for /ɛ/(m<u>e</u>n) *Traitor! Take revenge! Hesitate! Fate! Hate! Get away! Play. Shame! Pray! Friend.*

/ɪ/ /iː/ *prince! flee! free! kill a king! Seems. It is. quickly!*

/oʊ/ *So alone! No home! no throne! Ghost!*

/ɜ/ *search further! learn to assert, learn to hurt! Curst! murderer! world, earth.*

/uː/ /ju/ *weak willed, refuse to collude with you! beauty's illusion! stupid! useless! puke!*

/uː/ *Through doom to truth! Look for proof! Prove it's true! You fool!*

/aɪ/ *vile, I, mine, smile, lie, try.*

/ɔɪ/ *destroy! joy! Avoid! Void!*

/aʊ/ *crowd, vow, how? Coward!*

7. When you are confident in this sequence of vowel transformations, move back and forth in any order. Resist the temptation to move to the next before your instrument is thoroughly transformed.

8. Steps 1–5 can be replaced by the simpler process of working with a full-bodied gesture that expresses Hamlet 'carrying the weight of the world on his shoulders'.

Mapping a character's soul journey using a progression of vowels

Chekhov shows how to use a sequence of PGs to map the inner journey of a character.[14] Actors fluent in the language of the vowels can translate that map into a vowel-sequence that encapsulates the inner journey and provides strong entry points into the text. This vowel-map may well reveal a fundamental soul or vowel tendency within the character – an aspect of the work we will develop later.

In order to demonstrate this process, I have reduced the complex journeys of two characters to a few outstanding features. Once again, the choices I suggest are not definitive but illustrate the possibilities. The map that follows is no substitute for the layers required to build a complex character. In fact, it is a culmination of the character creation work described in *The Art of Acting* and the intimate relationship with vowels developed through *The Art of Speech* as well as in this chapter. Trying out the following suggestions for Lear and Olivia or arriving at your own map for these or any other characters assumes that preliminary work. The completed map would be a full-bodied, integrated speech and movement sequence, threaded with moments of the text that can be used at any time to warm up to your character, either for rehearsal or performance.

Vowel exploration 14 – mapping the soul journey of King Lear

- Lear's soul-journey starts with arrogant power or *hubris* /iː/(me)
- moves into growing bewilderment and hurt /ɜ/(he<u>r</u>d)
- that alternates with rage /eɪ/(d<u>a</u>te) [formed with placement for /ɛ/(m<u>e</u>n)]
- releases into madness /ɛə/(d<u>are</u>) and /u/(sh<u>oe</u>)
- and re-emerges as the newborn child /aː/(st<u>ar</u>) and /ɜ/(he<u>r</u>d).
- Lear grows in compassion and self knowledge /iː/(m<u>e</u>) and /ɔː/(<u>awe</u>)
- and devotion to the spirit who redeemed him. /ɔː/(<u>awe</u>)
- His increasingly refined sensibilities /ju/(imb<u>ue</u>) /ʊɪ/ (sw<u>ee</u>t)
- follow her in death across the threshold /uː/(sh<u>oe</u>)
- and his spirit is released /ɛə/(d<u>are</u>).

Vowel exploration 15 – Mapping the soul journey of Olivia

Olivia's journey in *Twelfth Night* is very different.

- She begins in the /ju/(imb<u>ue</u>) of arrogance which is a mask however to protect
- her integrity /iː/(m<u>e</u>)
- and vulnerability /ɜ/(he<u>r</u>d)
- and her longing for a true meeting /ɔː/(<u>awe</u>).
- When the mask is pierced /ɜ/(he<u>r</u>d)
- she is without defences /aː/(st<u>ar</u>)
- confused by the new sensations and the identity of the one she loves /ɜ/(he<u>r</u>d)
- but finally able to unite with him /ɔː/(<u>awe</u>) and /aʊ/(<u>out</u>).

Chapter 3

Sound Experience (2)
Vowels as key to Laughing and Weeping

Laughing and weeping

The ability to weep or laugh convincingly on stage may be part of what constitutes an actor's talent, but actors who rely solely on personal emotional recall to fuel their performances may not find it easy to repeatedly invoke these levels of response. Unless we respond truthfully, we cannot be convincing. Yet even if it proves possible, for instance, to weep with extreme grief night after night during a long season of performances, it's psychically draining to keep drawing on such intensity of personal emotion without an objective way to access and contain it. Steiner has suggested that the soul states that result in laughing and weeping can be accessed objectively by working with specific vowels.[15]

To appreciate the wisdom of his insights we must explore the psycho-physical process that happens in us when we laugh or weep and identify its archetype. Then we can learn to activate the reflex consciously that in our everyday experience kicks in unconsciously. The intimate relationship between emotion and what happens in our body when we laugh or weep is not straightforward. We know that linking tears to grief or sadness, and happiness to laughter is too simple, for we can laugh in moments of great pain or cry with joy. Sometimes we don't know whether to laugh or cry, and there are times when we laugh until we cry, or vice versa. Weeping can occur on a scale anywhere between a snivel and a gut-wrenching howl, and laughter anywhere between a slight chuckle and a side-splitting shriek.

We also know that what is funny to an audience will mostly not be funny to the character/s involved who, on the contrary, are often in excruciating pain or torment. It is well known that Anton Chekhov wrote his great full length plays to be performed as comedies and disagreed with Stanislavski who viewed the characters and their predicaments as tragic. Their altercation demonstrates our complex relationship to these responses.

Whatever the degree or cause of our response, we want to investigate the processes by which our physical, etheric and astral bodies, sometimes gently, sometimes violently, reorganise their interaction in order to regulate and re-establish equilibrium between our inner life and outer circumstances. The explorations in Chapter 2 have developed our ability to translate vowels into experience and back again. This ability enables us to recognise the processes that culminate in tears or laughter as vowel-states.*

Weeping

Exploration 1 – weeping

Observe yourself and others weeping. Regardless of context, particular emotions or levels of intensity, identify the psycho-physical stages of the process. The following is my subjective stream of consciousness attempt:

An event or word breathed in before my so soft soul, unready, could mount defence or stop that lung-startling, searing breath, excoriating flimsy organs, skin too frail to wrap a membrane round this tiny bit of everything, keep intact delusion of my separate self, protect it from the vasty deeps.

Now that tide of life sweeps over me, inside me on a gasp. Life I did not want to know has sought me out and lodged within. Soul not ready to digest, to recognise, to feel this thing, accept this bit of universe, this pain, belongs to me.

Keep it at bay, keep me from feeling it! Hold my breath while desperate, faster than thought, I weigh the options! Pain! Too high a price to pay for selfhood. Better to stop breathing, hold my breath until I die, rather than let my bodybound spark of consciousness, clung to so dearly, become driftwood in the flood.

Unless you find the strength right now to cough it up, to push it back, that unfelt gasp solidified inside you, frozen, swallowed whole, unless . . . you find the courage to release it, and feel it as you breathe it out. Or will you hold it still? Pressure building, no acceptance, no release! Better to stop breathing, not to feel!

Urgent now the choice!

Either feel the pain or press the dead breath deeper, years-of- not-relenting pressure-into organs, unresisting bones, illness crushing life that streamed through living cells.

Or can my body push the undigested lump of frozen feeling, breath solidified, back to where I dare at last to feel?

However terrible, not worse than this forever deadness! Then heave it from your lungs, cough up that frozen stone, release the melting waters of emotion, ready to be known, not so awful understanding after all, distilled in tiny drops, cascade and join the greater flow of life again, belong.

---

* And will in turn prepare us to explore how the styles of tragedy and comedy were born from the wisdom of the ancient Greek Logos mysteries in *The Actor of the Future 3*.

The release of tears accompanies the breathing-out that raises our emotion into consciousness, granting insight into what is felt. It shows how our soul, which functions in us through the airy element, is woven with our life/etheric-body which functions in us through the watery element.

It's easier to observe all the stages of this process in situations where the soul takes longer to accept and integrate experience. But slow or quick, we can extract the following pattern from our observations. There is an interruption to the normal rhythm of our breath. We gasp in air, again, again, and hold it while the tension builds and presses ever deeper down into the body. When it cannot take in any more or hold it longer, the body pushes back, expelling it in bursts. Each release is followed by a further sharp intake of breath that in its turn is held until the weeper is forced by necessity to gasp it out: a series of cascading spasms that occurs only when the peak of pressure has been reached. If a bout of weeping is prolonged this process establishes a rhythm of its own.

Having identified the archetype of the psycho-physical dynamics taking place we can recreate it in a full-bodied sequence according to our Chekhov principle. If we polish this movement sequence into a little work of art, it provides us with a template that, in combination with our tools for character development, enables us to access and truthfully portray the many levels and degrees of weeping experienced by different characters in different circumstances.

We are ready to explore how this template calls forth a response from our vowel-sensing instrument; a first step towards the integration of our soul experience of weeping, with language.

Exploration 2 — vowels and the archetype of weeping

1. Imagine and express full-bodily that you are *floating* in the sea of life, at one with it, riding its waves and carried by its currents.
2. Now imagine being battered by great tidal waves. They engulf you and sweep you away.
3. Gasp in your breath and hold it to prevent you swallowing the wave. Stop breathing and hold that gasp inside you. You will die if you do not breathe again but if you breathe again you will only take in water. Meanwhile your body continues to be swept up in the tide of life.[*]
4. Make a conscious choice to fight, push back against the tide. Gather all your

---

[*] *The Art of Acting*, Chapter 1: *floating*.

strength into a full-bodied gesture and when you sense your strength is great enough to push it back, and you cannot hold your breath any longer, tip the balance and push your breath out as you push back against the wave.

5. You will experience the reflex to gasp in again. Once the reflex is activated let it take its course. Surrender to the impulse to gasp in and release, gasp in and release.

6. Observe how the reflex attracts particular sensations or emotions.

7. Work with these according to the process for *qualities and sensations.*[*] Layer the weeping reflex with each quality in turn and in varying degrees of intensity.

8. Pay attention to the body-of-sensations aroused by the tension-and-release stages of the full-bodied weeping template. Identify which full-bodied vowel-states most express the tension[†] and which express release.

9. When you have made your own discoveries, experiment with Steiner's indication that release into weeping can be accessed by attuning to the German vowel ä to which the nearest English vowel is the diphthong /ɛə/(d<u>a</u>re).

10. Recreate the tension and release with the full-bodied vowel sequence : [tension − /ɛ/(m<u>e</u>n) into release /ɛə/(d<u>a</u>re)]. Once this is established reduce the movement from level 10 to level 1 without losing the intensity.

Exploration 3 – vowels and weeping – artistic application 1

We are now ready to apply this template to the moment where King Lear weeps in Act 2 scene 4:

> What! Fifty of my followers at a clap,
> Within a fortnight? . . . Life and Death! I am ashamed
> That thou hast power to shake my manhood thus,
> That these hot tears which break from me perforce,
> Should make thee worth them . . .

1. Identify the sequence of interactions culminating in the wave that finally engulfs the king. Choose one or two Chekhov tools to access his intensities. Having endured the humiliation of Goneril's deliberate rejection and attempt to strip him of authority, Lear learns she has dismissed half of his retinue and left him with 50 men. Apply your full-bodied template to this moment: *I am swept away by the wave of her action and I gasp it in, swallow it whole and let the pressure of it build inside as I*

---

[*] *Art of Acting*, Chapter 3.

[†] Suggestion: /ɛ/(m<u>e</u>n).

flounder in the maelstrom, not yet able to allow myself to feel the pain, humiliation, grief and so much else.

/ɛ/(m*e*n)

2. *Hold your breath and tension inside* (level 10) and when you can hold your breath no longer, find the strength to push back against the pressure. As it releases, release your breath and voice in /ɛə/(dare): *This lets you feel his grief.*

3. Explore and identify the *qualities and sensations* aroused by the interaction of this template with your work on Lear's character, and play with the words. Let them cascade, like his tears, between the spasms of his breath. Explore how Shakespeare's sense of phrasing, sound and rhythm support the pain's insistence to express itself in words within the broken stream of breath.

4. Once your full-bodied journey is secure, explore reducing it from level 10 and making it your 'actor's secret'.

Exploration 4 – vowels and weeping – artistic application 2 – partner work

Our second example is from Act 1 of Anton Chekhov's *Cherry Orchard*. Lyubov has returned to her family estate and is confronted by Trofimov, who had been the tutor of her son before he drowned. Seeing him, she is overwhelmed by the tide of grief she has repressed in the intervening years. Now she embraces Trofimov, pressing her stifled breath/grief into him, until the dam bursts. As her breath is released, so her grief cascades in his supporting arms. Play with the power of the template to call forth the depth of her emotion and support her language. When you have completed the process, A and B reverse roles.

> *Trofimov*: Petya Trofimov, I was Grisha's tutor … Can I have changed so much?
>
> *Lyubov*:   (*embraces him, quietly weeping*) My Grisha, my little boy … Grisha … my son … my little boy dead, drowned … Why? Why, my friend?

We are now ready to condense our integrated body/voice template into a mantra that invokes an experience of weeping that is both truthful and artistic.

Exploration 5 – vowels and weeping – partner work

1. A and B throw a beanbag back and forth. Build in intensity and imagine that the bag thrown at you is a blow of fate delivered by each other.

2. Let your whole body tense as you grip the beanbag tightly, at the same time inhaling sharply with the shock. Holding your breath, contract your whole instrument around the beanbag/'source of pain'. Increase the pressure as you press the shock more deeply into the unconscious realm inside you.

3. When it becomes unbearable, release your breath and beanbag together, letting them drop to the earth.

4. As soon as you release your breath, obey the reflex to gasp in again. Repeat the sequence of pressure and release again. Gasp in, hold, release. Gasp in, hold, release.

5. Explore how the depth and quality of weeping is determined by how much breath is taken in and the depth to which you let it penetrate. It can be shallow, penetrating no more deeply than the shoulder blades, or very deep, pushing down below the diaphragm into the abdomen and even down into the feet. Another factor that affects the quality of weeping is time and rhythm: whether it manifests in quick short spasms of breath or longer, deeper ones. Play with the whole range of possibilities.

6. Integrate these breath and movement sequences with the vowels that most effectively encapsulate the stages of tension and release. Besides the already mentioned tension of /ɛ/(men) what also works for me is /ɜ/(herd) [nearest to German oe or ö] and uttered as a glottal stop, or /ju/(imbue) [nearest to German ü] that then releases into the diphthong /ɛə/(dare) [nearest to German ä].

7. During this process, observe what emotions surface. Allow yourself to feel them. This is what you want and it demonstrates the psycho-physical process is working; full-bodied permeation leads to reliable sensations and emotions that because they are accessed objectively, can be equally objectively relinquished.

Exploration 6 – vowels and weeping

If a scenario suggests itself within the sequence of sensations, follow its impulse, but don't manufacture one. Focus on the process of weeping and resist getting caught up in a situation that distracts you from the purpose of the exercise, which works effectively without a predetermined context.

1. Warm up a *quality and sensation*, for example: sadly, shamefully, bitterly, compassionately, angrily, joyfully, hopefully.[*]

2. Layer each one with the stages of *vowel exploration 5*.

---

[*] *The Art of Acting*, pages 176–179.

Exploration 7 — vowels and weeping

1. Replace the beanbag with a series of objects, e.g. a letter, ring, photograph, handkerchief, ball, piece of furniture, garment, candle, etc.
2. Repeat the process of explorations 5 and 6. Sometimes allow the object to inspire the quality and sometimes let the quality inspire your connection to the object.

Exploration 8 — vowels and weeping

1. Apply the stages of *vowel exploration 5* and experiment with weeping while you speak. As you release the diphthong /ɛə/(d<u>a</u>re) [nearest to German ä] from the tension of /ɛ/(m<u>e</u>n) try simple words and phrases like *no, yes, it's too late* and *I never knew*, letting them emerge within and permeated by the vowel quality.
2. Experiment until you can coordinate breath, sounds, words and imagination so that weeping does not obliterate or blur the clarity of what you say.
3. Experiment with simple words or phrases that arise, for example: *no, oh no, I never knew, if only I had known*, allowing them to cascade like the tears themselves, within the /ɛə/(d<u>a</u>re) quality. Once again, your goal is verbal clarity within the distortions weeping generates.

Exploration 9 — vowels and weeping

Apply your vowel explorations of weeping to specific characters. Unless you've worked on one of these before, don't attempt to build a complex character, but make just a simple choice such as PG layered with a *quality and sensation*. You need to be anchored in the character enough to practice speaking text while weeping. Here are some examples to get started.

- Sonia and Vanya at the end of *Uncle Vanya* by Anton Chekhov.
- Andromache in *The Trojan Women* by Euripides.
- George at the end of Act 3 and Martha at the end of *Who's Afraid of Virginia Woolf?* by Edward Albee.
- Coriolanus with his mother before he marches on Rome. Act 5, scene 3 of Shakespeare's *Coriolanus*.
- Miss Quadling at the end of *Night on Bald Mountain* by Patrick White.
- Desdemona in several moments from Shakespeare's *Othello*, particularly the willow song scene, Act 4, scene 3.

- King Lear in Act 2 scene 4 (see exploration 14) and Cordelia in *King Lear*, Act 1 and Act 4 scene 1.
- Imogen in Act 4, scene 2 of *Cymbeline* when she wakes up beside what she thinks is her dead husband's headless body.
- Pericles and Marina when they recognise that they are father and daughter in Act 5 scene 1 of *Pericles*.
- Faust when he is called back from suicide by the Easter bells. Goethe's *Faust* Part 1, end of scene 1, night in Faust's study.

We have worked to integrate bodily reaction, soul sensation, breath and vowel-quality so that through these complex layers of sensation we can still speak clearly. Once this integration has become instinctive, the process of tension and release infused with the vowel shift will trigger weeping. Emotion will be released without invoking it directly. In this way we achieve objective subjectivity; we can be emotionally truthful and, at the same time, fully in control.

When I weep, an impression from the world I am not yet ready to receive has already lodged in me. I bury it deep within my body until my soul is ready to allow it into consciousness. When I laugh, I alternate between *wanting* to receive an impression and holding it at bay until I'm ready.

Laughing

Exploration 10 – laughing

Observe yourself and others when you laugh. What causes you to laugh and what are you actually *doing*? Identify the common factors in each context. Here is my subjective stream of consciousness attempt.

Not again! Disaster! Something said or done, something shocking, unexpected, absurd, ungraspable always seems to happen to ... why me? the shock to normal consciousness, poor soul, accustomed to a universe predictable – one that plays it by the all agreed and recognisable, the understandable by everyone, every NORMAL (that is) everyone, the sensible, the indisputable, the proper rules.

Push it away, O self, this, this time too absurd, too unbelievable reality, hovering just outside the box of yes! Appealing universe of nonsense and absurdity, imperfection infinitely more enjoyable – and is it possible for god too to enjoy a tickle ? Occasional relief from infinite perfection, chuckle beckoning, can't suppress it any longer giggle, not dis-

astrous utterly to take it in, but yet how can I know for sure that death is not the end
and this might be the end of me and then? ... but on the other hand ... push it away ...
no let it in ... no heave it, breathe it far away ... don't let it in, not yet inside me, still a
chance to stay intact, call the shots, control reality, allay the fear of what? That this
might be the death of me? ... But in a universe of rational reality it has not killed me yet
... this ... totally ridiculous, so why not let it in? To hell with rationality and anyway,
just look at me! Still here to tell the tale my almost-died-of-laughing-but-I-didn't, will-my-
sides-yet-hold-me self? Will you stop it!

My subjective mapping of the laughing process, identifies the gesture and sensation of
reaching out to grasp the impression with the vowel placement /ɒ/(d<u>o</u>t) [which in its
longer form of /ɔ:/(<u>awe</u>) is frequently transformed into the diphthong /oʊ/(n<u>o</u>) by
English speakers]. But, before the embrace of this diphthong /oʊ/ can be completed,
the self establishes a boundary between itself and what it cannot grasp, and flings it
away again. The impression is rejected. My instrument recognises this sensation as the
vowel gesture /ɛ/(m<u>e</u>n) which in its longer form is transformed into the diphthong
/eɪ/(d<u>a</u>te) by English speakers.

   The energy required to reject the impression before it can lodge itself inside my soul
activates my diaphragm and the will-placement in my mouth. In spasms, gentle or
extreme, of /h/and glottal stop[16] I nudge or fling the discomfort from my soul pro-
ducing the ripples or explosions known as laughter. This dialogue of alternating
gestures (embrace it – fling it away – embrace it – fling it away) continues until my
soul feels ready to receive the original impression. As the strength of the rejecting
spasm lessens, the laughter subsides into ever more accepting sighs of integration.

Exploration 11 – vowels and laughing – partner work

1. A and B throw a beanbag to each other.
2. Endow the beanbag with different qualities such as a spider, dead rat, used tissue,
   wormy apple, rotten egg, half-eaten sandwich etc. As it touches you, react to it as
   something that is so awkward, startling, unexpected or unpleasant, that you hurl it
   from your space instinctively.
3. From your now-safe distance, reach out to it, approach it, examine it, but even as
   you pick it up, reject it once again.
4. Try this with many different tempos and levels of intensity, responding to the
   impulse that each object stimulates. Always work full-bodily.
5. Integrate the sequence of vowels:

/ɔː/(awe) – reaching out to catch and grasp

/ɛ/(m<u>e</u>n) or /eɪ/(d<u>a</u>te) – establishing a boundary, followed by rejection

6. Expand your gesture of rejection to a full-bodied push or fling and use it to support the activation of your diaphragm to in turn support your breath to form a glottal stop or /h/.

7. When you have coordinated all the elements, layer the process with a sequence of *qualities and sensations* such as mischievously, nervously, openheartedly, cynically, resignedly, joyfully, playfully, etc, at differing levels of intensity.[*]

8. Replace the beanbag with other props.

9. Analyse the qualities and stages of response when someone causes you to laugh. Explore how these relate to the full-bodied template you developed through steps 1–6.

When the vowel sequence (/ɔː/(awe) /ɛ/or /eɪ/) has been firmly anchored in the psycho-physical process (embrace/reject), a simple increase in the speed of alternating /ɔː/and /ɛ/ will activate the same sensation sequence in the lips and mouth that laughter does. As with weeping, this allows the reflex to 'kick in' enabling us to laugh when we choose, and control the way we integrate our laughter with our other choices.

The consonants /p/ and /k/ also encourage the explosive release of breath and voice that happens when we laugh. Use *Poppycock!* to practice this release on a word. Observe the cascade of laughter that follows in its wake.

Exploration 12 – vowels and laughing

Layer the processes of exploration 11 with a character choice that enables you to play with the following examples.

Romeo and Juliet, Act 1, scene 3
The nurse's loud and energetic laugh dominates the space. Perhaps to begin with, Juliet and her mother resist joining in but in spite of themselves cannot help responding, each with very different qualities.

King Lear, Act 1, scene 4
The fool's humour makes Lear laugh in spite of himself.

---

[*] *The Art of Acting*, Chapter 3, Qualities and Sensations.

Henry IV Part 1, Act 2 scene 4
Hal and Falstaff enjoy role-playing Hal's return to court to be rebuked by the king.

Twelfth Night, Act 2, scene 5
Sir Toby Belch, Sir Andrew Aguecheek and Fabian are helpless with laughter at Malvolio's yellow stockinged, cross-gartered reading of the fabricated letter from Olivia.

A Midsummer Night's Dream, Act 2, scene 1
Puck enjoys recounting his pranks to the fairy.

The Cherry Orchard, Act 1
Lyubov's part joyous/part-desperate return to her family estate provides numerous examples of laughter that masks the underlying tragedy.

Chapter 4

Sound Experience (3) — Character-types and vowels

Blood/nerve-sense polarities

Steiner observed that certain human beings live more in the passions and feelings that well up deep within their souls, while others are more awake in their sense perceptions of the world. We experience the former as 'warm blooded' while the latter, who predominantly function through their nerves and senses, appear to us as 'cooler'.[17]

Some may be victims of their tendency while others ennoble its potential. The warm-blooded type can be so self-absorbed and preoccupied with their own inner dramas that they barely register the world outside themselves. Yet someone who ennobles this potential through inner work contributes deep empathy and warm and passionate involvement to the world. On the other hand, the nerve-sense type can degenerate into a highly nervous, agitated person, constantly reacting in a knee-jerk way to every outside stimulus without the means to process their experience or integrate it with their inner life. Yet when such types develop the potential offered by their constitution they evolve into human beings who can see and analyse a situation clearly and objectively.

Probably most of us possess both tendencies in some degree or other and will veer in one direction or the other depending on the situation. Some of us will learn to balance them and reap the benefit that each potential offers. It's important that we do not judge either tendency by the negative aspects of its functioning or regard those who exhibit it as incapable of growth or transformation. Like all our tendencies, these polarities are simply opportunities to gain experience and each potentially can decline into decadence or be refined into its higher possibilities.

Each type provides us with another useful framework for identifying and expressing aspects of a character. It is the I AM Presence in a human being that is able to work consciously with these polarities in order to ennoble them. The simple processes described in *The Art of Acting*[*] will serve to activate this presence in us, making it available for these next explorations.[18]

Steiner observed that the long vowels, /a:/(star), /ɔ:/(awe), the English diphthong /oʊ/(no) and /u:/(shoe) and the diphthongs, /aɪ/(life), /aʊ/(out) and /ɔɪ/(joy) are

---

[*] See pages 118–119 and 248–252.

warm and full. Their warmth originates from deep within our constitution, permeates the world around and spreads across large surfaces. In contrast, others like the long vowel /iː/(m__e__), the English diphthong /eɪ/(d__a__te), and all the short vowels such as/ɛ/(m__e__n), and /ɪ/(s__i__p) and /æ/(m__a__n) sound sharper edged; some pointed, staccato, some flat, some thin, they arouse alert sensations of awakened clarity. We sense that these sharp reactions to the world remain closer to the *surface* of our soul.

Based on observation of these tendencies in life, we will first use Chekhov's tools to lay a psycho-physical foundation for each tendency: one that supports and integrates with Steiner's observations.

Exploration 1 – vowels and blood type – individual and partner work

1. Warm up *radiating*. When you are thoroughly permeated with the fire element, layer it with a *slow tempo* and *legato* dynamic.[*] Then, imagine the warmth radiating through your blood to fill every cell of your body. Sense how the warmth and fire from within wants to pour into the world.
2. Pour it full-bodily.
3. Now integrate it with your *heart-centre*.[†] First work with your undefended heart and focus on your I AM presence. Integrate these choices with the speech placement exercises on the lips.[‡]
4. When you have warmed up your voice, introduce the vowels mentioned earlier: the /aː/(st__ar__), /ɔː/(__awe__), /oʊ/(n__o__) and /uː/(sh__oe__), and penetrate the world with their warmth.
5. Layer radiating fire with the defended heart.[§] Imagine that the fire instead of streaming freely out into the world in a constructive, focused way is blocked and turns in on itself. It becomes so inwardly consuming that you hardly pay attention to the world around you. Anything you do become aware of only adds fuel to the fire within. Let the pressure build until it finally explodes, consuming the surroundings.
6. Express this 'high blood pressure' full-bodily, while playing with the Speech texts and vowels in step 9.

---

[*] *The Art of Acting*, Radiating: pages 64–66 and Legato: pages 104–107.

[†] *The Art of Acting*, pages 136–140 and 159–162.

[‡] Quoted at the end of step 9 they have been introduced in *The Art of Speech*, pages 133–135.

[§] Ibid., page 163.

7. At some point, layer your I AM presence so it permeates and calms the tempest through its active stillness.[*]

8. Moving full-bodily, alternate between the passionate, radiating, giving soul and the passionate, self-absorbed, tormented soul, exploring how to use these vowels to express both the evolved and unevolved examples of this blood-type character; the first pours blessing on the world out of its warmth and inner richness while the other churns around inside itself or pours its burning torment out into the world, consuming everything that comes into its path.

9. Integrate the exercises for these vowels.[†]

/ɒ/(dot) /ɔː/(awe), /ɔə/(door), and /uː/(shoe)
storm wolf roars forth
through door and tomb
bold wolves bored
through door and tomb
doom taught wolves bored
through door and tomb

/ɑː/(star)
the parcel master asks mail
rather marshal crafty Karl

/ɑː/(star)
A bra da ka bra

10. Use them as texts for improvising as you move around the space alternating these two possibilities.

11. Pair up, A and B alternating roles. Continue to improvise full-bodily but enter into dialogue, exchanging the vowels and their exercises as your text.

Exploration 2 — vowels and nerve-sense type — individual and partner work

1. Warm up and layer *staccato* and *fast tempo* with the *head centre*.[‡] Integrate these with an animal who demonstrates strong nerve-sense tendencies; perhaps a bird or deer or rodent whose senses are utterly attuned for fight or flight.[§]

---

[*] *The Art of Speech*, page 151.

[†] Ibid., pages 59–61 (only the vowels referred to in step 3).

[‡] *The Art of Speech*, pages 104–107 and 146–149.

[§] *The Art of Acting*, pages 168–169.

2. Sustaining your full-bodied work, teacher/partner A threaten or attack the class/ partner B with /k/, /t/, /d/, /s/, /f/. Class/B react with /iː/(m<u>e</u>), /eɪ/(d<u>a</u>te), /ɛ/ (m<u>e</u>n) or any of the other shorter vowels.

3. Warm up the vowel exercises for the single sounds supported by your full-bodied work.[*]

4. Layer your I AM presence and experience it penetrate and calm the nervous agitation, leaving you clear and objectively awake. Sustain your full-bodied nerve-sense activity and move back and forth between a nerve-sense person permeated with the I AM presence, and one enslaved to their reactions.

5. Improvise with a partner and then within the group, exploring how these two nerve-sense characters, one evolved, one unevolved, interact. Exchange the vowels and their exercises as your text.

> /eɪ/(d<u>a</u>te)
> lay bending various trays
> facing days labour
> various labour trays
> lay bending facing
>
> /ɪ/(s<u>i</u>p), /iː/(m<u>e</u>) and /eɪ/(d<u>a</u>te)
> quickly finished veered each
> it irritates labours phases
> it irritates labours phases
> veered each quickly finished

Exploration 3 – playing with vowels and both types – individual and group

Vowel explorations 1 and 2 have provided us with four possibilities of character:

> *Blood type ennobled through the I AM presence.*
> *Blood type without the I AM.*
> *Nerve-sense type ennobled through the I AM presence.*
> *Nerve-sense type without the I AM.*

1. Divide into groups of four. Prepare so that all four types are represented in each group.

---

[*] Quoted at the end of step 5 they have been introduced in *The Art of Speech*, pages 59–61.

2. Working full-bodily, improvise the range of interactions that arise between the four types in your group. Exchange the vowel exercises as your text.

3. Swap roles until you each have sampled every type. Observe and compare your responses in each interaction.

4. Rejoin the other groups and continue interacting in the larger group. Continue to swap roles so that there are always an equal number of each type within the group. Sometimes you will engage with the same type as your own, either more evolved or less, and sometimes different. Observe and compare your responses.

5. Share your observations in the group.

Exploration 4 – playing with vowels and both types – individual/group

The following words and phrases demonstrate how these vowel tendencies can express the blood/nerve-sense types. They make a bridge between the basic vowel exercises from *The Art of Speech* and their application to artistic texts that we will look at later.

1. Improvise full-bodily as you integrate these words with steps 1–4 from *vowel exploration 27*.

> Blood without I AM
> O Woe! You wound my soul! My heart is pounding! Doom and gloom!

> Blood with I AM
> Calm down! Don't frown so much!
> You'll drown in your own sorrow.

> Nerve-sense without I AM
> Hither and thither! In such a dither! What's the date?
> He made me late! What a fate! In such a state!

> Nerve-sense with I AM
> Think clearly and then speak! Take a break!

Exploration 5 playing with vowels and both types – partner work

Explorations 1–4 prepare us to explore the exercises Steiner gave to express the interaction of these types.[19] Although translation affects the efficacy of the vowel sounds of the original, I consider it important to include them. Not only have the phrases in *exploration 4* been based on them, but they make a bridge between the archetypes and their application to the complex characters we will consider next. By including them, perhaps they will inspire you to create your own. Begin each inter-action only when you have completed your full-bodied/speech warm up for each type.

A: *blood type with the I AM*
B: *nerve sense type without the I AM*

A: Marked you the pallor of that countenance?
B: I didn't see anything strange in his face.
A: You must look rather at what is crass.
B: Take not my feelings of self from me.
A: Hardly enough on guard are you.
B: I will not take it that you say this.

A: *blood type without the I AM*
B: *nerve sense type with the I AM*

A: True it is. I have offended him.
   Can you blame me for it?
   Hardly was I in the house
   – the door was not yet to –
   Stung me then his most scornful look.

B: Learn to take this life a bit more as it is.
   Don't you see the misery of people everywhere
   Who, in their ignorance, make mistaken decisions?
   – many a heart misleads the head –
   And they, instead of progressing, forever stumble.

A: Ah well, I'll make it good again.
   But can I also hope
   That he'll retract his sharpness?
   How far harsh looks can stab one –
   It bored deep down into my soul.[*]

Exploration 6 – first step towards artistic application of vowels and types

Appendix A contains more dialogues for simple blood/nerve-sense characters .

1. Warm up with the preparations suggested in explorations 1–5.

---

[*] For an alternative English rendering by Mechthild Harkness, see Appendix A.

2. Choose one or two Chekhov tools to create a sketch of the character. For example: animal study, visualisation and incorporation, expansion and contraction, PG and objective. Layer these with the type.

From soul type to individual soul

We are ready to integrate these types with more complex characters who cannot be reduced only to that single tendency. In my own work, I have found that the choice of blood/nerve-sense type contributes a rich layer to a character and confirms its validity by interacting fruitfully with other choices. Exploring type develops skills to create a psycho-physical-vocal basis for a character and makes its greatest contribution when we weave its threads into the complex fabric of the other choices we have made. If you have not worked on these characters before, begin by approaching them as types. Then use your Chekhov tools to layer them with more complexity. Otherwise layer the types with your pre-existing choices.

Exploration 7 – vowels and blood/nerve types advanced application – partner work

This first piece of dialogue from Act 1, Scene 5, between King Lear and his fool suggests the interaction of the nerve-sense type with the I AM (Fool) with the blood-type without the I AM (King).

Fool: Shalt see nuncle, thy other daughter will use thee kindly. For though she's as like this as a crab is to an apple, yet I can tell what I can tell.

Lear: What can'st tell boy?

Fool: She will taste as like this as a crab does to a crab. Canst tell nuncle why one's nose is in the middle of one's face?

Lear: No! Why?

Fool: Why? To keep one's eyes on either side of one's nose, that what a man may not smell out he may spy into.

Lear: I did her wrong.

Fool: Canst tell how an oyster makes his shell?

Lear: No.

Fool: Nor I neither, but I know why a snail has a house.

Lear: Why?

Fool: Why to keep his head in. Not to give it away to his daughters and leave his horns without a case.

Lear: I will forget my nature. So kind a father ... Monster ingratitude!
Fool: If thou wert my fool, nuncle, I 'd have thee whipped for being old before thy time.
Lear: How's that?
Fool: Thou shouldst not have been old before thou hadst been wise.
Lear: Let me not be mad, not mad, sweet heaven. I would not be mad.

The next text from Bernard Shaw's *Saint Joan* suggests the interaction of the nerve-sense type without the I AM (Dauphin) with the blood type with the I AM (Saint Joan).

Charles: ... I cannot do it. I am not built that way; and there's an end to it.
Joan: Blethers! We are all like that to begin with. I shall put courage into thee.
Charles: But I don't want to have courage put into me. I want to sleep in a comfortable bed and not live in continual terror of being killed or wounded. Put courage into the others, and let them have their belly full of fighting but let me alone.
Joan: It's no use Charlie; thou must face what God puts on thee.... Thou must fight Charlie, whether thou will or no. I will go first to hearten thee. We must take our courage in both hands; aye, and pray for it with both hands too.
Charles: Oh do stop talking about God and praying. I can't bear people who are always praying. Isn't it bad enough to have to do it at the proper times?
Joan: Thou poor child, thou hast never prayed in thy life. I must teach thee from the beginning.

Vowels as expression of an individual soul

Identifying the fundamental soul quality of a character

Steiner suggested that a vowel can be a key that unlocks a character's fundamental soul disposition.[20] His examples may seem abstract, simplistic or imposed if we use them as a substitute for developing a nuanced character. However, when integrated into a more complex character they contribute an essential element.

The processes described in *The Art of Acting* and *The Art of Speech* transform our psycho-physical instrument into an organ of perception both for the soul gestures and dynamics that constitute specific characters and for the gestures of the vowels. By means of this new organ – our sensation- body or Chekhov's 'sensitive membrane' – we begin to sense that they are not two different worlds that must be joined but expressions of a single reality.

In Chapter 2 we used King Lear and Olivia from *Twelfth Night* to explore how a vowel sequence can provide a map or template for the significant stages of a character's inner journey that will enable us to recreate them.

It's the soul's nature to be in constant movement in relation to the world and in any situation we may move through a range of emotions. Now we want to see whether, through those shifts and changes, vowels can help identify a character's more fundamental disposition.

King Lear

Here, for example, I will try to convey how vowels helped me find and experience the essence of King Lear's soul. As I use my tools to understand and build the layers of the King, I feel my body-of-sensation stir, begin to sense like him ...

Unquestioning certainty of contours, authority to do as I will, bristling of reaction at the slightest hint of opposition, right to thunder at resistance, bully and demolish. I sense my instrument attuned to /ɪ/(s<u>i</u>p), /iː/(m<u>e</u>), /ɛ/(m<u>e</u>n), /eɪ/(d<u>a</u>te)? *This is no procession of mere passing moments of response but reveals something fundamental in my soul, the contours of my speech as well, colouring, giving edge to my voice* ... and as a str<u>a</u>nger to my heart and m<u>e</u>, hold th<u>ee</u> from th<u>i</u>s for<u>e</u>ver ... b<u>e</u>tter thou hadst not b<u>ee</u>n born than not to have pl<u>ea</u>sed m<u>e</u> b<u>e</u>tter ... <u>e</u>very <u>i</u>nch a k<u>i</u>ng. *Yet this fixed, immutable persona is not the all of me. Shattered, I sense the something more begin to stir, some part that longs to reach out and connect, to truly know another* /ɒ/(d<u>o</u>t), /ɔː/(<u>awe</u>) and /oʊ/(n<u>o</u>). How dost my boy? Art c<u>o</u>ld? *What will it take to release this more of me, allow me to evolve?* ... I did her wr<u>o</u>ng. *At last to know myself:* I am a very foolish f<u>o</u>nd <u>o</u>ld man ... F<u>o</u>ursc<u>o</u>re and upward, n<u>o</u>t an hour m<u>o</u>re n<u>o</u>r less ... N<u>o</u>r I kn<u>o</u>w n<u>o</u>t where I did l<u>o</u>dge last night ... I am <u>o</u>ld and foolish ... *and embrace reality:* N<u>o</u>! n<u>o</u>! n<u>o</u>! n<u>o</u>! n<u>o</u>! Come let us away to prison ... Thou'lt come n<u>o</u> m<u>o</u>re ... O after O after O. This theme will be explored again in Chapter 6.

Shakespeare's unerring genius for matching language and experience helps cultivate our growing organ of perception for the match of vowel and soul. The very vowels uttered in key moments by his characters confirm our insights. Our discoveries however must not tempt us to 'poke' that vowel with crass or shallow emphasis when it occurs. Rather we have learned how to radiate a vowel quality, permeating an entire character or passage with its substance. Now, by attuning to its quality, our voice/body instrument transforms into a vessel for another's soul.

Approaching the planetary beings – vowels as a bridge to higher worlds

Step-by-step, as we explore the relationship between the vowels in speech and gesture and our life of soul, we may start to sense that soul is something more than our subjective feelings and emotions: that these come from somewhere larger than our finite selves. A universal Soul, perhaps? We sense that inwardness is not an accidental side-effect or property of matter but *exists* within a macrocosmic inwardness that is no more perceptible by outer means than is our microcosmic inwardness. Its functioning may register on instruments that measure brain and nerve activity but cannot be *experienced* except by inwardness itself.

Material thinking and perception would reduce our inwardness to measurable cellular secretions and electric impulses. Disciplined devotion to the vowels, no less attentive to phenomena, opens our perception of the macrocosmic inwardness that, not disdaining those cellular secretions or electric impulses, but engaging with our corporeal nature, makes use of them to bestow its gifts and faculties on human souls. Empirical evidence based on outer measurement may reveal the footprints of its passing but does not reveal the source and content of the consciousness that work like this can verify, no less empirically.

As we master this chapter of our work with character, intimations of this deeper mystery begin to stir. To journey further requires that we develop organs of perception for the higher levels of cognition Steiner designated *Inspiration* and *Intuition*.[*] These alone can grant empirical experience that deep within each human character its own beingness is woven through with vaster psychologies than earthly personality alone can generate.

By examining our own experience with rigour, we may learn to trust what we begin to sense; a spectrum of feeling-life exists that is pure and objective, in comparison to which, most of our personal emotions seem, like Hamlet's do to him, *muddied*, dis-ordered, out of harmony. Could it be that our greatest poet was not merely painting pretty pictures in this passage from *The Merchant of Venice*, but describing a reality that once was, and still might be, experienced?

> Look how the floor of heaven
> Is thick inlaid with patines of bright gold.
> There's not the smallest orb which thou behold'st
> But in his motion like an angel sings,
> Still quiring to the young eyed cherubims:
> Such harmony is in immortal souls;
> But while this muddy vesture of decay
> Doth grossly close it in, we cannot hear it.

To imagine the influence within our soul of swirls of gas or lumps of matter stuck up there in space, is certainly *more than cool reason apprehends*. Such a view of planets is

---

[*] *The Art of Acting*, pages 42–43, and *The Art of Speech*, pages 24–25.

enough to dismiss any notion of astrology. Yet quite apart from their influence on life itself, no one can deny that the rhythmic cycles of the sun and moon through day and night and throughout the year affect our inner state. If these arouse in us the range of sensations, thoughts, feelings and emotions that the whole history of poetry bears witness to, why might not all the planets just as surely, just as intimately, influence the way we think and feel?

Figure 51 Archetypal eurythmy gestures for the planetary beings

Through Eurythmy, Steiner has given us a process to develop our body-of-sensation into an organ of perception able to discern how the scale of our microcosmic inwardness, experienced as vowels, is generated by the macrocosmic beings of the Planets, whose activity within us opens up these pathways in our soul. Chekhov's psycho-physical technique reveals how full-bodied gesture grants access to the inner life of character.[*] On this basis, we may regard the planetary gestures discerned by Steiner's more evolved perception as *cosmic psychological gestures* (CPGs).

---

[*] *The Art of Acting*, pages 207–216.

Along with their accompanying vowels they grant access to the inner life of the divine creative beings who inspire our consciousness,[21] and allow us to behold our character-creations through their lens.

Figure 52 Archetypal eurythmy gestures for the cosmic vowel sounds

We learn that a character's psychology is partly the creation of the macrocosmic aspects of the Self that pour their activity into the unique soul configuration of that character. We learn to recognise their greater planetary gestures in the characteristic gestures that identify a human being.

For English-speaking actors, research into Shakespeare's characters reveals the fusion of his insight into character with the sounds of which his words are woven. Through this we start to sense the higher consciousness that has given birth to them and creates the magic that still has power to enchant us. We stand at the next theshold of our work as actors – to be satisfied with portraying character as understood till now – or, with Shakespeare's, Steiner's and with Chekhov's help, to take another step towards the acting of the future.

Chapter 5

Our High Work Masters[22] (1)
Vowels and the Planetary Beings

The Planetary Beings

Fool: The reason why the seven stars are no more than seven is a pretty reason.
Lear: Because they are not eight?
Fool: Yes indeed: thou'lst make a good fool.

In the following excerpt from the lecture, *What has Astronomy to say about the Origin of the Earth?* given in Berlin in 1911,[23] Steiner points to the abyss between material perception of the stars and planets, and the realm of *being*, an abyss which, if anything, has only widened since he spoke these words.[24]

> Imagine the human brain enlarged . . . to such an extent that we could walk about in it and look at the movements in it in the same way as we look at the movements in the celestial bodies. If in these movements of our brain we do not perceive anything of the psychic counterparts of these movements, we need not be surprised that when standing within such an enlarged brain – namely the universe – we cannot find the bridge between the movements of the stars in the heavenly spaces and the possible activities of soul and spirit which extend throughout the world spaces. These have the same relation to the movements of the stars as our thoughts, feelings and soul experiences have to the movements of our own brain substance.

The work we are about to undertake will help create the bridge we cannot find by staring at material phenomena alone.[25]

The ancient Greeks used the word 'planet' to designate the moving bodies in the heavens. To their physical perception, the earth on which they stood appeared to be the still centre around which moved the planets: Moon and Mercury and Venus, Sun and Mars, Jupiter and Saturn.[26] The Greek perspective of an earth centred cosmos has been labelled geocentric. Since the Renaisssance, advances in mathematics and technology have led to the replacement of the geocentric paradigm by the heliocentric view; the body that forms the centre of our solar system is the sun, which is a star, and the bodies that orbit it (including earth) are planets. The number of these planets continues to increase as advances in technology allow us to see ever further into space.

In this framework the moon is not a planet but the earth's satellite. The continuing debate as to whether Pluto should be designated as a planet demonstrates that scientists are still not finally decided on what constitutes a planet. Nonetheless, the heliocentric view is now accepted.

We may ask why Steiner chose to base his eurythmy explorations of the planets on this more ancient geocentric view. There is a much more fundamental difference between the two paradigms than a merely physical perspective. For the geocentric framework arose out of the direct perception the ancients still possessed that the stars and planets related to the earth were spiritual beings who serve the evolution of the human being. Their visible bodies (and their interpenetrating spheres delineated by their orbits and extending out as far as and including Saturn) were only the material indicators of their activity and consciousness.

As physical perception replaced the old clairvoyance and was increasingly confirmed through the research and discoveries of scientists like Galileo (1564–1642) and those who followed, it proved impossible for the materialistic scientific mind to cling any longer to the last remnants of this ancient paradigm: that the underlying fabric of the cosmos was composed of the activity and consciousness of beings. The geocentric cosmos of beings was replaced by a cosmos of material bodies that move around the sun, according to abstract calculable laws, in vast immensities of empty space.

In his poem *The Pulley*, written when the shift in paradigm was just beginning to take hold, the English mystic poet George Herbert (1593–1633) expressed the huge inner revolution taking place as human consciousness increasingly beheld the finished works of nature denuded of divine creative power. He pictures God creating human beings and, in a last gesture to ensure His creatures would not abandon their Creator utterly, bestowing on them every blessing but the gift of rest:

> 'For if I should,' said he
> 'Bestow this jewel also on my creature,
> He would adore my gifts instead of me,
> And rest in Nature, not the God of Nature:
> So both should losers be.'

Steiner recognised that the temporary triumph of the materialistic paradigm is a necessary stage in humanity's development. However, when, through the new art of Eurythmy he gave a pathway to explore the inner nature both of the planets and the constellations of the zodiac, it is not surprising that he based this on the being-oriented geocentric framework.

Through the processes of Speech formation and Eurythmy human beings can develop organs of perception through which we will perceive again, but consciously, the beingness of all creation which humanity had once perceived unconsciously[*]

He understood that we can do this healthily only if we start from the standpoint of ourselves as ego beings, at the centre of our own experience. The ego's challenge is to recover universal consciousness in freedom and without loss of the selfhood it has struggled so long to achieve. That self will be able to maintain its integrity so long as its experience is scrutinised and filtered by the rigour of its own intelligence, wrought in the fire of the self's knowing of itself in the act of knowing. Without this integrity of self to anchor us in our encounter with the macrocosmic consciousness our microcosmic consciousness would risk obliteration.

From Steiner's perspective then, the older paradigm is not simply an expression of primitive naivety to be replaced by our current more sophisticated knowledge. Rather, that former, more intimate human-centred viewpoint is re-evaluated for its equally valid contribution to our understanding. As the material perspectives of the cosmos continue to expand we can be deceived into thinking that the vast amounts of information fed back to earth by the latest scientific instruments will eventually culminate in all there is to know. But if we want to apprehend the consciousness that has condensed itself into the material appearances – not only of our immediate heliocentric planetary system but of the rhythms and configurations populating ever further distances – Steiner suggests our starting point must be to penetrate with new spiritual scientific consciousness the former geocentric paradigm of beingness. Material science now posits multiple, peripheral perspectives. Yet what does it contribute to our lives to be informed of other universes if we do not really know our own? Just as some planets appear to move in a retrograde rotation before they resume their forward path, before we can progress, not just in quantity of information but in wise experience, perhaps we too must first go back and rediscover that our own, nearest cosmos is inhabited with beingness. Only then will we come to know ourselves as meaningful participants in more distant communities of macrocosmic inwardness rather than mere ciphers lost in vast and empty space.[†]

---

[*] *The Actor of the Future 1*, Epilogue.

[†] I am aware that the cosmic paradigm underlying this investigation is the one that has informed the evolution of the western culture within which this present work seeks to illuminate the trajectory of western drama and performance practice and point to its next evolutionary step. The transition from the 20th to the 21st century made many of we 'westerners' aware that the Mayan culture for example had its own cosmology; it arose out of their perception of a different community of Beings who participated in the cycles of its civilisation and worked within a different trajectory. Likewise the indigenous cultures of many continents have cosmologies that arise no less from their clairvoyant perception of the planetary beings and the constellations that have guided their experience, than did the paradigm we are working with arise out of the perception of the ancient cultures that have flowed into the western stream. This

Contd

Steiner understood that actors and eurythmists in our present stage of evolution can only engage in the practical disciplines required if we work in the human/geocentric paradigm: that I in my body am the centre of my own activity and consciousness. Only from this standpoint can I healthily attempt to penetrate as far into other spheres as my organs of cognition will allow, because my consciousness of self remains intact.

The classical form of drama emerges from this geocentric paradigm, based on a central protagonist around whom orbit other characters. Their lives and journeys are viewed through the lens of their relation to the central character. Shakespeare's *Hamlet* is a typical example. But in *Rosencrantz and Guildenstern are Dead*, Tom Stoppard explored an alternative perspective when he made Shakespeare's minor characters the central protagonists in the drama of their experience of Hamlet in their lives.[27]

Each perspective has its own validity. In the multiple universes some scientists now postulate there may be many dramas, each with its own cast constellated round a different central character. But we may also respect and learn to re-evaluate the one in which the human being is the central protagonist on the stage of planet earth. In this scenario the spheres of activity penetrating and surrounding us are packed with the love, unfinished business, and purposeful dynamics of macrocosmic beings constellated in intentional communities to serve our evolution: beings with souls greater than our present separated consciousness conceives, whose spheres of influence expand to the celestial rim and whose vast charismas and psychologies transcend our own.

Recently I watched a documentary in which an astrophysicist described how science has identified the chemical reactions by which the elements that constitute our universe first appeared and then evolved into increasingly complex forms of matter. He went on to demonstrate that human beings can be reduced to the same complex chemical components of which the stars are made and concluded that, like the stars, we are also 'nothing special'. I wrote this in response to his astonishing conclusion.

The Stuff that Stars are Made of

Experts inform us
we're just made of the same stuff as stars —
that's all we are —
nothing special —
nothing to write home about.

---

book in no way claims to represent the only valid cosmology but in a pragmatic way accepts that we can only start from our own experience. Then by developing the organs of perception that the path suggested here makes possible we can use them to explore whatever other cycles of experience our destiny presents us with.

Greater minds than mine
have done the sums
the chemical analyses
and now pronounce
precise choreographies
meridians of meeting
angles of probable collision and dissent,
in abstract lines and formulae:
a universe of mindless things
revolving mindlessly
in patterns
strangely mathematically precise
through empty space.

Yet when a star is born
chatter quietens
foil wrappers stop mid crackle
a hush descends.

She steps on the stage;
a Goddess-illumining the night.
Widening spheres
fill with her imminence.

Dull retinas
blindly staring into interstellar space,
bombarded by celestial intensities
hypothesise that
after all
there might be something there —
strings
dark matter
darker energy.

Colossal mechanisms
constructed to register its wavelengths
after years detect a hiss.

But only the infinite unmeasurable heart
can sense the Presence
translate the static into
meaningful communication
the unmeasurable music of the spheres.

In this spirit we shall use Eurythmy to explore the planetary beings that compose our solar system, whose activity and consciousness make possible our human soul experience.

Cosmic Psychological Gesture (CPG)

We have learned through the process bequeathed to us by Chekhov how a gesture can express and penetrate a human character's psychology. If we approach the Eurythmy gestures for the sounds of speech and the zodiacal and planetary beings, with the organ of perception developed through this former process, it enables us to penetrate into the inner life of the macrocosmic beings whose greater souls are woven into ours. Since these gestures allow us to access and explore the psychology of macrocosmic beings I will expand Chekhov's terminology and refer to them as Cosmic Psychological Gestures (CPGs).

Eurythmists learn to penetrate their instruments with the very consciousness that formed and condensed them out of the cosmic life. They do this by entering into the divine creative movements of the macrocosmic consonants and vowels reflected in our earthly speech. To become an instrument for the divine creative Being of the Word, eurythmists penetrate so deeply into it that the dense material body can reveal the cosmic movements out of which it has condensed and which continue to enliven it. To do this, eurythmists must inhabit their bodies differently from actors who, with some exceptions, incorporate specific earthly characters within specific earthly circumstances.*

Those of us following this path towards the future art of acting must however first experience these gestures eurythmically if we are to sense that each nuance of our inner life is not an arbitrary consequence of biological advancement. Only then will the first sensations of the cosmic consciousness that streams into the human soul, granting us our inwardness, awaken as experience. Then we must be able to return again to earth, bringing that awareness with us as we weave it into the creation of an earthly character inhabiting an earthly body.

Therefore to prepare a path for this awareness, ideally actors must be guided first by a eurythmist who can show us how to stir our life/etheric body into movement and awaken in our subtle body-of-sensation a sense for how the gestures condense out of cosmic activity and consciousness. Without this experience our gestures risk

---

* Refer to *The Actor of the Future 1*, Chapter 5: The Century of Research and Epilogue: The Crucible of Art. and *The Actor of the Future 3*, Chapter 3: Other states of being.

becoming fixed prematurely into static signs that have been hardened into earthly muscular activity and cannot cultivate a sense for the living macrocosmic soul.

CPG exploration 1 – vowels and planetary beings

1. Led by a eurythmist, explore the gestures of the following planetary beings and the vowels: beginning with the most open vowel, shaped furthest back in our mouth, and proceeding in the order of their placements in our mouth from back to front.[*]
2. Explore how the sensations generated by each gesture inform you of the inner nature and intention of a being.[†]

---

[*] *The Art of Speech*, Chapter 1.

[†] *The Art of Acting*, Chapter 4, pages 206–216 for the basic exploration of psychological gesture as a means of accessing and expressing the objective of a character.

Figure 53 Archetypal eurythmy gesture for /a:/ – Cosmic /a:/

Figure 54 Archetypal eurythmy gesture for the planetary being, Venus.

Figure 55 Archetypal eurythmy gesture for /ɛ/ and /eɪ/ – Cosmic /ɛ/ and /eɪ/

Figure 56 Archetypal eurythmy gesture for the planetary being, Mars

Figure 57 Archetypal eurythmy gesture for /iː/ – Cosmic /iː/

Figure 58 Archetypal eurythmy gesture for the planetary being, Mercury

Figure 59 Archetypal eurythmy gesture for /aɪ/ – Cosmic /aɪ/

Figure 60 Archetypal eurythmy gesture for the planetary being, Moon

Figure 61 Archetypal eurythmy gesture for /ɔ:/ and /oʊ/ – Cosmic /ɔ:/ and /oʊ/

Figure 62 Archetypal eurythmy gesture for the planetary being, Jupiter

Figure 63 Archetypal eurythmy gesture for /uː/ – Cosmic /uː/

Figure 64 Archetypal eurythmy gesture for the planetary being, Saturn

Figure 65 Archetypal eurythmy gesture for /aʊ/ – Cosmic /aʊ/

Figure 66 Archetypal eurythmy gesture for the planetary being, Sun

The gestures of vowels and planetary beings[*]

Each CPG becomes a path to ever deeper knowing of a Being whose contribution to the spectrum of our soul experience also manifests in our capacity to speak that vowel. Approached in this way the eurythmy gesture for each vowel that unlocks that aspect of our own inner life can subsequently do so for a character.

We cannot but be humbled as we sense the presence of these High Work Masters. They have wrought within our bodies the organs and channels by which their actions, rhythms and secretions can be at once discrete and yet can interact and mingle. By doing so they allow us to experience their work within our souls. Material biology and chemistry have shown that all emotions and expressions of our inwardness are processes that take place in our bodies, concluding that these processes are causal. Yet it could be argued equally that the physical processes observed are the effects of consciousness and simply demonstrate our functioning is psycho-physical.[28] The eurythmy gestures offer actors pathways into the infinite dimensions of the soul, at this stage unavailable through personal emotional recall. Through them we can experience how those infinite dimensions and our personal emotions interpenetrate.

When we have experienced the eurythmic gestures we can explore how these cosmic influences metamorphose into the incarnated earthly sensations and experience explored in Chapter 2.

Relationship of infinite and personal dimensions of a vowel

CPG Exploration 2 – vowel and planetary being

Speak the vowel during any of these steps, when the impulse to express it vocally arises from the full-bodied penetration of your instrument.

1. Based on the work in Chapter 1, respond to an object, plant, fruit, letter or whatever, in the quality of /ɑː/(st<u>a</u>r).
2. Permeate your whole instrument with /ɑː/(st<u>a</u>r).
3. Sustain the sensation while you stand, walk and enter a space.
4. Express the vowel in a full-bodied gesture of your own.
5. Inhabit the eurythmy gesture /ɑː/(st<u>a</u>r).
6. Integrate this gesture with your own.

---

[*]To discourage us from thinking of the planets as conglomerates of gas or liquid or lumps of matter revolving mindlessly in space, I refer to them as planetary beings.

7. Pay attention to the body-of-sensation that arises while you move back and forth between these levels of expression of the vowel.

8. Integrate this body-of-sensation with your inmost core of being. Sustain it and imagine that this nuance of your inner life is not an accidental something but a gift bestowed on you by a greater Someone (or Being) in the universe.

9. Imagine that Someone (or Being) pours their soul substance into yours, making it possible for you to sense what they sense.

10. Imagine that /ɑː/(st<u>a</u>r) sensation expands into the cosmos until it fills the periphery.

11. Become that Someone. Step into that role. Look down and radiate this macrocosmic /ɑː/(st<u>a</u>r) towards the earth.

Partner work

12. Take it in turns to be the human being who receives /ɑː/(st<u>a</u>r) into your soul on earth and the Being in the cosmos who radiates it to your human soul on earth.

Individual work

13. Create a movement sequence that weaves back and forth between the roles. As you move from the role of cosmic Being in the pure eurythmic gesture to a human being expressing everyday experience with human gesture, explore the two different ways of inhabiting your body.

14. Pay attention to the changes in sensation as you shift from peripheral consciousness to focused earthly consciousness and back again, moving through each stage of the continuum.

CPG exploration 3 — /ɑː/(st<u>a</u>r) and Venus

Speak the vowel during any of these steps, when the impulse to express it vocally arises from the full-bodied penetration of your instrument.

Individual

1. Begin at the cosmic end of the continuum. Permeate your whole instrument with /ɑː/(st<u>a</u>r).

2. Make a conscious transition from the gesture for the archetypal /ɑː/ into the gesture for the planetary being Venus. Pay attention to the journey of sensation.

3. Move back and forth between the gestures /ɑ:/ and Venus.
4. Explore the Venus body-of-sensation generated by the CPG. What is this being doing, intending to communicate, wanting human beings to experience? Express these sensations in your own words, finally condensing them into a sentence beginning with: *I want to* . . .

Partner work

1. Take it in turn to be the human being on earth (B) and the planetary being Venus (A).
2. A: radiate to B alternating vowel and planetary gestures.
3. B: Stand neutral and available within A's field. Sense your whole instrument respond as you receive A's substance. Let it permeate your soul until your body is imbued with its substance and grows into A's gesture.
4. Devise a speech/movement sequence that expresses your reciprocal relationship.
5. Reverse roles and repeat steps 1–4.

Individual

6. Working on your own again, recreate the journey of movement and sensation as you (the human being) imagine receiving the substance Venus radiates to you.
7. Working on your own again, recreate the journey of movement and sensation as you (Venus) radiate your substance into human souls.

Is there a more perfect expression of this planetary gesture than Juliet's words to Romeo in Shakespeare's play?

> My bounty is as boundless as the sea,
> My love as deep. The more I give to thee
> The more I have, for both are infinite.

CPG exploration 4 – /ɛ/(m<u>e</u>n), /eɪ/(d<u>a</u>te) and Mars

Repeat CPG explorations 1–3 but now in relation to /ɛ/(m<u>e</u>n), diphthong /eɪ/(d<u>a</u>te) and planetary being Mars.

CPG exploration 5 — /iː/(m<u>e</u>) and Mercury

Repeat CPG explorations 1–3 but now in relation to /iː/(m<u>e</u>) and planetary being Mercury.

CPG exploration 6 — /aɪ/(l<u>i</u>fe) and Moon

Repeat CPG explorations 1–3 but now in relation to /aɪ/(l<u>i</u>fe) and planetary being Moon.

CPG exploration 7— /ɔː/(<u>awe</u>) and Jupiter

Repeat CPG explorations 1–3 but now in relation to /ɔː/(<u>awe</u>) and planetary being Jupiter.

CPG exploration 8 — /uː/(sh<u>oe</u>) and Saturn

Repeat the steps of CPG explorations 1–3 but now in relation to the vowel /uː/(sh<u>oe</u>) and planetary being Saturn.

  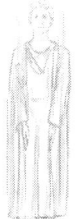 

CPG exploration 9 — /aʊ/(<u>out</u>) and Sun

Repeat the steps of CPG explorations 1–3 but now in relation to the vowel /aʊ/(<u>out</u>) and planetary being Sun.

New sensibilities, new planets

If our intellectual capacity is still evolving why might not our feeling life as well be also in a process of development? There may be feelings waiting to be felt, requiring sensibilities not yet developed or only now beginning to develop. Beethoven and Liszt are just two composers who knew that much of what they wrote would be appreciated only in the future. Ears cannot hear what souls are not ready to experience. Yet audiences now consider the sensations awakened by that music lie within their comfort zone and it is new generations of composers who challenge the boundaries of our experience. Are we not always expanding into new dimensions of our feeling life?

Does the continuing discovery of planets in the outer universe suggest we are ready to expand our inner universe: their outer bodies only the material forms of beings who

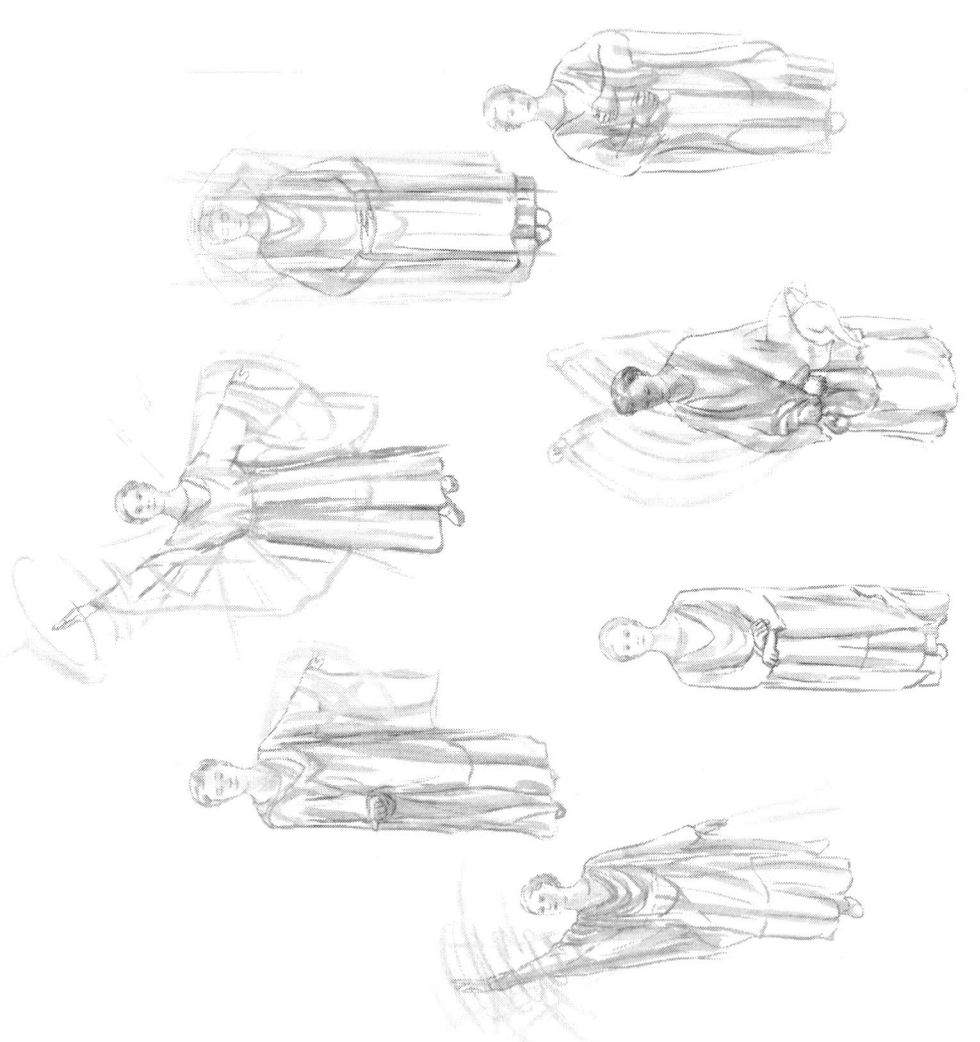

Figure 67 The planetary beings

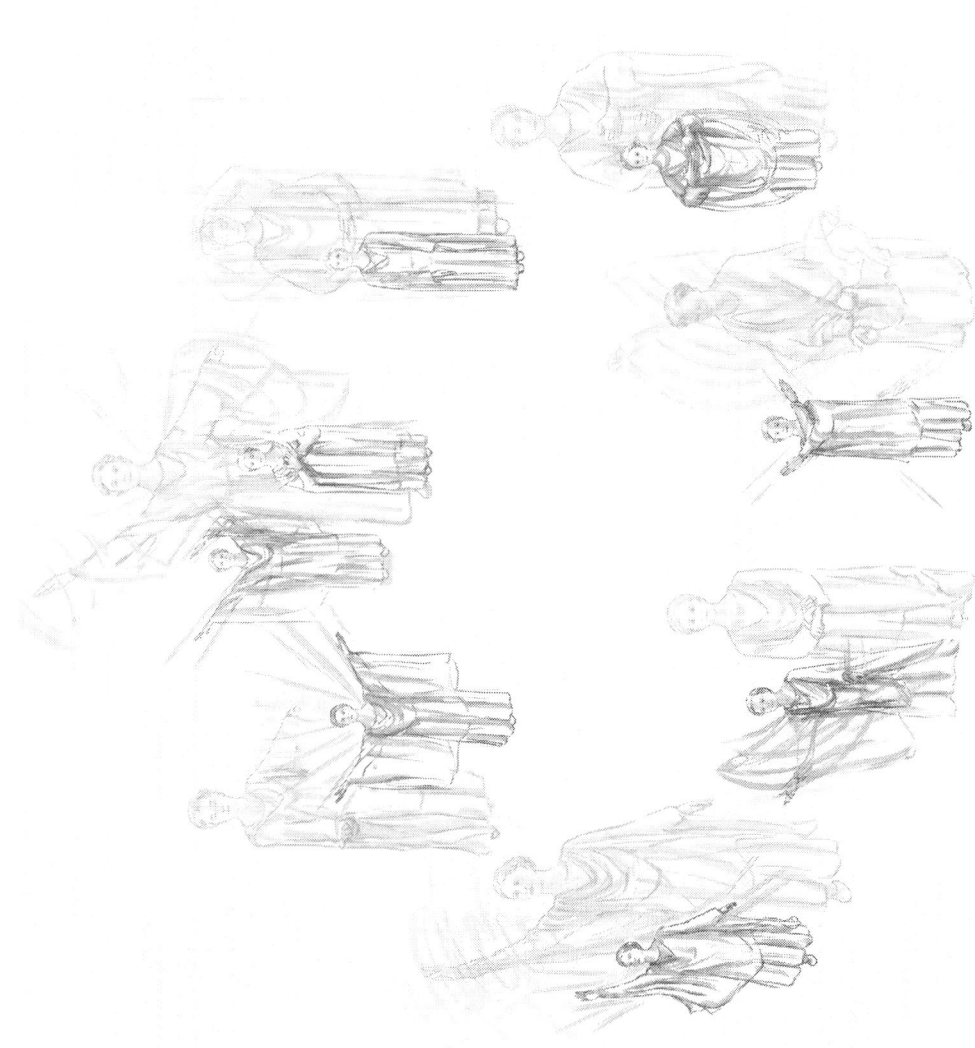

Figure 68 The circle of planetary beings radiate their presence through the Cosmic Vowels

stir new sensibilities within the human soul, bestow new faculties that only now we are ready to make conscious, just as we have only now perceived their outer forms?

And if we are ready, might we consider this expansion to be no more an arbitrary outcome of biological advancement than the states of soul explored already. Might these new sensibilities also be the gift of planetary beings who accompany our evolution?

We cannot help but question the link between these new sensibilities and the planets that lie beyond the boundary of the Saturn sphere, regarded by the ancients as the limit of their geocentric cosmos. In that context Uranus and Neptune and Pluto, identified only since the geocentric paradigm has been replaced, are certainly outsiders. Yet if we are to be consistent, our evolving sensibilities cannot accept there are exceptions to the state of beingness and demand we find a way to investigate the inner nature of these planets too.

At the same time we observe that there are vowel placements whose relationship to the planetary beings of our geocentric universe are not included in the range revealed by Steiner's research. These include the German oe (ö) and ue (ü). As explored in *The Art of Speech** neither of these appear in their pure form in most spoken forms of English and in SRP (Standard Received Pronunciation) correspond most closely to the vowel /ɜ/(h<u>er</u>d) and the diphthongs /ju/(imb<u>ue</u>) and /uɪ/(s<u>wee</u>t).[29]

Might these be connected with the planetary beings Uranus and Neptune or with Pluto?

Just as these supersensible companions must have been there in the heavens before we could perceive their presence so too these vowels are not new. They appear in many languages. Perhaps however it is only now that we are ready to consciously explore the dimensions they awaken in our souls.

Perhaps these vowels will provide us with some clues.

Pushing the boundaries

The vowel /u:/(sh<u>oe</u>), sounds from the most forward placement of our lips and signifies that we have reached the boundary of Saturn who marks the edge of our geocentric universe. Yet before the microgesture in our mouth that marks the boundary of /ɔ:/(<u>awe</u>) can transform and reach this furthest boundary of /u:/(sh<u>oe</u>) our soul must cross the two vowel thresholds mentioned earlier.

If Steiner did connect these vowels, German oe (ö) [English /ɜ/(h<u>er</u>d)], and German

---

* *The Art of Speech*, pp 19, 55–57.

ue (ü) [English /uɪ/(sw<u>ee</u>t) and /ju/(imb<u>ue</u>)] and the diphthong /ɔɪ/(j<u>oy</u>),[*] as well, to planetary beings, I do not know of it. His way of working was to always wait till someone asked a question before providing answers and often such questions were the stimulus for his further explorations. For whatever reason we are left with the tantalising facts that there are more vowels in our octave than planets in the ancient geocentric universe and that science has identified more planets in our solar system than Steiner has related to the vowels.

This begs the question: can we connect the recently discovered planets to these vowels? That Steiner also gave no gestures for the planetary beings, Uranus and Neptune, though both had been identified before his birth, prompts us to use our own evolving organ of perception to explore their objectives, search for CPGs that might embody them and for their possible connections to these vowels.

In the lecture cycle, *The Spiritual Hierarchies*, Steiner speaks of Uranus and Neptune (Pluto had not yet been identified) as the bodies of spiritual beings whose spheres of activity, while initially connected to earlier stages of the evolutionary cycles that finally condensed into the geocentric model of the universe, later withdrew from it. If this is the case, clearly they have once again been drawn into its field, presumably with tasks the human race would not have been prepared to consciously engage with until now. What is clear is that Uranus and Neptune and Pluto are planetary beings of a different order than those we have explored thus far. Might their activity relate to the challenge of our time? Perhaps these vowels that lie between our impulse to embrace reality /ɔ·/ (<u>aw</u>e) and our final ability to penetrate it with full consciousness /u:/(sh<u>oe</u>) provide a clue.

Inhabiting the gestures Steiner gave for these arouses strong sensations. And if we could articulate these glimmers of awareness arising in our post-Kali Yuga souls, might we sense the presence of Beings who first appear to us as adversaries? Threatening , shattering old structures and securities, they confront us with what we do not want to face. Yet when we rise to meet the challenge we will understand that they have served our further evolution. Someone calling to us thus:

Human Beings! There are things unrecognised within your comfort zones of custom and tradition, still unacknowledged, but stammering to find a voice, crying out to be included, er? /ɜ/(h<u>er</u>d). The heresies of history will no longer be controlled, suppressed, forced into pseudo unity, a happy ending only for the few, that is premature because so many are excluded.[†]

---

[*] See end of this chapter for an exploration of this diphthong.

[†] *The Actor of the Future 1*, Chapters 2 and 4.

Figure 69 Archetypal eurythmy gesture for the German oe (ö), nearest to /ɜ/ – Cosmic /ɜ/

Figure 70 Archetypal eurythmy gesture for German ue (ü) nearest to /ʊɪ/ and /jʊ/ – Cosmic /ʊɪ/ and /jʊ/

Uranus

As our inner world expanded so did our perception of the outer world include the first 'new' planet and in 1781, Uranus was identified and named.[30] Astrologers discern that it heralded that aspect of our present time in which the despised and rejected, those excluded from community, find their voice and will not stay silent till they too are welcome at the wedding feast?[*] Is it a coincidence ... er ... that we express the doubt or hesitation ... er ... that challenges the status quo ... er ... interrupts the flow of thoughts ... er ... linear progression, with its awkward stutter ... er ... with this next vowel in our octave, /ɜ/(h<u>er</u>d)?[†] Is it possible this vowel is the soul gesture of a Cosmic Being who nudges us, speaking on behalf of the outsider; shattering the centuries of structures made by those with the power to control what will no longer be controlled until its voice is heard ... er ... first in individuals and then in whole communities?

Let us recall that the pure vowel (as it manifests in the German oe, ö) is formed when we sustain the microgesture of the lips in /ɔ:/(<u>awe</u>) while inside the mouth the jaw, tongue and hard palate assert the microgesture of /ɛ/(m<u>e</u>n). This conflicted placement is clearly the expression of a conflict in the soul; one part wanting to embrace and accept and another wanting to reject or keep a boundary between the world and self. We sense this conflicted state in the widening gulf between the stated policies and ideals of governments and institutions, the waves of reform attempted over many centuries, and the harsh realities in which so many live. We reach out wanting to embrace and trust the words of experts, the brilliant minds who seem to offer the solution. Yet in our modern and postmodern age we have learned to doubt the power of thought to find solutions amidst the contradictory phenomena and information that confront us. We do not trust that those authorities we looked to once for answers are committed to the welfare of any but themselves.

How easy is it then, for those who feel they have been h<u>ur</u>t to h<u>ur</u>t in turn. Yet within this shadow-side of doubt, we find its nobler counterpart: the willingness to examine one's opinions, refrain from jumping to conclusions, and to probe the deeper questions of reality, the blessing of uncertainty.

Neptune

And still the frontiers of our consciousness expand, demanding exploration, not suppression and control. To penetrate and understand what once had been rejected and cast out demands refining of the self and of the senses. Astrologers discern that

---

[*] This is a central theme of *The Actor of the Future 1*.
[†] *The Art of Speech*, Chapter 1 for the section on the octave of the vowels.

this capacity to hear the urgent calling of our times to understand and not to persecute is connected with the influence of Neptune, first identified in 1846.[31] And can we sense the connection of this new capacity with the vowel (German ue (ü) and its English counterparts, the diphthongs /uɪ/(s<u>wee</u>t) and /ju/(imb<u>ue</u>*)?

The German ü is also the result of conflicted microgestures in the mouth. This time however in ü the lips maintain the tiny, focused, rounded gesture of the /ʊ/(t<u>oo</u>k), while inside the mouth the tongue and jaw and teeth ridge tense to form the /i:/(m<u>e</u>).

It is as though, through penetrating its experience – /ʊ/(t<u>oo</u>k) – the ego wakens to its most intense sensation of itself, – /i:/(m<u>e</u>) – which then in turn can penetrate its own experience more consciously. This utmost refinement of the sensing self is either a response to the antipathy we feel towards a world that is not worthy of that self (ew! pew!) or to the sympathy when some exquisite beauty prompts us to refine what is not worthy in ourselves and strive towards our infinite potential. It is as though the choices forced upon us by the sheer intensity with which evil now declares its field of action on the earth allow us no escape.† We must strive for this sharper sensing of our own imperfection in the presence of the I AM Self. If we are not to succumb to Neptune's shadow side of hatred, the flame of our true self must awaken.

On the basis of these thoughts and questions apply steps 1–8 of *CPG exploration* 2 to the following vowel placements, using the images to guide your journey.

Uranus exploration – /ɜ/(h<u>er</u>d)

---

*We have spoken already in Chapter 1 of *The Art of Speech*, of the metamorphosis of the pure vowel (German ü) into the English diphthongs; /ju:/ and /wi:/.

† The theme of evil is explored in Chapter 4 of *The Actor of the Future 1*, and the chapter on the age of the consciousness soul in *The Actor of the Future 4*.

Neptune exploration — /ju/(imb<u>ue</u>)

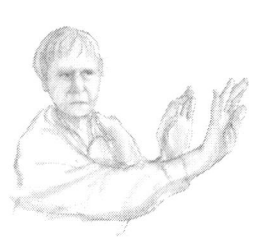  

New tasks

The depth and number of connecting pathways of sensation flowing through my instrument while working with these vowels from the macrocosmic to the human level support my insights into their connection with the planetary beings Uranus and Neptune. That Steiner did not suggest their planetary gestures prompts a research task that actors and eurythmists might undertake together: first, to articulate the objectives of these Beings who inspire us to these further reaches of our souls[*] and then to search for CPGs that could embody them. Here are my attempts at identifying their objectives:

Uranus: *I AM that being in the cosmos, part of the greater Self, that inspires you to evolve. I want to stir up your complacency, make you question everything – all opinions, judgements, prejudices that support your sense that you belong because you have excluded what is different, and what you do not understand.*

Neptune: *I AM that being in the cosmos, part of the greater Self, that inspires you to evolve. I want to refine your senses and your understanding until you develop powers of discernment that enable you to recognise the difference between good and evil, pleasure and pain, joy and sorrow, peace and torment; to rightly penetrate your own reality.*[32]

The sensations of discomfort experienced by English speakers who must contort their mouths to achieve the pure placements of the French and German vowels alert us to

---

[*] We know from the explorations into PGs and objectives in Chapter 4 of *The Art of Acting* that identifying the objective must precede the finding of a PG.

the effort still required to integrate these two outsiders of our planetary system. Perhaps they suggest why the more phlegmatic aspect of the English-speaking soul that seeks conciliation and wants to smooth things over, lets these vowels slide into diphthongs.

Between the gesture to embrace and reconnect of /ɔː/(awe) and the gesture that penetrates resistance /uː/(sh<u>oe</u>) and arrives at final union that is fully conscious, we cannot bypass, slip around, slide or jump across, or in any way avoid the stumbling block and challenges of evil. The conflicted microgestures of those vowels prepare us to engage with the complex issues of our time. Only by penetrating the resistances will the coiled spring of /ɔɪ/(j<u>oy</u>) be able to release into the joy of resurrection. We shall explore this diphthong in the next chapter. For now we will continue to explore the relationship between the archetypal cosmic gestures of the vowels and planets and the human gestures we observe in life. It is time to strengthen our ability as actors to sense how the macrocosmic gestures are transformed as they penetrate the psycho-physical constitution of an earthly human character.

CPG exploration 10 – human and cosmic gesture

Speak the vowel during any of these steps, when the impulse to express it vocally arises from the full-bodied penetration of your instrument.

1. Spend time observing other people's gestures and your own. Explore them full-bodily until your body-of-sensation reveals which vowel qualities they manifest.
2. Begin each practice session (initially led by a eurythmist) moving through the circle of planetary gestures and accompanying vowels. Pay attention to the body-of-sensations they arouse.
3. Focus on one. Treating the planetary gesture as a CPG, explore the objective generated in your body-of-sensation.
4. Then explore the connection between the planetary gesture and the vowel. Can your body-of-sensation discern why someone having that objective would express its soul nature through that specific vowel?
5. Explore how the pure archetypal planetary gesture is modified when you penetrate your body with the muscular tensions of the everyday behaviour of a human being living on the earth. Observe the variations in sensation that arise as the archetypal form is bent or distorts into its human counterparts: by altering the angle of your head for example, raising or twisting your shoulders, tensing the muscles of your hands, contracting or expanding the space between your legs or feet, standing on

your toes. Pay attention to all the changes in sensation and the feelings or emotions that are generated. Pay attention to the shift in sensation when you transition back to the eurythmic gesture and back again into its human counterparts.

6. What sorts of moods or memories or situations surface through the human gestures?

7. Return to the archetypal full-bodied gesture and explore how it modifies when you layer it with different *qualities and sensations, expanding and contracting, qualities of movement, centres, objectives, atmospheres, imaginary bodies,* etc.

8. At the end of each session, once again move through the circle of eurythmic gestures for the planetary beings.

Relationship of *character* to vowel and planetary being

Through such explorations our instrument becomes increasingly responsive and more skilled in recognising how a character's particular, intimate physical and vocal mannerisms bear the imprint of their macrocosmic counterparts:[*] and how the archetypal forms of the CPGs are modified as they pass through the lens of a human character's particulars.

It is unlikely that the full-bodied (level 10) gestures here portrayed will be seen in a performance. However, these archetypal gestures for the planetary beings and their accompanying vowels expand the actor's range of sensibilities. For the first time we have the conscious means by which the multi-dimensional nature of the human being can penetrate the human-centric work on character.

Unless the preparation processes described are undertaken faithfully, the next step of applying them to character creation could easily become the imposition of a concept rather than the exploration of artistic intuitions arising from the depths of our sensation body. As always, our choices are confirmed when the intuitions that arise from this layer of our work integrate with all our other choices and enrich them. Then we are surprised by the further paths of exploration they suggest and how they expand our vision of the character beyond its everyday perspective of itself. When our experience is anchored in the full-bodied gesture work we are free to experiment with our by-now-familiar process of reducing outer movement without diminishing intensity.

---

[*] Steiner's descriptions of the vowel gestures can be investigated and corroborated by an unbiased exploration of:

1) the material described in Chapter 1 of *The Art of Speech,*

2) this present chapter, and

3) the principles described in *The Art of Acting* for developing an archetypal full-bodied gesture.

These preliminary steps cultivate the organs of perception that allow us to explore the integration of these newly budding faculties with those arising from our prior work with character development.[*] These are the first baby steps along a path of character creation that consciously incorporates the planetary influences in our human souls.

Can we identify a character's predominant soul tendency and recognise the planetary being whose work it is to generate that tendency and how that might express itself in vowel qualities of speech and gesture? Work at this level demands such interweaving layers of evolving sensibilities that it defies attempts to formalise the process. However, to illustrate the possibilities, I share what I discovered when I worked with this dimension to create the range of Shakespeare's characters in *King Lear*.[33] Chapter 6 assumes the reader's knowledge of the play.

---

[*] *The Art of Acting.*

Chapter 6

Our High Work Masters (2)
Vowels and the Planetary Beings in Shakespeare's
King Lear

The creative process can never be determined by a set of rules but nonetheless is permeated by the rigorous intelligence that artistry demands, confirming, modifying or rejecting its discoveries which even in rejection, lead to further insights. I hope that in this chapter, my stream of consciousness, more subjective style inspires the reader's own exploration and demonstrates the protean nature of artistic intuition. A process that is anything but linear, instead it leaps from impulse to idea, idea to revelation, and revelation to another impulse, all according to its own inner truth: sometimes beginning here, sometimes there, back and forth from gesture to character, to vowel, to text, to planetary being: obeying a logic that springs from realities not merely intellectual, yet in a rigorous and ongoing interaction with the actor's mind. Each heading is intended only to orient the reader and be thought of as a summary of my discoveries. I did not begin with predetermined ideas or connections nor did my explorations necessarily unfold in the order here presented.

Such an exploration of the vowels and planetary beings is the fruit of the fundamental work to build a character.[*] It emerges out of and in turn contributes to it but is not possible without its firm foundation. Although this fundamental work is implicit in the work that follows, mostly I have chosen not to share those specific acting choices with the reader in order not to influence a colleague's different choices.

Nor does the revelation of specific vowel qualities in Shakespeare's language imply the insertion of a shallow emphasis when speaking. As described in Chapter 2, it reflects a tendency of soul imbuing all a character says or does as a key in music permeates a passage with its colour, flavour, fragrance, its specific nuance of experience.

King Lear, the vowels and planetary beings

I make my full-bodied journey through the gestures of the vowels and planetary beings, speaking when the impulse arises.

---
[*] *The Art of Acting.*

I make my full-bodied journey through the layers of prior preparation for the characters: such as centres, qualities and sensations, PGs, fragments of text and any other Chekhov tools.

I stand in the stillness with instrument attuned, available.

I feel the range of their dynamics and energies at work in my body-of-sensation. The layers of microcosmic character development and streams of macrocosmic soul potential interweave, attract and call attention to each other, begin to interact and speak with each other.

I sense an impulse to begin where it all began, reach back, down the unrestricted passage, back to the paradisal open throat; no obstacles obstruct the flow, no boundaries. /ɑː/(st*a*r)

Edgar – Venus – /ɑ:/

Figure 71 Cosmic /ɑ:/

Figure 72 Edgar: Armed, brother?

Figure 73 Cosmic /ɑ:/ radiates through Edgar

Figure 74 The planetary being, Venus

Figure 75 Edgar: But who comes here? My father poorly led.

Figure 76 Venus radiates through Edgar

Figure 77 Venus and Cosmic /ɑ:/

Edgar — Venus — /ɑː/ (st<u>a</u>r)

Could my arms, my mouth, a wider chalice open to receive, rearrange the solar systems of my atoms, galaxies of molecules: configuring my inwardness, to give and to receive the infinite outpouring love?

Resonating to that frequency my body-of-sensation senses an approach, a someone drawing near, open, without guile, his undefended heart too innocent to recognise deception, comprehend dissembling, devise survival strategies. A character arrives within my soul..../ɑː/...<u>a</u>rmed br<u>o</u>ther? *It is Edgar*

On his path to maturity, become a man, he will learn to keep his openness and yet defend and guide his blinded father...

B<u>u</u>t who c<u>o</u>mes here? My f<u>a</u>ther poorly led.

Instinctively I (Edgar) reach out to him, wary even as I check my back space for support ... give me your <u>a</u>rm ...

As I counsel him ... save him from despair, from suicide.

... thou happy f<u>a</u>ther, think that the clearest gods, who make them honours of men's impossibilities, have preserved thee ... Sit you down f<u>a</u>ther, rest you ... Here f<u>a</u>ther, take the shadow of this tree for your good host ... f<u>a</u>ther ...

The petals of his heart, (or is it mine), unwithered by betrayal and corruption, yet schooled in suffering, unfold into an open flower of compassion, a royal chalice. Someone in the universe bestows on him, (or is it me?), her infinitely giving, loving soul capacities, teaching him, or me, her secret way to give what we receive from the infinite renewing source. And as I sense my/ Edgar's gesture in her greater one, Goddess of all who love, and let it organise my soul, I play at the interface between the character's and actor's soul. Like Chekhov I feel myself outside the character, creating it. I feel myself expand into the heart of Venus. Lady, teach us how to Love! Teach me why I had to leave Your perfect paradise, fall from Your grace. Holding Your gesture, I am an all vibrating, listening, quivering ear. Your answer resonates: Would you have wished not to awaken and be kinged, become a man?

I sense the seismic shift in Edgar's soul, his receptive, gentle unsuspecting nature, rising to the challenge that confronts him ... how to face his brother and defend his honour?

Yet even when he moves towards the Martial /ɛ/(off<u>e</u>nd) . . .

Draw thy sword, that if my sp<u>ee</u>ch offend a noble h<u>ea</u>rt . . . thy arm m<u>a</u>y do <u>it</u> justice . . .

even as witness and reporter of his father's death

. . . O that my h<u>ea</u>rt would burst . . .

though made resilient through the struggle to birth his adult Self, /i:/(w<u>e</u>, s<u>ee</u>), he learns to make a healthy boundary with /ɛ/(off<u>e</u>nd, n<u>e</u>ver), /eɪ/(m<u>a</u>y) that never hardens into a defensive barrier, /ɑ:/(<u>are</u>, y<u>ou</u>ng, m<u>u</u>ch, h<u>ea</u>rt) . . .

We that <u>are</u> y<u>ou</u>ng, shall n<u>e</u>ver s<u>ee</u> so m<u>u</u>ch nor l<u>i</u>ve so long.

And still retains his fundamental /ɑ:/(heart) disposition of receptiveness.

As in life, not all characters evolve so clearly into a mature humanity. Some remain fixed in their pathologies or tendencies. Only some, like Edgar, fulfil the range of their potentials and maintain a subsequent stability. Another one is Kent.

Kent – Mars – /ɛ/ and /eɪ/

Figure 78 The planetary being, Mars

Figure 79 Kent: You slave ... You base football, player!

Figure 80 Mars radiates through Kent

Figure 81 Cosmic /ɛ/ and /eɪ/

Figure 82 Kent ... 'tis my occupation to be plain ...

Figure 83 Kent: Break heart, prithee break!

Figure 84 Kent: Knave! What a brazen faced varlet art thou ... you slave.

Figure 85 Cosmic /ɛ/ radiates through Kent

Kent — Mars — /ɛ/(m_en) /eɪ/(d_ate)

By the end of Edgar's journey I already sense my instrument vibrating with a different energy, attuning to a different quality of Being. This time a Someone whose love is fierce enough to wake us from our comfort-zone, to drive a wedge between and interrupt that perfect paradisal flow: a warrior for truth who bears the energy of inter-vention, opposition.

Mars erupts into the space, his gesture rearranging all the solar systems of my atoms, galaxies of molecules, reorganising all my sensibilities.

The body-of-sensations generated by his gesture scan, antennae-like, the range of characters vibrating at the edge of his magnetic field, seeking to detect — is one of them more fundamentally attuned to his disruptive planetary energy, called into presence by his reactive instinct to oppose: one who is committed to cracking what resists of outworn systems, habits and beliefs?

I am become that gesture and I sense its energies and form attract a now-not-Edgar inwardness into its field. A different sort of manhood penetrates my muscles. Suddenly the soul of Kent inhabits me, initiating separation, opposition, so that all the parts may see themselves reflected back.

Away, you kn_ave … kn_ave … kn_ave … sl_ave … thou unn_ec_essary l_etter, thou whoreson z_ed … aw_ay!

Trying my new voice, hard edged, firm, I speak my name and hear its vowel: Kent: /ɛ/(K_ent). *Extend its surface area into a dipthong* /eɪ/(…p_ation, pl_ain). 'It is my occup_ation to be pl_ain.'

And in Lear's kingdom I make a stand for truth. My heart is tempered to resist, oppose, do battle with the lie, expose hypocrisy and sycophants.

Thou kn_ave! Thou b_ase football pl_ayer! Aw_ay!
Kn_ave! What a br_azen f_aced varlet art thou … you sl_ave.

Love has forged a blade to slice through sentiment and tell it as it is …

All cheerless, dark and d_eadly. Thy _eldest daughters have fordone th_ems_elves and d_esperately are d_ead.

And later, warlike energy reined in, not emasculated but, Buddha like, tempered in compassion, unsentimental, present in my master's grief and death, utterly awake.

Break h_eart, prithee br_eak! He h_ates him, that would upon the rack of this harsh world str_etch him out longer.

The Fool and Cordelia — Mercury — /I/ and /i:/

Figure 86 The planetary being, Mercury

Figure 87 Cosmic /iː/

Figure 88 Mercury radiates through the Fool

Figure 89 The Fool: I'll teach thee a speech, Sirrah!

Figure 90 Cosmic /iː/ radiates into Cordelia

Figure 91 Cordelia: Seek, seek for him...

The Fool — Mercury — Vowel: /ɪ/(s<u>i</u>p) /i:/(m<u>e</u>)

Now with that wedge between myself and everything, the gift of Mars, Mercury orbits into sight. I step into his gesture and again my energies and inwardness are rearranged, restructured. I attune myself to /i:/(m<u>e</u>), I want to radiate myself into the world. My spine an upright staff, a rod of light, aligns itself to earth and heaven, creates a compass for the truth, no hair's breadth compromise. Its vertical /i:/... crossing the horizontal, tongue tensed against teeth and teeth ridge, projecting streamlined through a narrow slit of lips, permits no bending of the truth. Two characters, vastly different personalities and contours, condense around that central spine and crossbar, fading in and out, announce their presence in my soul:

Fool: I'll t<u>ea</u>ch th<u>ee</u> a sp<u>ee</u>ch s<u>i</u>rrah! ... I marvel what k<u>i</u>n, thou and thy daughters are. They'lt have m<u>e</u> wh<u>i</u>pped for sp<u>ea</u>king truth, thoul't have m<u>e</u> wh<u>i</u>pped for lying and sometimes I am wh<u>i</u>pped for holding my p<u>ea</u>ce. I had rather b<u>ee</u>n any sort of th<u>i</u>ng than a fool, but I would not b<u>e</u> th<u>ee</u> nuncle. Thou hast pared thy w<u>i</u>t on both sides, and left noth<u>i</u>ng in the m<u>i</u>ddle.

Inwardly, the Fool unceasingly adjusts the tension, pulling truth's thread taut. Outwardly he bends and twists, an extrovert who dances snake-like round the stiff unbending, healing Caduceus spine of truth.

Cordelia — Mercury — Vowel: /ɪ/(s<u>i</u>p) /i:/(m<u>e</u>)

Cordelia, the other, quietly at rest within truth's centre: I cannot h<u>ea</u>ve my heart <u>i</u>nto my mouth ...

Unafraid to exercise authority to serve compassion ... S<u>ee</u>k, s<u>ee</u>k for h<u>i</u>m ...

Or surrender it to serve a higher truth ... Proc<u>ee</u>d <u>i</u>n the sway of your own w<u>i</u>ll ...

Her clear perception pierces through the mask disguising evil but she too bears the healing staff of Mercury.

All blest s<u>e</u>crets of the earth spr<u>i</u>ng w<u>i</u>th my t<u>ea</u>rs. Restoration hang thy med<u>i</u>cine upon my l<u>i</u>ps and let th<u>i</u>s k<u>i</u>ss repair those violent harms that my two s<u>i</u>sters have <u>i</u>n thy reverence made ... These white flakes did challenge pity of them ... this thin helm ... mine enemy's dog, though he had bit me ... Shall we not see these daughters and these sisters ...

Such different personas, yet so resembling one another in their souls' most intimate configuration that through their deaths, in Lear's mind, their melodies have merged ...

And my poor fool is hang'd.

The Earl of Gloucester — Moon — /ai/

Figure 92 Cosmic /ai/

Figure 93 Cosmic /ai/ radiates through Gloucester

Figure 94 Gloucester: O you kind gods ... You mighty gods ...

Figure 95 Gloucester: Away and let me die … Alack, I have no eyes…

Figure 96 The planetary being, Moon

Figure 97 Gloucester: Away and let me die.

Figure 98 Gloucester: I am tied to the stake. I cannot fly.

Figure 99 Moon radiates through Gloucester

The Earl of Gloucester – Moon – the diphthong /aɪ/(life)

From back to centre of the mouth emergent from the rite of passage through the first three vowels from /ɑ:/(star) to /ɛ/(men) to /i:/(me), I stand reflecting on the dipthong /aɪ/: this time allow myself to slide from /ɑ:/ to /i:/. And this washing like the tide, from side to side, stirs in my body-of-sensation somehow, somewhere ... someone hovering and drawing near, someone swept up in the back and forth of life, in others' wills, powerless initially to stop the tide, assert the intervening /ɛ/(men).

And when he does, crushed by the iron fist of destiny, he cannot fly the savage reckoning, cannot comprehend what powers require this sacrifice! Quick now before the gates of heaven slam shut, barring you forever from the paradisal Venus love, can you retrace your gestures, reconstruct the process, try to understand what led you down that fateful slide?

Gather what your right hand once bestowed so openly, so trustingly, in front, and fearing to lose it, enclose it in your fist. Gather what your left arm once encompassed, stirring from behind, below, so trustingly, so openly. Lift it to the space in front, where you can see it, keep an eye on it, enclose it with your fist. Now slam the gates. It feels forever, no return, no looking back as fists lock, press equally downwards to the earth, upwards to the heavens; each holds each in check. Sense in that density, destiny solidify, summoning the Self. Is it yet too late? In that tension, awful stillness. In that stillness, birth of Self.

Sensation stirring, half remembering a time before my birth: how a pity-taking moon withdrew the challenges to come, too hard and even worse things from my sight – beyond-bearing, undigestible – to a safe haven orbit, holding them at bay, guarding entry into earth's domain until I unsuspecting entered, took my chance. Then too late behind me shut the gate!

A character approaches. My molecules all rearranged again, stirring in my wrists sensation ... of a different presence ... arrival of a different self.

Someone who pays a savage price to bring that self to birth, to utter I. Bound at the wrists it is the Earl of Gloucester:

O you k<u>i</u>nd Gods! <u>I</u> am t<u>ied</u> to the stake. I cannot fl<u>y</u>. Alack <u>I</u> have no <u>eye</u>s! . . . with this case of <u>eye</u>s? . . . away and let me d<u>ie</u> . . . tempt me not to d<u>ie</u> before you please . . . O you m<u>i</u>ghty gods . . . in your s<u>i</u>ghts . . .

A terrifying birth! Midwifed by his exiled, disguised behind two layers son, Edgar summoning his father back from death's despair, calls his father's note:

R<u>i</u>peness is all.

King Lear and the Duke of Cornwall — Jupiter — /ɒ/, /ɔː/ and /oʊ/

Figure 100 The planetary being, Jupiter

Figure 101 Cosmic /ɔ:/

Figure 102 Lear: Let it be so! By all the operation of the orbs ... Propinquity and property of blood ...

Figure 103 Jupiter radiates through Lear and Cornwall

Figure 104 Cosmic /ɔ:/ radiates through Lear's soul

Figure 105 Lear: I am a very foolish fond old man ... nor I know not where I did lodge
last night ...

Figure 106 Lear: You have some cause. They have not.

Figure 107 Jupiter radiates through Lear

Figure 108 Lear: I will not swear these are my hands.

Figure 109 Jupiter and Cosmic /ɔː/

King Lear – Jupiter – /ɒ/(d<u>o</u>t), /ɔː/(<u>awe</u>), /oʊ/(n<u>o</u>)

To find my way directly from the moon to Jupiter, both fists, like a lotus, open, the right gently circling in a curve in front of, then behind the left.

Or condensing through the sphere of Mercury, imbued with his poor fool's healing energy; that joyously released into the great expanse, traversing cosmos arm – to venture forth, return and venture forth again – now circles in towards the centre, orbiting, containing it. How my hands sense their touching spheres brush pass! His gesture revolving round 'what is', encompasses a different inwardness, aligns my consciousness to his. I speak it. /ɔː/(<u>awe</u>).

Someone who feels every inch a king approaches. A presence easily inhabiting the structures of authority, greatly feared, greatly hated, greatly flawed, greatly loved and greater still his worth-fighting-for evolving self. His meteoric words flung into orbit by his gesture, wreaking havoc, smashing the planetary pathways of those who intersect with his, are conjured in my mouth …

By all the <u>o</u>peration of the <u>o</u>rbs from whom we do exist and cease to be, here I disclaim all my paternal care, pr<u>o</u>pinquity and pr<u>o</u>perty of blood, and as a stranger to my heart and me, h<u>o</u>ld thee from this forever …

Such hurling thunderbolts of heaven in his rage – assumption of right to dominate, mistaking outer power for true authority, all this sensation through the gesture, generated easily inside me. So also the self-embracing tears of pity, cascading shrivelled little Os …

<u>O</u> m<u>o</u>st sm<u>a</u>ll f<u>au</u>lt, how ugly dids't thou in C<u>o</u>rdelia sh<u>ow</u>.

And the first miraculous opening to knowledge of himself … gigantic O.

I did her wr<u>o</u>ng …

And as each petal of his heart unfolds, o after o after o after o … how his heart expands to hold the more and more …

… how now my boy, art c<u>o</u>ld? I am c<u>o</u>ld myself … Take physic p<u>o</u>mp, exp<u>o</u>se thyself to feel what wretches feel … <u>o</u>ff <u>o</u>ff you lendings … … … I kn<u>o</u>w thee well enough, thy name is Gl<u>ou</u>cester …

No no no life. If that her breath will mist or stain the stone, why then she lives. If it be so, it is a chance that does redeem all sorrows that ever I have felt.[34]

Fragile, newborn royal power, inner sovereignty, resurrected, strange hands orbiting a kingdom not of this world ...

I will not swear these are my hands ... where have I been? Where am I?

And Cordelia – she sees it too – responds in his own key ...

... in your own kingdom sir!

Duke of Cornwall – Jupiter – /ɒ/(dot), /ɔ:/(awe), /oʊ/(no)

Some sensation in this gesture, intimating more to be revealed ... alerts me. I inhabit it again. Someone else attracted to the sphere of Jupiter, begins to orbit closer: someone who aspires to kingship, but whose shrivelled heart, retracted, shrunk beyond reach of his own, another's pain, who has said no for now to his further evolution, someone who seeks power only to control and dominate.

The Duke of Cornwall whose little o's contract and crush ...

Let us withdraw, 'twill be a storm ...

Who says to Gloucester when he followed the old man forth ... and returned with news of Lear's desperate departure in the night ...

Shut up your doors, my Lord ... Come out of the storm

Who crushes, as his own heart has been crushed, all opposition in his cruel fist ...

Go seek the traitor Gloucester ... bind his corky arms ... though well we may not pass upon his life without the form of justice, yet our power shall do a courtesy to our wrath, which men may blame but not control ... Fellows, hold the chair ...

And plucks out Gloucester's eyes.

Figure 110 Cosmic /3/

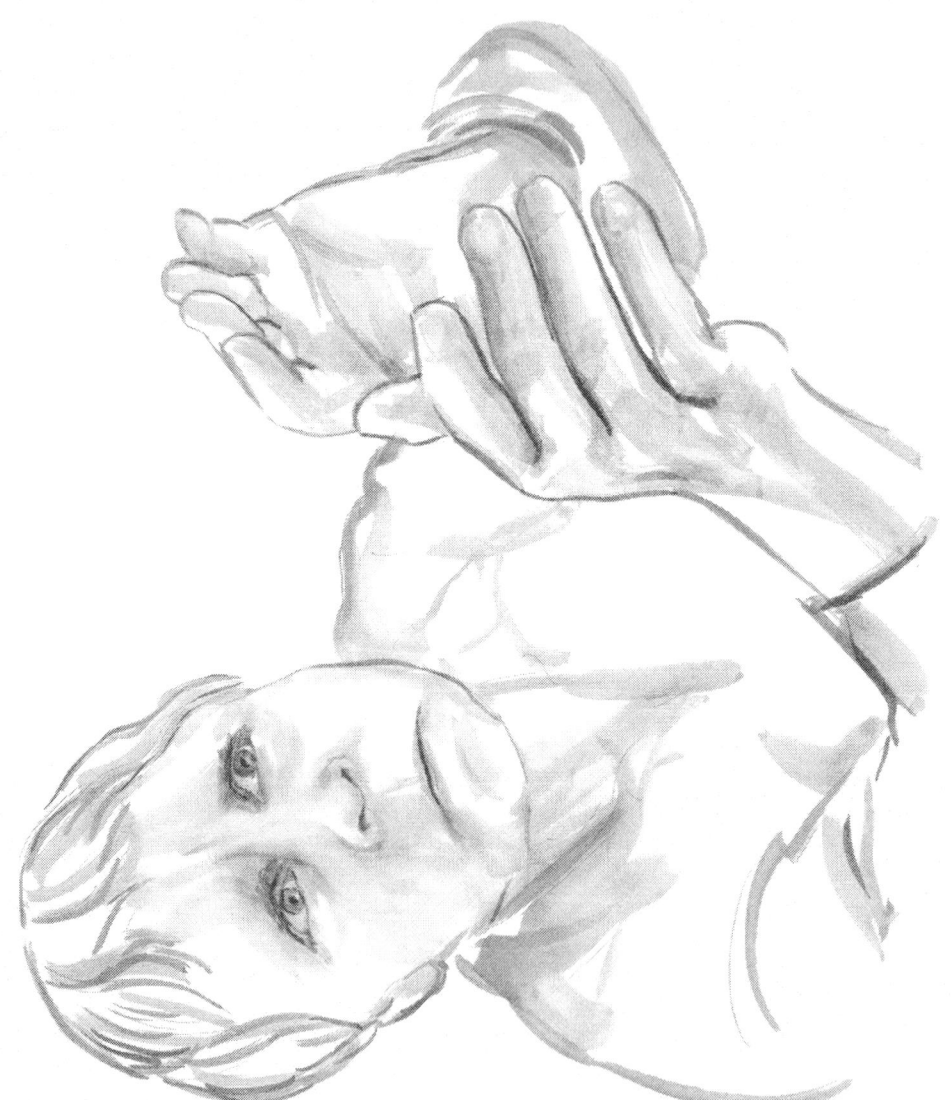

Figure 111 Regan: Dear, my Lord, be not familiar with her.

Regan — Uranus — /ɜ/(h<u>er</u>d)

I return to the eurythmy gesture /ɔ:/(<u>awe</u>). What am I holding? The world? The infant self? Whose? My own? Sensation that I hold my inner child. And if I revolve the tender inside surface of my arms and press them out, on their defenceless own to face the world — revolve the harder outside surface of my arms so they face in, awkwardly repulsed, not knowing how to nurture this dependent orphan thing.

Hardening sensation spreads into my face, nursing a hollow now. Hands and fingers prise its entrance open: sensation of wariness, not trusting of the world out there, to venture forth without support of someone else beside me. Big sister! Husband! Edmund?

Do I exist without them? Is there anyone inside me?

I speak the vowel /ɜ/(h<u>er</u>d): uncertain of my own place in the world, hoping someone hears me.

But if s/he is not heard, not tended to, how will the wounded one respond? A character approaches, nursing her hurt, still carrying her unacknowledged inner child, still waiting to be loved as much as she perceives her sisters are.
It is Regan . . .

> I am made of that self metal as my sister and prize me at her w<u>or</u>th . . . that's most c<u>er</u>tain . . . we shall f<u>ur</u>ther think on it . . .

And if she cannot be certain of her father's love . . .

> O s<u>ir</u>, you are old. Nature in you stands on the very v<u>er</u>ge of his confine. You should be ruled and led by some discretion which disc<u>er</u>ns your state, bett<u>er</u> than you yourself. Therefore I pray you that to our sister you do make ret<u>ur</u>n . . . Ret<u>ur</u>n you to my sister . . .

or Edmund's love . . .

> Dear my lord, be not familiar with h<u>er</u> . . . Witness the w<u>or</u>ld, that I create thee here, my lord and mast<u>er</u> . . .

what might she do?

Standing in the gesture /ɜ/ (er) I sense some ancient wound, something, do I even know what it is? Er . . . some ancient . . . kicked in the solar plexus something . . . /ɜ/ er . . . original betrayal. Always there, gouging a hollow where my heart should be, it inserts itself, comes between me and the world . . . others . . . life . . . separates me, keeps me wary, always watching for? . . . that thing! . . . keeps me aloof from feeling anything . . .

Sometimes I just want to do things to make someone feel my pain, know what I feel, scream my scream, so I can hear my own, feel it myself.

 *Edmund feels it too, that pain . . . that's why I understand him, why we understand each other . . . both of us have been betrayed, cheated by life, lack of our fathers' love. In this gesture, detatched, I can just watch for my chance, devise my strategies, dream of happiness.*

Goneril and the Duke of Albany – Neptune – /uɪ/ and /ju/

Figure 112 Cosmic /ju/

Figure 113 Cosmic /ju/ radiates into Goneril and Albany

Goneril – Neptune – /ʊɪ/(s<u>wee</u>t) /ju/(imb<u>ue</u>)

I move from/ɜ/(h<u>er</u>d) to /ʊɪ/(s<u>wee</u>t) and /ju/(imb<u>ue</u>). My lips curl back and forth between the pure German ü and the English diphthongs, trying to carry the more incisive placements of the purer vowel into the English, feeling the sensations shape my mouth as lips gyrate and twist in mockery – alternating /ʊɪ/(s<u>wee</u>t) and /ju/(imb<u>ue</u>). Someone drawing near!

The eldest unloved daughter, Goneril who feels herself abused . . .

He always loved our sister most . . .

And because she cannot p<u>u</u>rify the hatred in her soul will now in turn ab<u>u</u>se . . .

I'll not end<u>u</u>re it . . . Now by my life, old fools are babes again, and must be <u>u</u>sed with checks and flatteries, when they are seen ab<u>u</u>sed . . . retin<u>u</u>e . . . and not to be end<u>u</u>red riots . . . that <u>you</u> protect this course and put it on by your allowance, wh<u>i</u>ch, if <u>you</u> should, the fault would not scape cens<u>u</u>re, nor the redresses sleep, wh<u>i</u>ch, in the tender of a wholesome <u>wea</u>l, might in their working do <u>you</u> that offense, wh<u>i</u>ch else were shame, that then necessity w<u>i</u>ll call discreet proceeding . . . Epic<u>u</u>rism and lust make it more like a tavern or a brothel than a graced palace . . .

Feel those twisting, moulding lips until my whole body moulds and twists around them, muscles tense, moulding, twisting the eurythmy gesture, feel its refining sensing edges harden into schooled-in-bitterness, brutality. From inside now I sense her sense her way into her victim's weaknesses, refine her instrument of torture – words . She knows exactly how to use the truth to screw deeper into unprotected wounds, inflict the sharpest pain; using them to bully, crush and pierce the vulnerable places; once inside to twist their barbs, extract the maximum humiliation. I  *screw my mouth and feel the twisted mockery with which she spews the venom of that diphthong at her husband, Duke of Albany . . .*

Marry your manhood m<u>ew</u>!

Duke of Albany – Neptune – /ʊɪ/(s<u>wee</u>t) /ju/(imb<u>ue</u>)

And in the field created in my soul by her abusive use of /ju/ and /ʊɪ/, I sense his presence as her nobler counterpart, allow the light to penetrate the gesture once again, refine my senses and lift me up into into its crystal clarity.

I sense him inside me now, constantly at work to purify his senses, to penetrate what he perceives, until he recognises that it is the face of evil he has seen in the woman that he married and once loved . . .

O Goneril! You are not worth the dust <u>wh</u>ich the rude <u>w</u>ind blows in your face . . . She that herself <u>w</u>ill sliver and disbranch from her material sap, perforce must <u>w</u>ither and come to deadly <u>u</u>se.

It is as though they share the same potential. Albany ennobles it, using its powers to understand, discern the truth . . .

> <u>W</u>isdom and goodness to the vile seem vile . . . What have <u>you</u> done? Tigers not daughters . . . <u>you</u> are not worth the dust that the rude <u>w</u>ind blows in your face. . . .

Goneril only to whip what she derides and wring from the world the love she craves . . .

I have been worth the <u>wh</u>istle.

Edmund – Saturn – /uː/

Figure 114 The planetary being, Saturn

Figure 115 Saturn radiates through Edmund as he dies

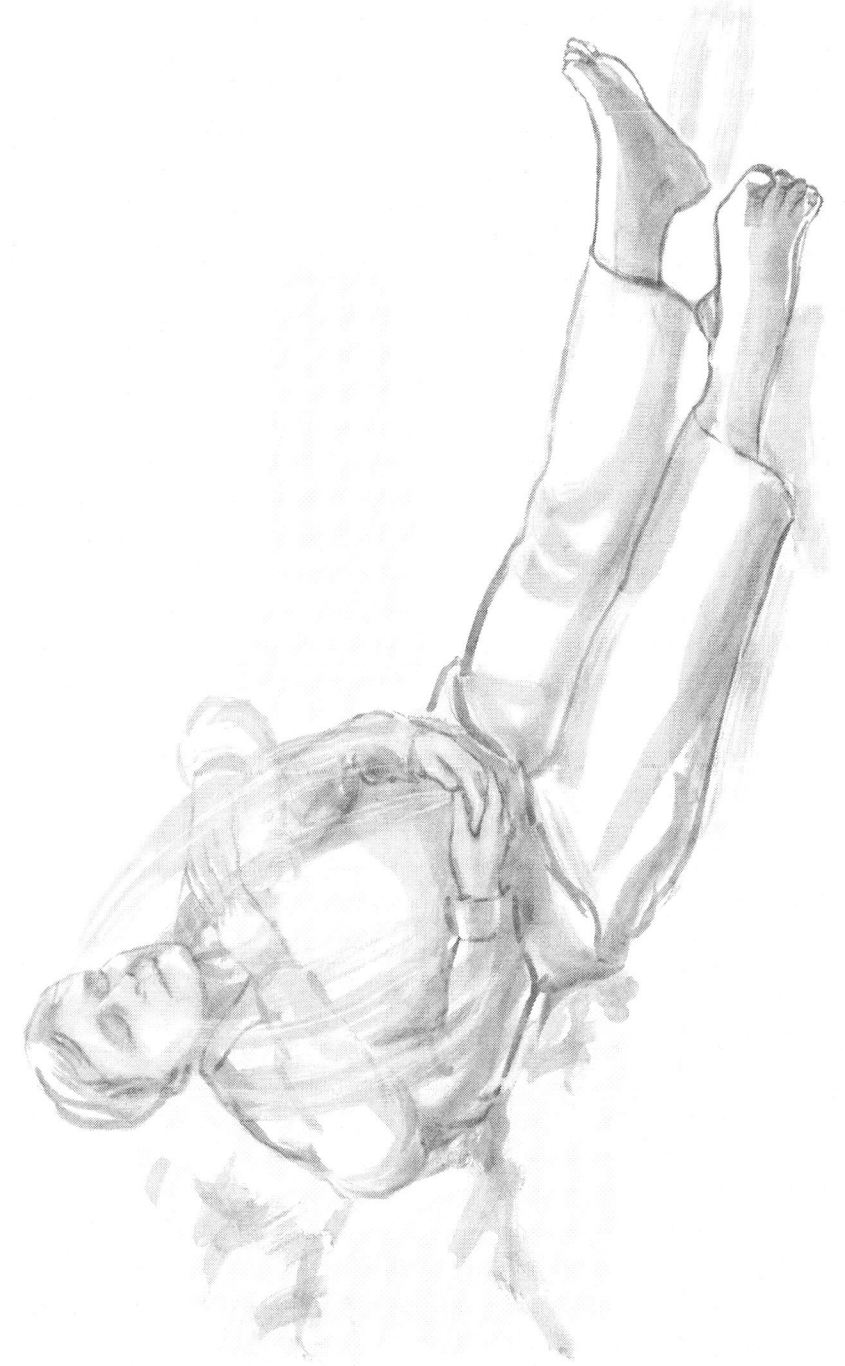

Figure 116 Edmund: The wheel has come full circle . . . Some good 1 mean to do . . . .

Figure 117 Cosmic /uː/

Edmund – Saturn – /u:/(sh<u>oe</u>)

Saturn... Hands curved, somewhat covering each other, moving between brow and abdomen, scanning the field, a sense of quiet scrutiny, deep and active contemplation ...

As I move into the gesture /u:/, a fierce intelligence inhabits me. It penetrates through everything and everyone, finds their weaknesses and knows exactly how to play them off against each other.

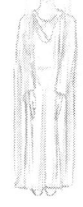

I survey the scene but weighed down by the dross of my perceived deprivation, all my powers are focused only on revenge, the play with brother's, father's ... f<u>oo</u>lish honesty ... the play with each sister's love until one died from being poisoned by the other who ... after sl<u>ew</u> herself.

Now wounded /u:/ and as death contracts me to the essence of myself the vast landscape of my life and all our lives expands towards eternity, and I can see things differently.

Hearing the story of my father's death, engineered by my own betrayal and told by the hated brother – whose property and title I coveted – I see I never recognised my father's love. I am Edmund, admitting my crimes to Edgar.

Thou hast spoken right, 'tis tr<u>ue</u> ... This tale of yours hath m<u>o</u>ved me and shall perchance d<u>o</u> g<u>oo</u>d. Some g<u>oo</u>d I mean t<u>o</u> d<u>o</u> spite of mine own nature ...

Heavy Saturn lead refined at last to pure and 'costing not less than eveything'[35] *simplicity! I complete the octave with these dying words.*

The wheel has come f<u>u</u>ll circle I am here...

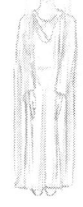

/u:/ the gift of Saturn; furthest out, the last we come to of the ancient planets! lips contracting, pushing forward to beyond the final boundary, culminating last of all the vowels, future of myself, refining to a laser focus, narrow beam of self to pierce the veil of my illusions, penetrate my past, bring it all to Saturn scrutiny, and clear at last. In my end is my beginning.

King of France — Sun — /aʊ/

Figure 118 The planetary being, Sun

Figure 119 Sun radiates through the King of France

Figure 120 King of France: This is most strange/That she, who even but now was your best
object . . . should in this trice of time/Commit a thing so monstrous to dismantle/So many folds
of favour.

Figure 121 The inward Cosmic /aʊ/

Figure 122 The inward Cosmic /aʊ/ radiates through the King of France

Figure 123 The King of France: O gods gods, tis strange that from their cold'st neglect/My love is kindled to inflamed respect.

Figure 124 The outward Cosmic /aʊ/

Figure 125 The outward Cosmic /aʊ/ radiates through the soul of the King of France

Figure 126 The King of France: Thy dowerless daughter, King ... is queen of us, of ours and our fair France.

King of France – Sun – diphthong /aʊ/(out)

Ready to begin again, sweep the whole range, alpha and omega, beginning and end. I move into the gesture of the sun, sensations of consciousness, multi-dimensional, embracing everything. I sweep it all, entire cosmos, past and future in recurring cycles, beginning and end containing one another. And could mere mouth encompass all of this or vowel capture in a second, split of time, the cycles of eternity? /aʊ/(out).

> *First the Sun gesture – arms for a moment, holding in suspense, suspend that infinite eternal cosmos-wielding swing. Not fix exactly – anyway not possible to catch a single ray – but yet to hold it long enough to, just to, capture, no, not capture or imprison but – maybe to have the eternal in my grasp just long enough . . . to what? – expand in wonder, then contract to probe, look through and in one mouth sweeping both together all at once . . .*
> */ɑ:/(st**a**r) and /u:/(sh**oe**)*

Try the left arm bending at the elbow, forearm parallel – not to fix, but for a flash, a moment, one single piercing ray of radiance suspend.

*Begin with /ɑ:/(st**a**r) and end in /u:/(sh**oe**) and on the way encompassing each other and everything between . . . words from Shakespeare's sonnet 116 surface in my body-of-sensation:*

> Love is not love
> That alters when it alteration finds . . .
>
>   . . .
>
> L**ove** alters not with his [time's]brief <u>hours</u> and weeks
> But bears it <u>out</u> even to the edge of d**oo**m

Reminding me of someone else's words:

> . . . Love is not l**o**ve
> When it is mingled with regards that stand
> Al**oo**f from the entire point . . .

The King of France arrives.

*The movement from /ɑ:/(st**a**r) to /u:/(sh**oe**) within his words takes me to the diphthong /aʊ/(out).*

> *I let this archetype arrange my sensibilities, create a field around me and within. A sun-like soul approaches, configured by the vowel of the sun. It is the King of France offering the chance to Burgundy to choose for love or property. . . .*

> Will you have her?
> She is herself a d**ow**ry . . .

*And only when Burgundy has had his chance and chooses property, love
bestows its crown:*

> Thy d<u>ower</u>less daughter king ... is queen of us, of <u>ours</u>, and <u>our</u> fair
> France.

Continuing to push the boundaries

And so the circle is complete. We have explored how a character's soul
disposition can be identified, configured and communicated through a vowel. We
have sensed that our microcosmic human souls are woven with potentials emanating
from a macrocosmic inwardness that calls us to evolve.

Figure 127 The circle of planetary beings radiating through the characters of King Lear

Pluto — /ɔɪ/

Figure 128 Cosmic /ɔɪ/

Beyond tragedy – Pluto – the diphthong /ɔɪ/ (j<u>oy</u>)

In *King Lear*, only once do we transcend the /ɔɪ/ of p<u>oi</u>son and destr<u>oy</u>: it is when Edgar tells us that his father, at the point of death, progressed from pain to j<u>oy</u>.

> … his flawed heart twixt two extremes of passion, j<u>oy</u> and grief, burst smilingly …

It is the scope of tragedy to end with death. Yet let us not forget the death of Socrates who held the cup of hemlock to his lips and 'readily and cheerfully drank the poison'.[36] And at the end of *Oedipus Tyrannus,* in the language of the mysteries, the chorus hints that something lies beyond.

> Only that joy is lasting that human beings carry with them through the gate of death.[*]

Joy in earthly life is a happy-ending attainable till now by very few. Can we imagine a consciousness existing in the universe whose mission is to carve the possibility for joy within our souls even as we wrestle with mortality? Is there a planetary being whose objective might be stated thus?:

I will to prepare your souls for joy. Therefore you must conquer fear of death. Only through death can death be overcome. I am the Lord of Death.

To fulfil my objective you must recognise that what or whom you blame as the cause of your unhappiness is a part of yourself you cannot yet embrace. If you must destr<u>oy</u> it to learn it is only your illusion of your self you have destr<u>oy</u>ed and in doing so you have destroyed nothing that is real, so be it.

I mirror back to you the destructive forces in your own soul. Until you acknowledge that the darkness you condemn in others is your own, embrace it with your left arm, sweep it all up with your right, there can be no resurrection, happy ending.

/ɔɪ/ Lips strain to do the same impossible; rounding forward to enfold /ɒ/(d<u>o</u>t) – something left behind, forgotten, something I must first go back to find – retrograde they call it – looping back behind the barrier of teeth to find the something of myself I left behind, /iː/ (m<u>e</u>) and bring it back with me …

Unable to complete the miracle unless the darkness is included too, sweep up in that embrace the all – not only nice – of me, and like a coiled spring release it to the future – /ɒ/ (d<u>o</u>t) /ɔː/(<u>awe</u>) wound through with/iː/ … /ɔɪ/ Destr<u>oy</u> … J<u>oy</u> …

And might this diphthong be the voice of Pluto, lord of death, first identified in 1930? Our consciousness only then beginning to be ready to perceive his call, not soon enough though to av<u>oi</u>d a holocaust, avert catastrophe. 'Couragio Bully Mon-

---

[*]My rendering; *The Actor of the Future 4.*

ster!' *What you fear is your own shadow. Embrace it or destroy our planet and the human race!*[37]

Only the vision of the future that Shakespeare gives us in *The Tempest* when Prospero admits *this thing of darkness I aknowledge mine,* allows us to move beyond the tragedy to the joyous light-filled /ɔɪ/ (j<u>oy</u>) of the divine commedia.[*]

O then, rej<u>oi</u>ce beyond a common j<u>oy</u>.

The diphthong /ɔɪ/ is a prophetic glimpse of the happy ending for which we yearn but must still strive to reach. With this in mind we can use the same steps 1−8 of the CPG exploration 2, in Chapter 5 in order to investigate it further.

The maps of Shakespeare's language and the clues that Steiner gave for reading them guide our souls to see and hear with other eyes and ears the infinity of beings in the heavens, invisible to earthly sight, inaudible to earthly ears, who nurture our evolving inwardness. In Shakespeare, words and soul are one.

Although the Hubble telescope reveals undreamt-of vistas in the universe, what we perceive through telescopes has not necessarily been penetrated with our consciousness. At this time of writing another multi-million dollar project to scour the universe for any signs of conscious life has been announced. Yet we often do not recognise or value the conscious life around us and within us all the time.

This work invites us to explore what traditional astrology and Steiner, in his very different way, affirmed: we will never ultimately understand the stars and planets if we deny their inwardness. Infinite expansion outwardly is only meaningful if it is accompanied by infinite expansion inwardly. How might the discovery of Chiron in

---

[*] *The Actor of the Future 3*, chapter on tragedy and comedy.

1977 or other planets still to be detected relate to our evolving sensibilities? Will we find a clue to their inwardness and to our own in vowels not yet explored?

As an actor, how rewarding to so attune my feeling-life and sound-producing instrument that sounds and feelings are experienced as one reality! To know it has not been given us to feel without means to express that feeling, that higher powers may speak through us when we speak, to touch an audience and reconnect them with the greater universe. Thus the ancient priestly task of actors is renewed appropriately for our time.

Chapter 7

Our High Work Masters (3)
Consonants and the Starry Beings of the Zodiac

Expanding the horizon of the consonants

In *The Art of Speech* we explored Steiner's indication that vowels express the range of inner life, and consonants the elements out of which the material universe condenses. Chekhov's psycho-physical techniques, beginning with the *qualities of movement*,[*] encourage us to go beyond a simplistic interpretation of this apparent division between outer form and inwardness. To an instrument attuned, all outer form is an expression of an inner state, and all inner states must at some point and in some degree express themselves in outer form.

As with the vowels, only a eurythmic exploration of the gestures will allow us to approach the inner nature of each consonant in such a way that it contributes to the process of character creation. It is assumed therefore that, ideally, an exploration of the consonants led by a eurythmist precedes and accompanies what follows.

Consonants and character

We have seen how the vowels create pathways of sensation which channel not only the changing moments of our soul experience but even fundamental tendencies of soul. Now we must discover how the consonants provide the channels through which the forces that define and shape our characters and destinies condense.

Exploration 1 – Consonant and character

1. Choose a range of contrasting consonants such as this sequence that expresses a progression through the qualities of fire, air, water, earth: /s/, /r/, /l/ and /g/.[†]
2. Wear a neutral mask to encourage you to work full-bodily. Warm up with the

---

[*] *The Art of Acting*, Chapter 1.

[†] *The Art of Speech* and *The Art of Acting*, Chapter 1.

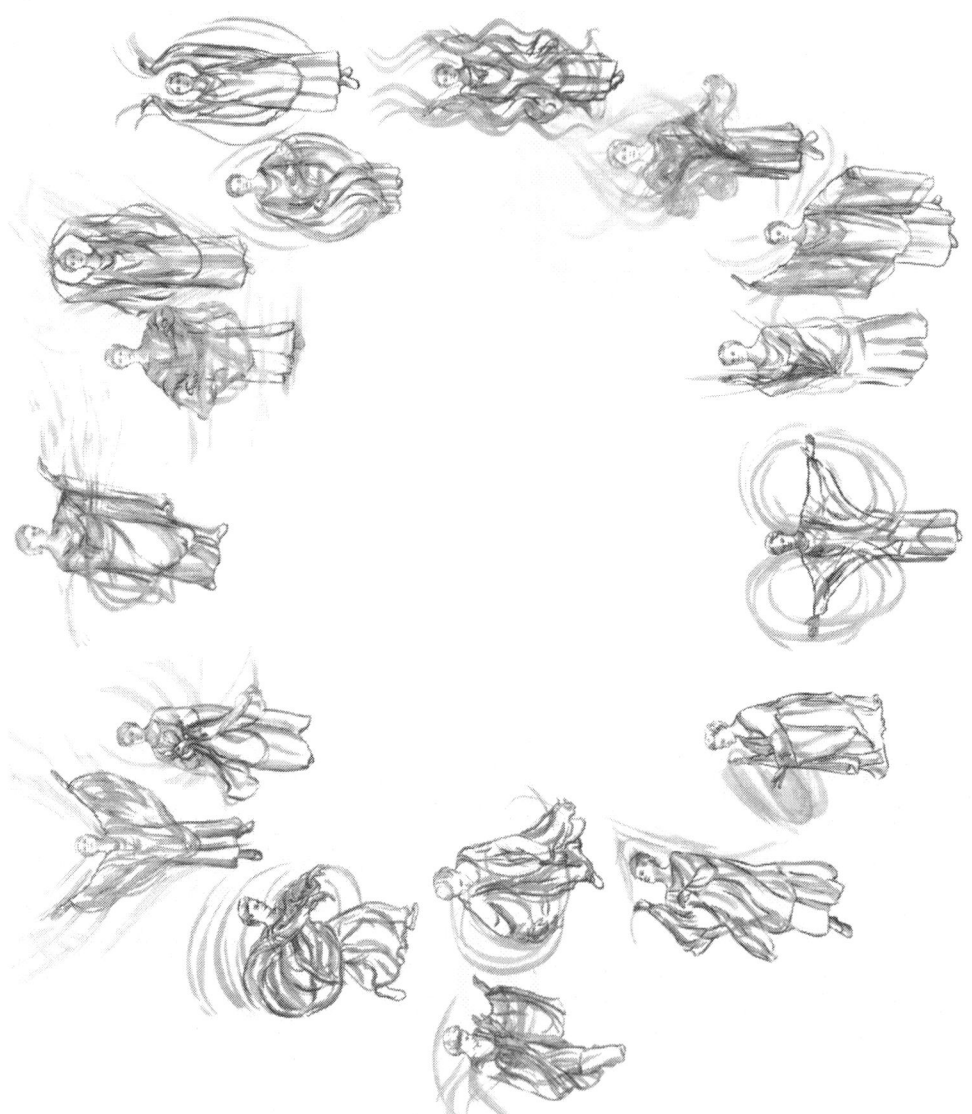

Figure 129 Archetypal eurythmy gestures for the Cosmic Consonants

appropriate *quality of movement*, then focus on the consonant of choice. If possible, listen to a colleague speak each consonant in turn while you allow the sound to penetrate your body and transform the way you move; this will include the muscular tensions in your speech organs.

3. Speak the sound while you move, so that it is born out of and integrated with your movement.

4. Have a partner observe the quality of integration and give you feedback.

5. Reduce the movement from level 10–1,[*] and explore how a consonant can imbue such naturalistic actions as walking, sitting, standing, kneeling, improvising with a prop, saying simple words like *yes* or *no* or *maybe*, with its character.

6. Sustain the body-of-sensation generated by each consonant's activity in turn and improvise a simple action sequence; for example: enter the room, switch on a light, search for something, read a letter, etc. Can you experience how differently an /s/ or /r/ shaped character, for instance, reads a book?

7. Repeat the process with each consonant until you have a sense of how each character behaves. Observe also that due to the intimate relationship between our soul and body the character's movement arouses and is fused with its psychology.

Exploration 2 – Consonant and character

Explore the range of characters summoned by each consonant. For example, character /f/ can set fire to everything around them, searing everyone with their untempered heat. However, when layered with the I AM[†] presence, character /f/ can also generate the force for change and be fired with the courage to leap across the barriers that separate the known and unknown, past and future, into a new cycle of becoming.

1. To access the range of character potential that a consonant can activate in your sensation body, layer it with the *defended or undefended heart, other centres, tempo and dynamic, expansion and contraction, qualities and sensations, archetypes, objectives and PGs*, etc.[‡]

2. In each class or practice use these steps to explore each consonant until you are familiar with them all.

Vowels lead us into different states of soul but do not condense or crystallise as deeply

---

[*] Chapter 1, exploration 1, *The Art of Acting*, pages 46–47.

[†] See Chapter 2.

[‡] *The Art of Acting*, Table of Contents.

into outer form as consonants which imprint their defining tendencies even into the
bodies they inhabit with a sense of permanence.

Exploration 3 – Consonant and character

1. Choose a character from a dramatic text on which you have already done foundation work. Using your full-bodied tools, warm up the basic layers of your
   character. Stand with your instrument attuned. Are there consonants whose basic
   qualities align with those layers of sensation to interact and fuse with them into the
   fundamental disposition of that character?
2. If more than one suggests itself attune your instrument to focus on each in turn. If
   the discoveries arising from your work confirm, fructify and integrate with your
   other choices, observe how that consonant becomes a binding agent that attracts
   the other layers of your work into its field and imprints its defining character on
   them.
3. Allow your body-of-sensations to suggest a moment in the life of your character and
   improvise it using movement only.
4. When you sense the impulse, speak the consonant and explore how it shapes your
   voice and speech.
5. Verbalise the subtext. Explore how the quality of consonant imbues your character's speech with its own defining features and contributes to an integrated body/
   voice/speech gestalt.
6. Do the same with words from the text.
7. Consolidate the integration of the consonant with the other layers of your character
   and the way it speaks the text.

The consonants and the Starry Beings of the Zodiac

> By all the operation of the orbs
> From whom we do exist and cease to be....
>
> *King Lear*, Act I, Scene 1.

We explored in Chapters 3 and 4 how the vowels lead us to experience the work of the
planetary beings in our souls. This experience confirms and deepens the claims made
in traditional astrology that the planetary beings work through our different organs
and secretions to create the conditions that allow us to experience an inner life. Now

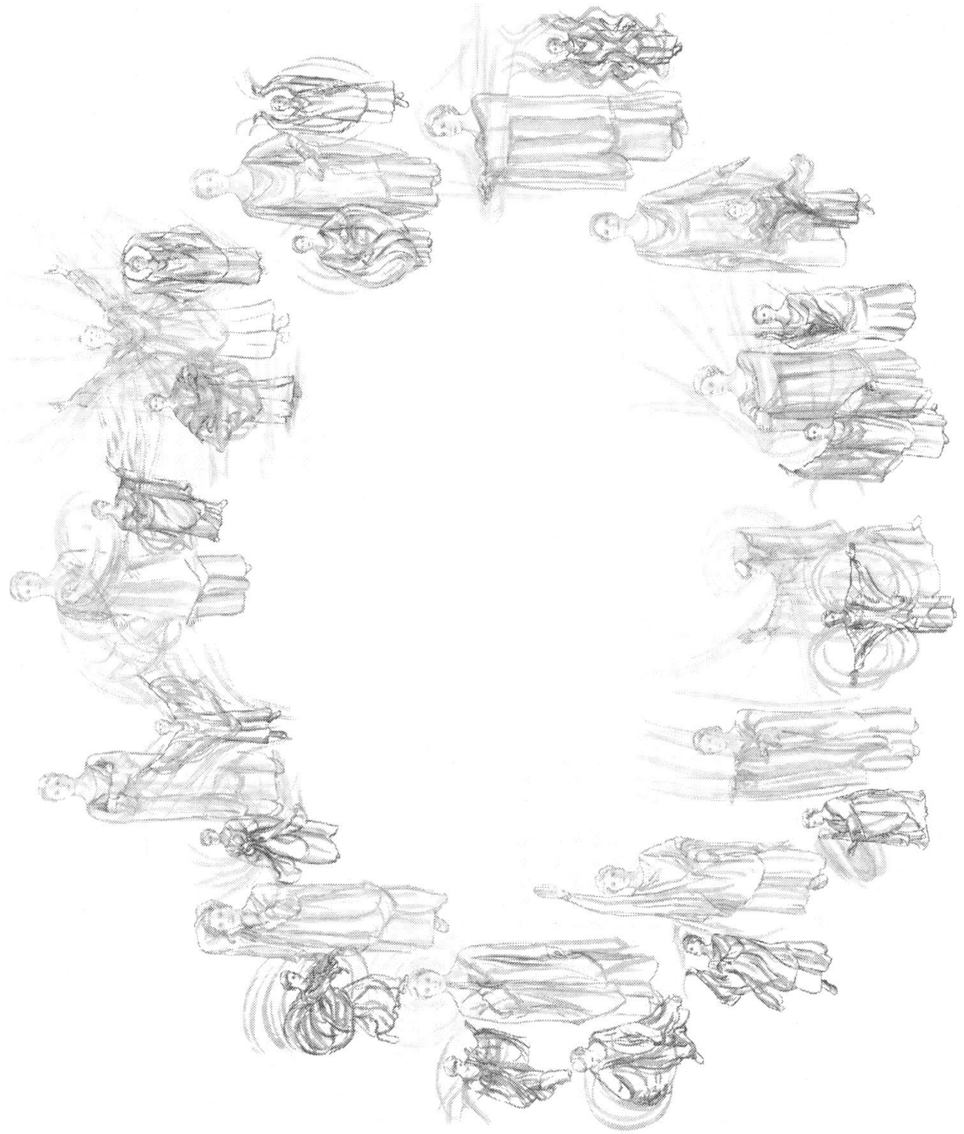

Figure 130 Starry Beings of the Zodiac with their accompanying Cosmic Consonants

we are ready to explore how the consonants relate to the divine creative beings whose visible bodies are referred to as the constellations of the zodiac.

These insights are revealed in the eurythmy gestures of the consonants and starry beings. If we approach them as CPGs, they allow us to explore the contribution each one makes to the range of potentials at work in human character and destiny. These starry beings work from supersensible dimensions to perfect each human entelechy. In cooperation with its moral, spiritual evolution over many lifetimes, they weave their influences through the planetary spheres, through the dynamics at work in human destiny, condensing them even into the specific psycho-physical constitution that serves as the vessel for the next life of that entelechy. This incarnating human being makes a life-long commitment, so to speak, to dwell in and utilise the possibilities inherent in this vessel. Just as the macrocosmic energies, gestures and dynamics of the planetary beings and their vowels are expressions of the Logos, the divine creative word, so too are the microcosmic sounds we call the consonants the human counterpart of the macrocosmic sounds emanating from the beings of the zodiac. Their influence condenses even into the forming of our speech organs which determine the distinctive qualities of speech and language of each human being. Therefore, the gestures of each starry being with its associated consonant/s hold the key to the clear delination of a character that radiates with supersensible dimensions.

Even the shallow caricatures that serve 'your star sign for the week' columns in a gossip magazine reveal in the commonality of elements described — with which the communal psyche still identifies, suspended as it is between sceptical and superstitious fascination — some glimmer of their more profound archetypes. We can use the tools developed in *The Art of Acting* to build a playful, basic sketch for the character-type based on the common elements associated with each constellation, both positive and negative. For example: the constitution of the Libran type cannot tolerate imbalance and disharmony, compelling them to strive for harmony and balance in their souls and their surroundings. Taken to an extreme this positive potential can lead to a 'peace at any price' approach to everything, a compulsion to be liked that results in an inability to know one's own mind or commit. The Gemini type has twin personalities, light and dark; the light one is extremely social, interested in everything, with a sparkling intellect, gifted in conversation and exchange of ideas but its nature can swing suddenly into the brooding inwardness of its darker twin. Geminis also can be indecisive, torn between conflicting choices, unable to make decisions and commit to them. Our developed bodies of sensation immediately sense how to transform such simple sketches into psycho-physical explorations that prepare the ground into which the seeds of Steiner's deeper insights can be planted later.

Exploration 4 – Consonant and constellation-type

1. Divide into groups on the basis of your dates of birth: all the Leos over here, all the Librans there, etc.
2. In each group, share what you understand about the type associated with your constellation, how it is expressed in you and others that you know. Build a profile of it. If there's a constellation type not represented in your group, build a profile together based on what you know.
3. Share your profiles with the class/ensemble.
4. Choosing tools that suggest themselves create a full-bodied working sketch of each.[*]
5. Share your preliminary sketches with each other, playing with the range of movement 10–1.
6. Sense which consonants align with the body of sensation arising from each working sketch and integrate them with your full-bodied explorations.

Exploration 5 – Consonant and constellation-type

1. Building on exploration 4, create a full-bodied working sketch (including consonant/s) for each constellation-type. Now each person in the group must choose to represent a different one.
2. Warm up full-bodily and sustain your choice while you move around the space responding to each other.
3. In pairs, improvise the interactions that arise between the different types. For example, an Aries and a Capricorn stuck in a lift together, or a Cancer and a Leo type caught in an avalanche, or a Gemini and Aries type go for couples' counselling. From time to time transition back to level 10 so your work is always anchored in your body-of-sensation.

Exploration 6 – Consonant and constellation-type

If there are enough of you, improvise the former situations in a group of 12, in which each type is represented.

---

[*] This refers to the tools outlined in *The Art of Acting*: qualities-of-movement, tempo and dynamic, expansion and contraction, centres, PG, imaginary bodies, archetypes, visualisation and incorporation, etc.

Exploration 7 – Consonant and constellation-type

Compare your discoveries about the consonants with Steiner's insights as revealed in the next exploration.

Through eurythmy gestures we are ready to explore the deeper mysteries inherent in these types. By alternating these with free play based on observation, we develop a sense for the relationship between character, full-bodied archetypal gestures of the consonants and the macrocosmic beings who pour their substance into the creation of a human being with its distinctive qualities and possibilities of destiny.

As with the vowels and the planetary beings, the eurythmy gestures about to be explored must be more than static symbols of an abstract theory. Ideally therefore we should initially be led by a eurythmist so they stir our life/etheric body into movement. Then we may sense how they condense out of, and at the same time expand us into, their cosmic substance. Only the pure eurythmic gestures can transform our body-of-sensation into an organ of perception for the presence and activity of higher beings. Without this experience the gestures risk being hardened into earthly muscular activity that excludes the macrocosmic life, fixed prematurely into static signs that we can be in danger of applying as an intellectual formula or set of tricks.

This next exploration, then must be undertaken many times. It is also important to absorb the many lectures in which Steiner shares his insights into the working of these cosmic beings.[*] These will then begin to penetrate the substance generated through your instrument with clarity.

Exploration 8 – Constellation archetype and consonant

1. Led by a eurythmist focus on the gestures of each consonant in turn and its associated constellation.
2. Treat each gesture as a CPG. The pathway of sensation that it generates enables you to feel your way into the consciousness and dynamics of intention of a being.
3. Penetrate each constellation gesture until you sense how the will embodied in it is connected to the will embodied in the gesture/s of its corresponding consonant/s.
4. For our present purposes we begin with Aries, the sign embodying the archetype of new beginnings. According to the tropical system of astrology, the return of spring coincides with the sun entering the sign of Aries at the March equinox. Then we will proceed, in the order of the signs through which the sun moves in the course of a year.[38]

_____
[*] See Bibliography.

Constellations of the Zodiac and the Cosmic Consonants

Figure 131 Aries radiating through Cosmic /w/ and /v/

Figure 132 Taurus radiating through Cosmic /r/ 'rolled r'

Figure 133 Gemini radiating through the inward and outward Cosmic /h/

Figure 134 Cancer radiating through Cosmic /f/

Figure 135 Leo radiating through Cosmic /t/ and /d/

Figure 136 Virgo radiating through Cosmic /p/ and /b/

Figure 137 Libra radiates through Cosmic /ts/ (German z)

Figure 138 Scorpio radiating through Cosmic /s/

Figure 139 Sagittarius radiating through Cosmic /k/ and /g/

Figure 140 Capricorn radiating through Cosmic /l/

Figure 141 Aquarius radiating through Cosmic /m/

Figure 142 Pisces radiating through Cosmic /n/

The relationship of the archetypal gestures of the constellations and their consonants to human gesture

Just as the archetype of 'rose' appears in myriad forms particular to climate, breeding and geography, so the twelve archetypes of the zodiac individualise as they weave their potentials into the creation of specific human beings/characters and the destinies unfolding through their circumstances and relationships. We will recognise the echos of these cosmic archetypes in the 'ordinary' gestures we observe around us as our body of sensibilities, immersed in the archetypal gestures, begins to resonate with the connections.

As we move back and forth between the infinite and personal dimensions of consonants and constellations, our ability to differentiate between inhabiting our instrument eurythmically or as human being/character, incarnated into earthly circumstances and conditions, will strengthen.

Exploration 9 – Constellation archetype and consonant

Connecting our earthly experience of consonants to the macrocosmic consonants.

The following exploration is also intended to be undertaken many times in order to expand and deepen these discoveries.

1. Building on the first 2 explorations in this chapter, choose a consonant, create its character and then explore how it stands and sits, moves, enters a space and relates to an object: a letter, flower, knife or ring, etc.
2. Inhabit the eurythmy gesture for the consonant. As you transition into it, pay attention to the shift from your earthly human body into your eurythmic instrument.
3. Move back and forth between these levels of expression of the consonant, paying attention to the changes in sensation.
4. Focus on the earthly gesture and its character. Sustain it and, while you move, imagine that this shape, determining your character, is bestowed on you by a greater Someone in the universe.
5. During this process, when the impulse to express it vocally arises from the full-bodied penetration of your instrument, speak the consonants.

Exploration 10 – Constellation archetype and consonant

Connecting our experience of the macrocosmic gesture of a constellation to our earthly experience

1. Treat the eurythmic gesture of a constellation as a CPG and incorporate it.
2. Identify the objective that declares itself through your body of sensation. What do you want to contribute to the destiny of human beings?

Partner work

3. Work together, taking it in turns to be the human being who is shaped by that forming gesture and the being in the cosmos who shapes the character on earth.

Individual

4. Create a one-person movement sequence that weaves back and forth between the roles.
5. As you move from the role of Cosmic Being in the pure eurythmic gesture to a human being inhabiting their body on the earth, explore the difference. Pay attention to the changes in sensation as you shift from peripheral consciousness to focused earthly consciousness and back again, moving through each stage of the continuum.

By now you have an instrument attuned to multi-layers of sensation, able to sense the pathways that connect them and respond to their interacting impulses. Now we learn to recognise the echoes of these macrocosmic gestures in the ordinary gestures we observe around us.

Exploration 11 Constellation archetype and consonant

Investigating the continuum between the macro and microcosmic gestures of consonant and constellation

1. Pay attention to the gestures you observe around you.
2. Recreate them, and pay attention to the body-of-sensations each one generates in you. Enter each gesture as deeply as you can until you sense what it expresses.
3. Put it into words.
4. Explore each macrocosmic consonant in turn. What is it expressing?

5. Put it into words.
6. Sustain the gesture and feel the shift in sensation as you make the transition into your human body on the earth. How many different ways can you modify the gesture by changing details of direction, head or hand position for example, while maintaining the archetype's integrity?
7. As you do so, pay attention to the changes in sensation. Do these gestures remind you of any of the everyday gestures you explored?
8. Reverse the process. Play with the everyday gestures until they reveal the archetypes concealed within.

Once we can recognise the cosmic archetypes within our ordinary gestures we are ready to apply this work to character creation. This readiness is the sign that the work we have undertaken in the ways suggested with eurythmy, Speech Formation and Chekhov's psycho-physical technique has transformed our body-of-sensation (or sensibilities or Chekhov's *sensitive membrane*) into an organ of perception. This organ enables us to recognise artistic truth in the choices we have made when they link up with each other, are deepened, suggest new possibilities, surprise us with connections we could never have predicted, and confirm that a Someone beyond our power to invent, not manufactured out of whim or cleverness or arbitrary interpretation, exists as a participant within a meaningful creation and pours its blessings, opportunities and challenges into our human lives.[39]

Following are two examples of the sorts of processes that enable such investigations and that might be part of workshopping a play. Both assume the actor has begun to cultivate this organ of perception.

Exploration 12 – Consonant, character and constellation

1. Choose a character already worked on with the processes described in *The Art of Acting*.
2. Move in a full-bodied way through the layers of gestures and dynamics out of which, thus far, your character is woven. You can visit them in any order and/or combination.
3. Scan the field of sensation accessed by these gestures until your *sensitive membrane* resonates with the field of sensation accessed by the gesture of a constellation and/or its accompanying consonant/s.
4. If the field of sensation generated by your character resonates with the field of sensation generated by the gesture of more than one consonant or constellation, this provides opportunity for finer tuning: more investigation on the way to a

clearer choice of constellation, or realisation that there may be more than one cosmic influence at work in a specific character.[40]

5. Once you have arrived at a working hypothesis, test it out. Explore full-bodily how the cosmic influence penetrates each detail of the character's behaviour and the words they speak.

Exploration 13 – Consonant, character and constellation

With characters you have created in the past or currently are working on, and for whom you already have an intuition that a specific constellation and/or consonant might be an influence, steps 1–3 above can be reversed.

1. Warm up the eurythmy gestures for that constellation and its accompanying consonant.
2. Observe if your full-bodied work attracts that character into its field. Experiment with text and character, exploring how the cosmic gestures and the human, deepen and enrich each other.

Intuition of the influence of a specific constellation and/or its associated consonant/s may precede our other work to build a character. Whether it be the character, the consonant or constellation that comes first, if we start our full-bodied work, the pathways of sensation generated will lead us to discoveries which, if our intuition is a truthful one, will strengthen and confirm each other. These discoveries can then be investigated further with the Chekhov tools and will in turn, deepen and confirm the former work. If our investigations do not confirm the outcome that we first intuited, the discoveries we make along the way will still contribute to the process and prove fruitful in other unexpected ways.

When we treat the gestures for each constellation and its consonant/s as *cosmic psychological gestures* (CPGs), each has the power to release the inspiration for many characters, a range of selves within the spectrum of possibilities provided by that constellation. For, as in life, each set of starry beings bestows on us a range of challenges and possibilities by which we undergo initiation. Some who set out on the path of a specific constellation's possibilities may give birth to or have already given birth to the I AM higher self within them. This allows them to successfully complete that level of initiation by evolving to the highest, noblest level of those possibilities. Those who use those same opportunities only to serve their baser instincts will fall into the decadence specific to that type.

In the English language this wisdom is woven mysteriously, inextricably into

Shakespeare's plays. Through them we can investigate how the divine creative beings at work in human lives and destinies permeate even a character's speech and language tendencies. His plays provide the perfect exercise material for English-speaking actors to achieve a high degree of speech and acting integration. Once this integration is achieved we can apply it to the characters in other dramas.

Viewing characters through the lens of the constellations does not limit human beings to twelve narrow choices or imprison them in static formulae. Rather, in combination with the many character-creating tools bequeathed by Chekhov, we discover how a single archetypal gesture expands into a vast range of potential characters. It reveals to our body-of-sensation the deeper layers woven into their biographies and how they influence a character's way of moving, speaking and relating to the world. Here, for example, are four very different characters for whom the shaping powers of Scorpio and /s/ bind their otherwise distinctive qualities into a gestalt and illuminate their differences within these greater dimensions of themselves.

Characters in the key of Scorpio shaped by the sound gesture of Cosmic /s/

Shakespeare's unerring intuition for the perfect match of character and sound allows us to sense how different characters, each in their different ways, can be created in the key of Scorpio and shaped by the sound-gesture /s/.

Figure 143 The starry being, Scorpio

Figure 144 Archetypal eurythmy gesture for Cosmic /s/

Figure 145 Scorpio radiates through Cosmic /s/

Figure 146 Scorpio expresses its nature through Cosmic /s/ and radiates its influence into a range of characters

Hamlet

Figure 147 Hamlet: Seems Madam? Nay it is. I know not seems.

Hamlet's speeches are woven through by /s/. His first words are:

Seems Madam? Nay it is. I know not seems.

His last:

The rest is silence.

As we move through his other speeches, we cannot help but hear that they are saturated with this consonant and therefore with its qualities, for instance:

... seems to me a sterile promontary ... what is this quintessence of dust?

...I have heard that guilty creatures sitting at a play have, by the very cunning of the scene, been struck so to the soul that presently they have proclaimed their malefactions. For murder, though it hath no voice, but yet will speak with most miraculous organ...

 Following this clue I prepared my instrument with the eurythmy gesture for the constellation Scorpio and its associated /s/. Then I condensed their macrocosmic being into the body of a human character on earth. I sense how my left arm and hand drawn earthwards, serve to steady me, enabling my right arm and hand to slice through space.

 I found that these gestures immediately synthesised with other layers of the character I had been working with and organised them into its gestalt. I sensed, embedded in the very language that he speaks, how /s/ reveals the sub- and super-text of a character impaled upon his own rapier intellect, stung by his own scorpion tail.

/s/ is the weapon with which he not only stings those around him into consciousness but is compelled to pierce through all illusion in himself. Sexuality, unable to fulfil itself in love, turns on itself and stings itself to death even as it savagely attacks every expression of it that he sees around him. He struggles to evolve from the scorpion who attacks out of impotence, to the soaring eagle who fulfils the destiny of his high calling and his noble nature ... *what should such fellows as I do, crawling between earth and heaven?*

I sense how /s/ penetrates the very form of my body, providing a custom-fitted dwelling for the character. This organising principle, permeates not only his customary way of gesturing but even the muscles of the larynx and organs of articulation, giving birth to a distinctive quality of speech, laser sharp and like a scalpel, slicing through each layer of deception.

Prospero

Figure 148 Prospero: I have bedimmed/The noontide sun, called forth the mutinous winds/ And twixt the green seas and the azured vault/ Set roaring war ... There stand, for you are spell stopped.

Over the years I have explored Prospero from *The Tempest*, seeking a way to access the macrocosmic levels of his character that are embedded in the language that he speaks. These must be woven through the 'all too human' aspects of his personality so the audience can understand the complex struggles of a character who is both great and small but who wrestles to transform his smallness.

In my daily practice with the cosmic archetypes I am suddenly arrested in my journey through the zodiac. Moving into Scorpio and /s/ my body-of-sensations is transformed. Suddenly I sense the presence of someone who wields power over all the elements and channels it through magic mantric spells. I do not need to try to feel how this would feel. It is inside me.

> There stand for you are spell stopped... Ye elves of hills, groves, standing stones and lakes, and ye that on the sand with printless foot do chase the ebbing Neptune...

I sense how /s/ enables him to pierce his inner life with clarity of insight and recognise his faults, his own need for forgiveness.

> Those being all my study ... to my state grew stranger ... and rapt in secret studies ... Sit still and hear the last of our sea sorrow... This thing of darkness I acknowledge mine... And my ending is despair unless I be relieved by prayer, which pierces so, that it assaults mercy itself and ends all faults.

That same /s/ which he had learned to use in order to impose his will has been refined at the end into an instrument that pierces through the very nature of illusion.

Of the four examples we explore, Prospero most nearly accomplishes the Scorpio initiation. From the heights of the eagle, his towering intellect penetrates the karma of relationships allowing him to finally transform his impulse for revenge into forgiveness and stop projecting his repressed sexuality on those around him. He renounces the power of 'rough magic' and surrenders it in the service of a higher magic, the alchemy of moral transformation.

Through the Scorpio gesture I feel how Prospero's attention is directed back to earth. He has learned at last to govern the kingdom of his soul. He is ready to return to Milan and govern those earthly things for which he is responsible.

Goneril

Figure 149 Goneril: Sir . . . dearer than eyesight, space . . . I had rather lose the battle than that sister/Should loosen him and me.

The imaginary body of a python has been a potent tool in working with the character of Goneril from *King Lear*. As I feel her body undulate seductively I find myself sliding into /s/ and remember that, like Hamlet, the first sound she utters is /s/... *Sir*!... With it she insinuates her way into her father's favour

> ... dearer than eyesight, space or liberty ... beyond all manner of so much...

And later uses it to sear with scorn:

> ... not only, sir, this, your all licensed fool, but other of your insolent retinue ... I had thought ... to have found a safe redress; but now grow fearful, by what yourself too late have spoke and done, that you protect this course, and put it on by your allowance, which if you should, the fault would not scape censure, nor the redresses sleep ...

Later still its coils tighten to secure her ends:

> I had rather lose the battle than that sister should loosen him and me ...

Goneril has let her sexuality degenerate to serve her lust for power. Scorpion-like, she stings her enemies to death: literally poisoning her sister and, with her jealousy, everyone with whom she interacts. Without the forces of her heart to mediate between her sharp intelligence and degenerate will, in this life she will not achieve the Scorpio initiation.

The queen in *Cymbeline* is similar to Goneril. In pursuit of power she also uses sexual machinations, will and sharp intelligence to manipulate her husband and everyone around her.

> *Queen*: Peace! peace! ... Sweet sovereign, leave us to ourselves ... Tis not sleepy business; but must be looked to speedily and strongly ...

Like Prospero, she has explored the path of magic but in her case does not evolve beyond the use of it to serve her lusts. As with Goneril, the queen's gesture draws her inexorably down towards the earth, where she will lose herself. When all her scheming fails, she 'stings herself to death' by poisoning.

Chapter 8

Our High Work Masters (4)
Consonants and the Starry Beings of the Zodiac in Shakespeare's *King Lear*

The world of Shakespeare's plays and the circle of the zodiac

In the 1970s I attended workshops in Dornach led by Sophia Walsh. She pioneered a way of working with the macrocosmic gestures of the zodiac and consonants as a basis for developing the twelve archetypal characters in Steiner's *Mystery Plays*. Since then her work has continued to inspire my experiments with the contribution that the planetary beings and vowels, consonants and zodiac can make to character creation, particularly as it is revealed in Shakespeare's plays.

The utterly complete-within-itself universe Shakespeare conjures in each play has always fascinated me. This sense of wholeness is true of every great dramatic work, indeed of every work of art, yet the degree to which it manifests in Shakespeare seems to me unique. Each set of characters emerges with an integrity of action, language and psychology. The tapestry of their lives and interactions seems to spring complete from some macrocosmic, organising sensibility, as though woven from the very source that shapes our destinies. Sophia's work handed me the keys to unlock this mystery.

Can musicians play the music that compels us to surrender to its mysteries if they do not understand how composers have created the desired effects? Again, again, the same set of keys, tones and intervals, the same range of tempi, determine what is possible. Again, again, the infinite chambers of our inwardness unlocked by that finite range of keys and intervals, astonishes. Again, again, that finite range of consonants and vowels! We are amazed at their capacity to arouse an infinite range of thoughts and feelings, to break us open, and to heal. Did Shakespeare know *how* he could do this? Actors certainly can speak his words without an inkling of this knowledge. Yet can they stimulate the levels of response we are referring to, without it?

Over the years, I have felt myself in the presence of this mystery whenever Shakespeare's words begin to sound; I have witnessed countless others sense it though the promise might be only partially fulfilled in readings or performances. How he does it has occupied me through my life. If the work that follows confirms that the High Work Masters who shape our language also shape our destinies, then perhaps we can sense the source of his magic. Is it because the whole cosmos of divine creative beings contribute their potential to each play that each world that Shakespeare makes feels total and complete?

Expanding to the whole play

Just as the chamber presentation of *King Lear* was the laboratory in which I researched the working of the vowels and the planetary beings so it also allowed me to investigate the working of the consonants and constellations of the zodiac. I found myself astonished at the depths of character and integrity of insights that were consistently revealed; they confirmed the levels of divine creative wisdom unconsciously or consciously at work through Shakespeare's 'genius'. Almost as soon as I began, the twelveness leapt out at me from every detail of action, character and language. Yet at many points I was aware I could have made quite other choices and that a different world, no less complete, would have then arranged itself. There is room for many readings of a great work of art. Individual musicians play the same composition differently, interpreting, emphasising this or that as it reveals itself through their unique artistic intuition. It is in this spirit that I share my contribution to the understanding of a mystery *that hath no bottom.*

Method of working

My engagement with this play had begun with study at university, lecturing about it, working on scenes and characters with students and myself on numerous occasions and finally directing two productions, one with students, one professional. Clarity demands that I refine into its essence the challenge to create all characters myself which was the culmination of this lifelong journey with the play and which took three years to complete. Like most such endeavours the process was in fact chaotic, leaping from doubt to intuition, back again to doubt, one intuition leading to another – across gestures, interactions, characters, language and different levels of investigation. There were months of intensive work interspersed with times of dreaming. Before I began this aspect of my research, I had already done much of the fundamental work to build each character using the tools described in *The Art of Acting*. My speech instrument was tuned to working with the formative powers of the consonants. Years of eurythmy had deepened my preparedness.

Although I believe the following conditions make such an exploration possible, they do not imply a fixed order or dogmatic process:

- Thorough immersion in the text.
- Work with Chekhov's tools for character creation.[*]

---

[*] *The Art of Acting.*

- Work with the eurythmy gestures for each constellation of the zodiac and its associated consonants: treating them as CPGs that grant access to the inner life of the Macrocosmic Beings who bestow on us the possibilities from which we weave our lives and destinies.
- Play with how these archetypes reveal themselves in everyday, more naturalistic gestures. As indicated in *The Art of Acting*, Chapter 4, and in Exploration 10 of Chapter 5, these nuances can be achieved by distorting the archetypal gesture one feature at a time (e.g.: level or angle of head, feet, arms, hands) allowing the effect to resonate and stimulate recall of a gesture seen or felt in others or oneself, paying attention to the shifts in sensation; all the time allowing words or phrases, longer passages of text to declare and insert themselves into the field created by these gestures.

As in Chapter 6, the following investigation of *King Lear* summarises my discoveries and is written in a stream of consciousness, subjective style to suggest how creative intuition works. It may be useful to read the explorations out aloud and try to recreate their journey.

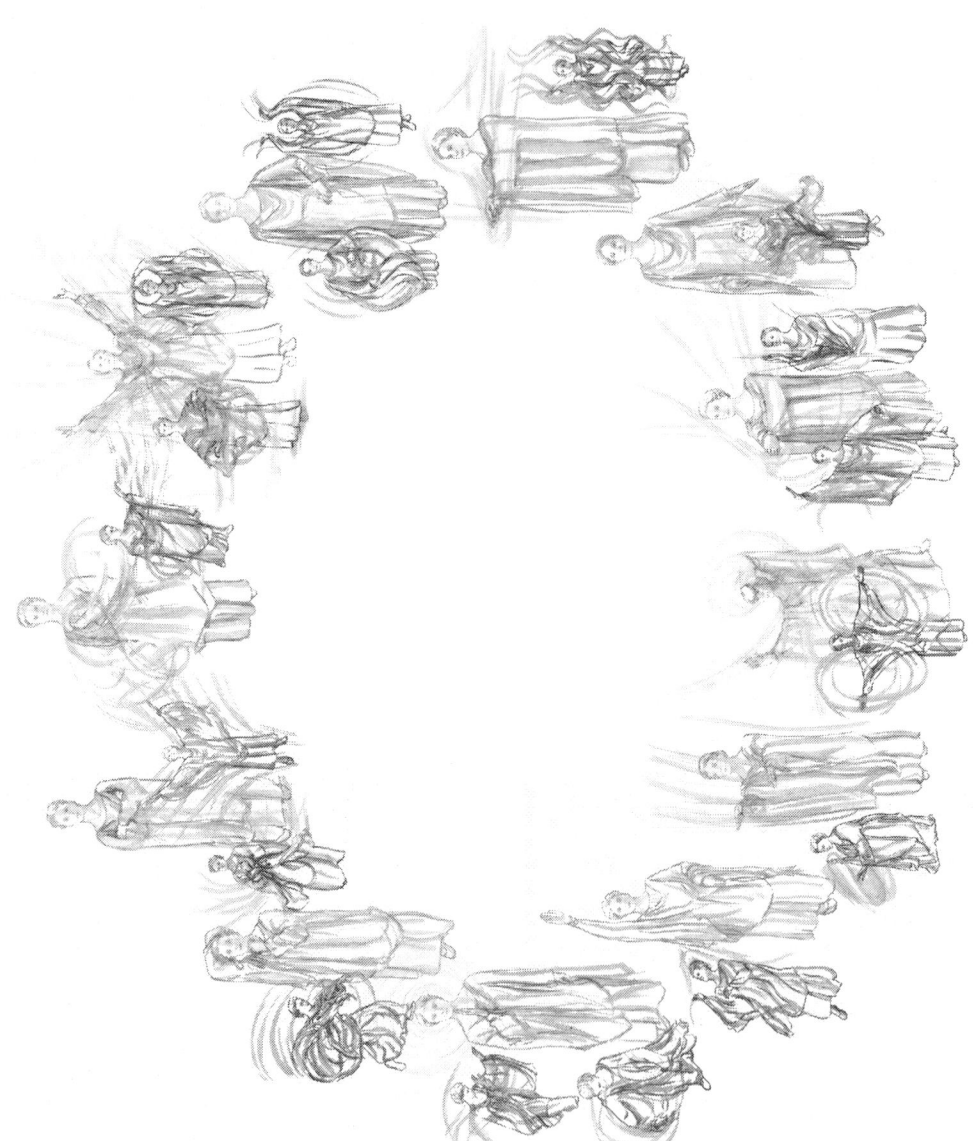

Figure 150 Starry Beings of the Zodiac stream through the Cosmic Consonants

King Lear – Leo – /d/ and /t/

Figure 151 The starry being, Leo

Figure 152 Leo radiates through Lear

Figure 153 Lear. For by the sacred radiance of the sun ...

Figure 154 Cosmic /d/

Figure 155 Cosmic /d/ radiates through Lear

Figure 156 Lear: Down thou climbing sorrow...

Figure 157 Cosmic /t/

Figure 158 Cosmic /t/ radiates through Lear

Figure 159 Lear: Beat at this gate that let thy folly in/And thy dear judgement out. . . .

Figure 160 Leo radiates through Cosmic /d/ and /t/

King Lear in the key of Leo, shaped by /t/ and /d/

Where to begin? Standing in an empty space. Body, mind and heart attuned. A flash of memory followed by dismissal – surely, connecting Lear's name with Leo is too obvious, an intellectual abstraction. Head or not, this memory from years ago won't leave me. At university, preparing for an essay on King Lear, *I am reading* Harley Granville Barker's, 'Prefaces to Shakespeare' *... Image of an old lion, no longer dominant, holed up in a cave, growling as he licks his wounds and savagely defends his fading power. Try it anyway! On all fours, digest the lion with my cells and muscles. Sustain the body-of-sensation and stand upright like a man, claws treading, rending empty air, still trying to control his universe, his kingdom. Fully stretched now into the periphery. Is this legitimate? Have I made it up? This almost Leo gesture.*

    Summoned by my body-of-sensation, words hover at the edge of consciousness; slide effortlessly into the dimension of his more-than-human rage. I expand into the hugeness of their power. What it must once have been! – striking terror in his subjects:

> Let it be so! Thy truth then be thy dower!
> For by the sacred radiance of the sun,
> The mysteries of Hecate and the night,

By all the operation of the orbs
From whom we do exist and cease to be,
Here I disclaim....

A whole passage peppered with /t/ and /d/; their consonantal power sounding from the constellation of the Lion. I sense my tongue prepare to use the /d/, so significantly placed, to batter the decisive verb into the space:

> Here I disclaim all my paternal care
> Propinquity and property of blood ...

    Lots of /d/, lots of /t/. Make a note of that! But don't jump too quickly to conclusions. Lots of /p/ as well ...

And as a stranger to my heart ...

No! I have not invented this! The heart, of all our organs, the focus in our bodies of Leo's forming power, mentioned so specifically, so soon!

And as a stranger to my heart and me
Hold thee from this for ever.

Intuition into overdrive! Try not to rush ahead, get too excited. References to Lear's heart leap off the page. Too many for coincidence.

But yet this heart shall break into a hundred thousand flaws or e'er I'll weep ...

> *Again, whole passages are peppered with /t/ and /d/ ...*
>
> O my rising hear<u>t</u>! <u>D</u>own ...
>
> *Another heart, another /d/...*
>
> <u>D</u>own thou climbing sorrow.
>
> *The eurythmic /d/ precisely mirrored as he pushes his pain down below the threshold of his consciousness.*

Is there any cause in nature makes these hard hearts?

And at the end Kent resonates in sympathy with Lear's heart:

Break heart, prithee break.

Hard to ignore, despite the many other sounds, the evidence now coming thick and fast!

Come no<u>t</u> be<u>t</u>ween the <u>d</u>ragon and his wrath ... My some<u>t</u>ime <u>d</u>augh<u>t</u>er!

/d/ ... /t/ ... There's /t/, not as the starting sound but in the middle. <u>D</u>augh<u>t</u>er ... <u>D</u>augh<u>t</u>er....

... and have his <u>d</u>augh<u>t</u>ers brough<u>t</u> him to this pass?

Kent tries to bring him back, sounding to him in his own key, risking his king's explosive wrath:

He hath no <u>d</u>augh<u>t</u>ers, sir...

The lion rends the space with claws that /t/ and futile beats the air with /d/

<u>T</u>rai<u>t</u>or! ... Nothing could have sub<u>d</u>ued na<u>t</u>ure to such a lowness but his unkin<u>d</u> <u>d</u>aughters

... /t/ ... /t/ Often more telling at the end of words.

Ou<u>t</u> of my sigh<u>t</u>!

Kindling the first spark of honest self-awareness.

I loved her mos<u>t</u> and though<u>t</u> <u>t</u>o se<u>t</u> my res<u>t</u>
On her kind nursery.

I move into the full-bodied macrocosmic gesture /t/. Can't help it! Fingers of both hands begin to beat, batter my skull, would split it open if they could. Words insert themselves into the action, /t/ striking, seeking for the skull's cleavage plane.

O Lear Lear Lear,
Bea<u>t</u> at this ga<u>t</u>e that le<u>t</u> thy folly in
And thy dear judgemen<u>t</u> ou<u>t</u>.

This is not about crass emphasis, battering a consonant each time that it comes along, leaving all the other words and sounds untended. This is learning how a consonant can permeate a verbal landscape with its gesture: provide the key that enables us to split or pluck or stroke each sound as it arises, imprinting an entire passage with its shaping power.

To use the sounds in minor key, creating dissonant chords that rend and tear:

Ou<u>t</u> of my sigh<u>t</u>! ...
<u>D</u>ry up in her the organs of increase
Tha<u>t</u> from her <u>d</u>eroga<u>t</u>e bo<u>d</u>y may never spring
A babe <u>t</u>o honour her. Or if she mus<u>t</u> <u>t</u>eem
Crea<u>t</u>e her chil<u>d</u> of spleen tha<u>t</u> it may be
A thwar<u>t</u> <u>d</u>isna<u>t</u>ured <u>t</u>orment <u>t</u>o her
<u>T</u>urn all her mothers pains and benefi<u>t</u>s
<u>T</u>o <u>d</u>arkness and <u>d</u>espair.

Using /t/ to tear its claws across the face of Goneril:

Tha<u>t</u> she may know
How sharper than a serpen<u>t</u>'s <u>t</u>ooth i<u>t</u> is
<u>T</u>o have a thankless chil<u>d</u> ...
Or with these nails I'll <u>t</u>ear thy wolfish visage

Or /d/ to push away, to harden:

... here I <u>d</u>isclaim ... the <u>d</u>ragon and his wrath.

Then resolving into major key ... use the light in /t/ to mark the dawning of self knowledge...

O I have <u>t</u>a'en <u>t</u>oo li<u>tt</u>le care of this ...

Or delicately brush away the drops that glisten on Cordelia's cheeks:

Be your tears wet?
Yes faith. I pray you weep not.

And with /d/ the growing definition of his new-found sight:

I did her wrong . . . I think this lady to be my child Cordelia . . . If you have poison for me I will drink it .

I know when one is dead and when one lives.
She's dead as earth . . .

My intuition seems to be confirmed. Lear is destined for initiation in the constellation of the Lion. He must ennoble the savage beast and purify the predator within his heart, become a true king to his subjects, serving instead of dominating them to serve his power.[*]

The evidence seems overwhelming yet even as I gather it, part of me observes another set of consonants: /b/ and /p/, paired equally, sounding a different key, creating a second theme. Have I been too hasty? Perhaps after all a different theme belongs to Lear?

Here I disclaim all my paternal care
Propinquity and property of blood

Explore the gestures . . . /p/

At first, arrogating pomp unto itself, exploding outward in a fury of offended pride, unable to look inward. Broken now, forced to look within, seeing responsibilities ignored.

Poor naked wretches, whereso'er ye be
That bide the pelting of this pitiless storm
How shall your houseless heads, your unfed sides
Your looped and windowed raggedness, defend you
From seasons such as these? O I have ta'en
Too little care of this. Take physic pomp.
Expose thyself to feel what wretches feel . . .

Born again, weaving between /d/ and /t/, showering over them the delicate effulgence of a different kind of /p/: perhaps not initially belonging to him but overlighting him with the sense of someone absent physically, who stirs sensations of her distant but still present presence, teaching him, even in her

---

[*] *The Art of Acting* on the ennobling of the beasts, page 189.

absence, an unfamiliar skill: to ask for the first time how another feels, feeling it condense into a /b/:

How now my <u>b</u>oy, art cold?

And /b/ and /p/ become a modulating bridge between the father and the daughter that he banished. I sense I have already moved into a different key and that his initiation is intimately bound with hers.

Cordelia – Virgo – /p/ and /b/

Figure 161 The starry being, Virgo

Figure 162 Virgo radiates through Cordelia

Figure 163 Cordelia: Good my lord, you have begot me, bred me, loved me./I return those duties back … Then poor Cordelia …

Figure 164 Cosmic /b/

Figure 165 Cosmic /b/ radiates through Cordelia

Figure 166 Cordelia kneels at Lear's bedside as he wakes out of his madness ... had you not been their father ... mine enemy's dog, though he had bit me ...

Figure 167 Cosmic /p/

Figure 168 Cosmic /p/ radiates through Cordelia

Figure 169 Cordelia: Restoration hang/Thy medicine upon my lips/And let this kiss/Repair those violent harms that my two sisters/Have in thy reverence made . . .

Figure 170 Virgo radiates through Cosmic /p/ and /b/

Cordelia – in the key of Virgo – shaped by /p/ and /b/

The gesture of /b/ leads me first to the embracing arms of one whose presence never left her father though he banished her.

> ... had you not <u>b</u>een their father, these white hairs ...

And now from /b/ to /p/ ...

> ... had challenged <u>p</u>ity of them.

Humble without pride from the beginning.

> Then <u>p</u>oor Cordelia ...

> ... Restoration, hang
> Thy medicine on my li<u>p</u>s, and let this kiss
> Re<u>p</u>air those violent harms that my two sisters
> Have in thy reverence made!

And are /b/ and /p/ her melody, could Virgo be her key? Thick and fast, examples leap at me:

> Good my lord, you have <u>b</u>egot me <u>b</u>red me, loved me.
> I return those duties <u>b</u>ack as are right fit,
> O<u>b</u>ey you, love you and most honour you.
> Ha<u>p</u>ly when I shall wed, that lord
> Whose hand shall take my <u>p</u>light....

Do they belong to her or Lear? Or does this interweaving of their consonants reveal a deeper mystery? Of two sound-scapes intermingling, as their themes entwine, he, the cello, (or is it bass?), playing music she, the viola, (or is it violin), has woken first in him, and then reversing, changing keys, major, then to minor, back again. Brief snatches to remind us she is never far away though physically removed to France. Mad on the beach at Dover he consoles the blinded Earl of Gloucester and invokes her melody:

> Thou must be <u>p</u>atient ... I will <u>p</u>reach to thee ... when we are <u>b</u>orn we cry ...

At last he wakes to find her there beside him.

> ... if you have <u>p</u>oison for me I will <u>d</u>rink i<u>t</u> ... <u>d</u>o no<u>t</u> a<u>b</u>use me ... <u>p</u>ray you now forge<u>t</u> and forgive ...

His consonants and hers, threads of their beings, woven inextricably. Kneeling there, sensibilities attuned, their notes resound, stirring their interwoven threads within me. Eurythmic, macrocosmic /p/ cascading, clothing me; sensations shower over me, purer than anything I can imagine. Have I ever in my life felt faithfulness like hers, who after death has won the right to guide him further in his own becoming?

Pure virgin soul, you have midwifed the birth of the second man in him. Eurythmic /p/ and /b/ invoke sensations delicate of daughter-become-mother helping his new baby self to stand and take his tentative first steps.

> ... will it p̲lease your highness walk?

Difficult to play someone so evolved, who, when we meet her, has already trod the path, what path? Shakespeare gives no clues to how she came to be in France's words

> ... herself a dowry

Lear's melody of /d/ entwined with hers. No clues to how she became incapable – not ever to exchange – not ever to trade love for worldly riches ... and the King of France so overjoyed – he never thought he would, he could, at last behold a kindred soul and spirit and have the opportunity to

> ... take up̲ what's cast away.

Difficult to play goodness, give me a devil any day! A character without a hint of journey, daddy's favourite it's true, but that does not explain or help me get inside her. Simply no biography for goodness, how she got to be that way, so perfectly arrived.

> ... and so I am ... I am.

Shakespeare more concerned to show the father's journey – every step of Lear's initiation meticulously crafted. But for his guide, his angel, not a clue. Yet how their music weaves together in his final lines, /d/ and /t/, /b/ and /p/...

> P̲ray you sir, und̲o this b̲utt̲on

And as he internalises her, weaving her notes into his, integrating in his final moments, her pure moral substance with his own ... the lion has become the lamb ... he is on his way to be a different kind of king: one without an earthly crown: one who rules not by abuse of power but by the gentle presence of the Self within.

An actor's ordinary tools don't help me access this. Personal emotional recall is futile. But standing in the macrocosmic gesture of the Virgin takes me to the quiet harbour of her soul, chastely indicates the sacred space within, the womb in which the spirit child is nurtured and prepared for birth.

Her gesture stirs in me sensations of the truth of her relationship with Lear, reminding me of Sonnet 116, the potency of love . . .

> That alters not with [time's] brief hours and years
> But bears it out even to the edge of doom. . . .

No source for this in any earthly biographical event; not mine nor hers. No back-story takes me there, refines emotions to such unsentimental depth of sacred feeling: sensations springing only from the life and consciousness of a greater Someone in the heavens now flowing through an earthly counterpart. Yet through the Virgo gesture substance flows, enabling me – for how else could I dare? – to speak:

> O my dear father
> It is thy business that I go about

Is this coincidence, how they echo words of Jesus in the Gospel, how they signal her allegiance; tell us of the power to which she has aligned herself?[41]

> No blown ambition doth our arms incite,
> But love, dear love, and our aged father's right.

Standing in her gesture, feeling her virgin soul, suddenly I sense her bridegroom has appeared beside me, standing easily, where he belongs. I take one step around the circle, slip into his place beside her and the macrocosmic gesture of the Scales.

The King of France – Libra – English /ts/ (German z)

Figure 171 The starry being, Libra

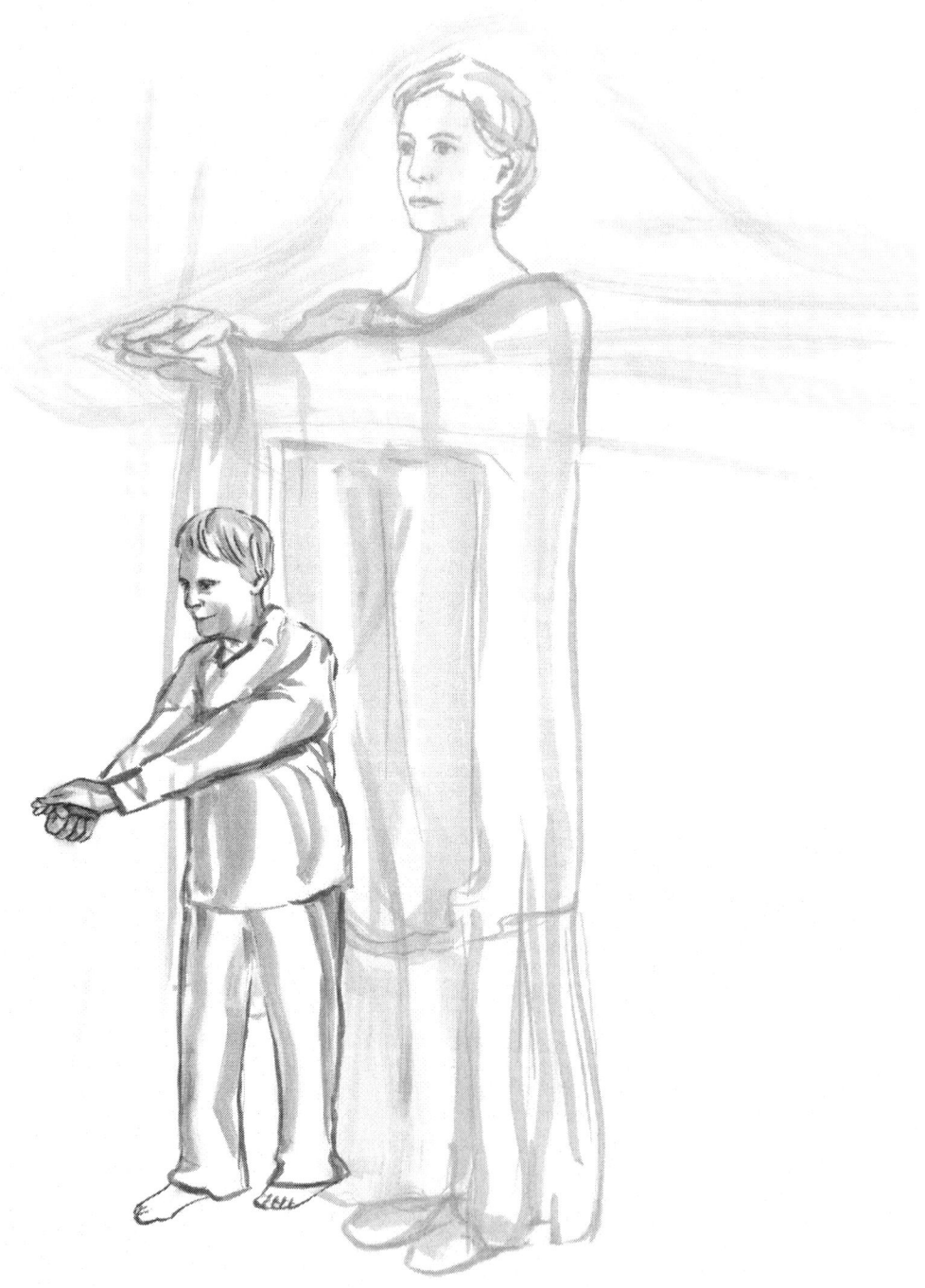

Figure 172 Libra radiates through the King of France

Figure 173 The King of France: Be it lawful I take up what's cast away . . .

Figure 174 Cosmic /ts/ (nearest to German z)

Figure 175 Cosmic /ts/ or German z radiates through the King of France.

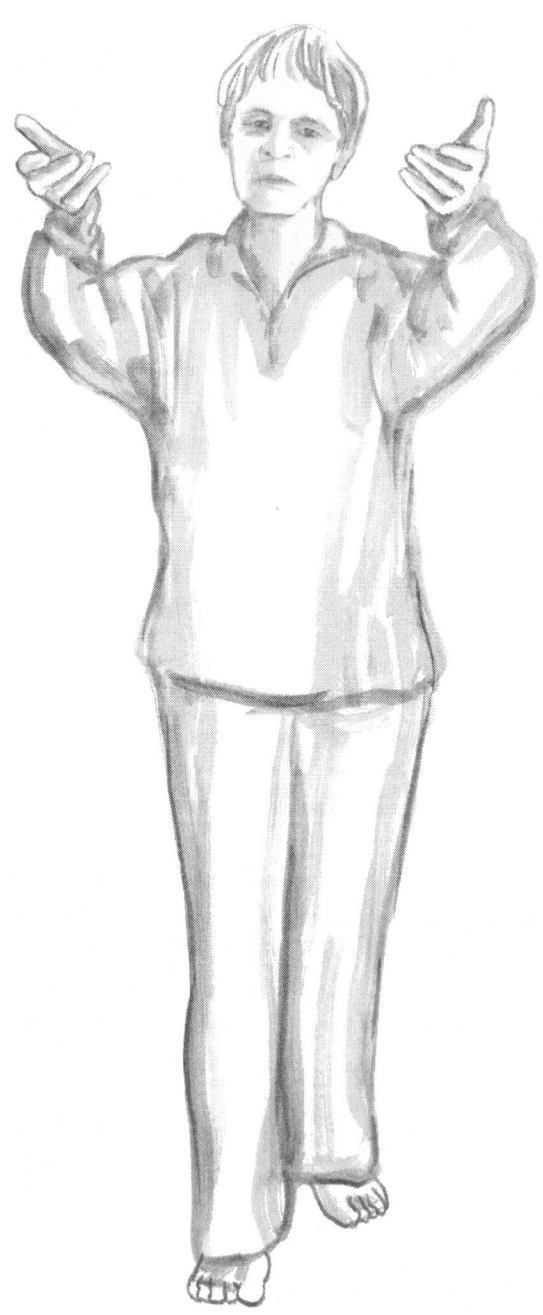

Figure 176 King of France: Queen of us, of ours and our fair France.

Figure 177 The King of France weighs Cordelia in the balance: Fairest Cordelia, that art most rich, being poor/Most choice forsaken, and most loved, despised.

Figure 178 Libra radiates through Cosmic /ts/ (German z)

The King of France — in the key of Libra — shaped by German z (nearest in English /ts/)

It shapes my soul, moves through me. If I let it guide me, descend into my human microcosmic form, I am holding the hands of my beloved where she kneels, petitioning Lear to see her truth. I have recognised my bride. Reaching down to grasp her hopeless cause I have felt our future. How can I not support her, raise her up?

Be it lawful I take up what's cast away.

The reaching down to grasp that heaviness, that seemed so hard for others, for myself could not have been more easy. It is the gesture for /ts/.

And as it raises us both from darkness into light, first with one hand, then the other, I find I balance this with that … and as I move the words insert themselves;

Fairest Cordelia, that art most rich, being poor,
Most choice, forsaken, and most loved, despised …

The chemistry of German z—fusion of earth and fire, searing heat, smelting of new metal cast, its gesture in eurythmy diving down into the density to lift that heavy load which, lifted, then dissolves, evaporates in light. And in English, not yet fusion, but meeting of earth and fire, /ds/ and /ts/.

… so many folds of favour … what's cast away

Love's not love
When it is mingled with regards that stand
Aloof from the entire point.

And could this be coincidence: the undeniable, the in-the- text-to-be-dis-covered similarity of sound between the two pairs of combining consonants and the crystal clear staccato sibilance of /ts/ in France and chance? Yet there it is … the unerring musicality of Shakespeare's sounds:

Thy dowerless daughter king, thrown to my chance,
Is queen of us of ours and our fair France.

The structure of my hips enabling me to lift and balance, stand upright, be a worthy bridegroom to this bride.

Leo . . . Virgo . . . Libra . . . I never planned it. It just seemed to happen that I moved around the circle in this way, found myself in this progression. Is there a wisdom in the order that is leading me unconsciously from character to character, around the circle, as though each one calls forth the next? What would happen if I just obeyed the impulse and continued in this way?

Stopped listening to the voice of doubt: surely it's too obvious! Just the sort of abstract scheme you wanted to avoid!

And yet it doesn't feel like a scheme. More as though some inevitable mystery is wanting to reveal itself. From the next place on the circle /s/ already summons me.

Goneril – Scorpio – /s/

Figure 179 The starry being, Scorpio

Figure 180 Scorpio radiates through Goneril

Figure 181 Goneril: Sir … dearer than eyesight, space or liberty … beyond all manner of so much, I love you.

Figure 182 Cosmic /s/

Figure 183 Cosmic /s/ radiates through Goneril

Figure 184 Goneril: He always loved our sister most ... if not I'll ne'er trust medicine.

Figure 185 Goneril: That were the most if he should husband you . . .

Figure 186 Scorpio radiates through Cosmic /s/

Goneril – in the key of Scorpio – shaped by /s/

Its gesture sucks me down. Sensations rouse and resonate. A character beckons. I retrace the steps that led this way and follow, sensibilities awake, as I move again from Virgo's guardian of sacred feminine through Libran balance of the hips, I find that I am sliding down the path of S, twisting down into the sexuality of Goneril. Drawn inexorably down – no bony structure holds me, no resisting upright as I deeper slide towards the earth.

Where to find the inner strength not to be drawn into the underbelly darkness? Surely no harm if I play – just for a moment, nothing serious, not for long – play with the possibility to let myself surrender to the downward pull into the dark, hips twisting now becoming sinuous. Before I know it, no strength left to wrest free, maintain my balance – how easy after all to slip then slide into the smoothly sloping sibilance of /s/ – my vertical much harder to maintain than I imagined.

It has led me down a pathway of sensation into a consciousness not mine. Suddenly! Unable to resist – Goneril inside me now – or is it I in her? She has arrived! Even my husband, struggling to escape my powers of sex-surrendered-to-the darkness-coils addresses me as –

. . . gilded serpent.

Nothing to block my downward slide towards the dark unless I rouse from deep-my-vertical-within, my own will to resist. Or is it mine and do I really want to be a human being? And was I ever? Do I even know what it is? Can I remember in its paradisal form, a gesture that stirred sensations of my head still crowned with stars? Forces of the eagle, power of intelligence to penetrate, illuminate the dark, use my creative power to conceive the good?

Was that conscious, the dual meaning of the word 'conceive'? Did Shakespeare hear it too? The serpent hiss into my ear . . . sss eat thisssss and you will never die . . . you will be a god.

Conceive and fare thee well.

My sibilant coils down inside my dear lord Edmund's ear and now we slide together down the slippery slope towards the glistening fruit of power and we have made the once still-to-be-decided choice.

Eliminate whatever stands between yourself and what you think you want. Use your intelligence to serve your lower nature. Use whatever is to hand: poison, sex, words, to sting your prey. But first make love, convince the world to trust. Then you can eat your mate. All this swept into

the vortex of your speech, into the sibilant, smooth-as-velvet, serpent hiss of the first word you speak:

S̲ir ...

Intelligence poised, you watch your prey, sense his weakness, how desperate the old man is. He doesn't care, doesn't love you, never did, wouldn't know what it means. But sensing just how much he needs to hear you say, in front of everyone, that you love him, how much he is willing to relinquish just to hear the words ...

S̲ir ... I love you more than word can wield the matter ... dearer than eye s̲ight, s̲pace or liberty ... beyond all manner of s̲o much ...

And you have made your choice, are on your way into the dark. Your path is set. Your husband, Albany, will one day wake and see beyond the mask of your seductive powers.

But do you understand the jealousy that drives you? Hiss out the unconscious revelation of your wound ... the feeling you have been deprived ... slicing the space with your self-justified attack ... seeking to defend your own self-interest. After all, it is only what you, what you both, deserve. You and your so-long-as-she-is-useful-to-you sister, Regan.

He alway s̲ loved our s̲ister mo s̲t and with what poor judgement he hath now ca s̲t her off, appear s̲ mo s̲t gro s̲sly ...

The blade of /s/ insinuates its sharp incisive sting into the texture of your words throughout the play. Perceiving threat from that now-no-longer-useful sister, poison her!

I had rather lo s̲e the battle than that s̲ister should loo s̲en him and me ... that were the mo s̲t if he should hu s̲band you.

Succumbing to your venom, /s/ courses now through Regan's veins.

... s̲ick o s̲ick ...

And you hiss back.

If not I'll ne'er tru s̲t medi c̲ine ...

With Edmund's death, and nothing to prevent your deeper slide towards annihilation, you stab yourself. Your jealousy still hissing through the message that reports your death.

... and her s̲ister by her is poi s̲oned. She confe s̲ses it.

Scorpio's gesture grants me from eagle height, perspective on the sad seduction of my wasted life. In death's crossing it enables me to see what might have been a different choice, too late now for this life but ... for my next and Lear's?

His curse still follows me, echoes down the centuries, still shatters me, makes me feel the terror of knowing, when he broke like that, that I had gone too far – no turning back. From this eagle height I feel a longing – remembering the hugeness of his pain and mine – that after all it might not be too late, evolving from that blasted fruit some hope – for my sexuality, capacity to bear a child: some possibility of healing in a future time, assurance of another opportunity to try again to love and make a different choice. I sense (or is it she?) the choices that this initiation offered me. Could I have chosen differently? Do I regret?

Regan – Sagittarius – /k/ and /g/

Figure 187 The starry being, Sagittarius

Figure 188 Sagittarius radiates through Regan

Figure 189 Regan: Edmund and I have talk'd,/And more convenient is he for my hand/Than for your lady's.

Figure 190 Cosmic /k/

Figure 191 Cosmic /k/ radiates through Regan

Figure 192 Regan: Pluck out his eyes

Figure 193 Cosmic /g/

Figure 194 Cosmic /g/ radiates through Regan

Figure 195 Regan: That's as we list to grace him ... You'll go with us ... Sister, go with us.

Figure 196 Sagittarius radiates through Cosmic /g/ and /k/

Regan – In the key of Sagittarius – shaped by /k/ and /g/

Retrace your steps around the circle, once again testing the progression. Artistic intuitions hum. No reason not to keep on moving this way round, step into the archer, Sagittarius. An image of a centaur comes to mind, then chaste Diana. Inhabiting the macrocosmic gesture, I sense the held-in-balance tensions of power eternally restrained, eternally preparing for release. My gaze is steady, focused down the ages, scanning vast peripheries of space and time, patient yet fully poised. No false impulse causes me to start, pre-cipitating chaos, risking that I miss the appointed meeting time and place.

I descend into my microcosmic earthly form, sense muscles tighten with old wounds demanding retribution, threatening my steady aim, making me impatient so the slightest provocation sets me off. Left hand, arm and shoulder pulling back the bow, right elbow straining forward pushes against restraining left, impatient to release the pent up savage impulse for revenge. Somehow I hold it in, keep my eyes on target, bide my time. Frus-tration, rage, not ready openly to show its face, releases pressure in exploding consonants. If words could kill! /k/ and /g/.

Move their gestures, feel them strike, eliminate your foe! /k/ and /g/, /k/ and /g/. Sensations resonate, begin to nudge, insist! The leading consonants of my two sisters' names! Cordelia and Goneril! A place to start. Pronounce their names, relishing the strong beginnings of each word ... Goneril ... Cordelia ... Suddenly an inside-gesture-flash: a someone else inside me, a consciousness possessed by incessant chanting of those names inside my head, obsessive mantra over and again, sometimes aloud, some-times inwardly. /k/... Cordelia ... I could kill her, strike her dead.

Gestures now release sensations thick and fast. Through clenched jaw it explodes, spewing hatred's subtext from my mouth. Father loves her best ... always gives her anything she wants.

/g/ ... Goneril ... seething hatred of her dominating will, won't give me any space, always suffocating me. Just because she's older than I am, and stronger.

Yes I learnt to elbow my way, make space for myself.

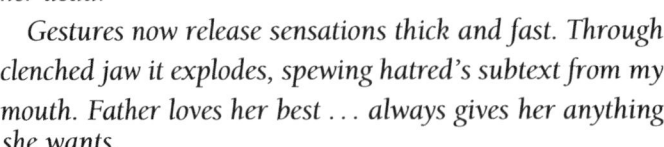

But I mustn't let her know how much I hate her, because I need her to stand up for me against my father when he blames <u>me</u> for what <u>she</u> did ...

I mean Cordelia /k/, when all the time it was Cordelia . . . /k/ . . . Cordelia. . . . Well, go along with Goneril /g/ . . . anything she wants, anything she says, but all the time make my own plans, watch for my opportunity. I have my own ideas. I'm the clever one after all, cleverer than she. I'll show them just how clever I can be. Gesture – a suit of armour holding tight my underneath-it-all-the-time incessant pain.

I just want someone of my own to love and who I know loves me. Husband? No, not Cornwall, but I need him too to hide behind, to do the nasty things on my behalf.

Mustn't let them know that underneath that holding-of-my-elbow tight control, that all the time, if words could shoot like arrows, kill, release straight to the heart those want-to-kill-them names and speak so it would kill them . . . Cordelia . . . Daddy's little girl . . . one clear chop! . . . /k/. Goneril . . . /g/ . . . push her away, get her out of my space, crush her, grind her into dust.

Gesture for the archer, firm thigh supporting all that held-back-in-the-elbow-murderous power waiting to release from the hand-sling that holds it

in, the bow releasing arrow to its mark . . . and kill them both. I wish I were as strong as Goneril, big bully, but I'm not! Alright, but smarter than she is, release my elbow from its sling . . . poke my way into the world, make a mark to get the love I need. Daddy! Daddy! Regan poked me Did not. Did! Did not! Did! Traitor! . . . /kkkk/ . . . poke out your eyes if I could, poke out someone's eyes!

Of course it was Goneril that SAID it first, always leaving me to do her dirty work but it was MY idea. I had it first, my lifetime's pus a seething boil inside me ready to explode, can't hold it in, aspire to centaur any longer human rising out of animal, a civilised veneer cracked open. After all a savage underneath!

Plu<u>ck</u> out his eyes!

For now, so much revealed. Test further! Yes, Regan has that uncanny arrow-like precision that makes Sagittarians so scary to be with . . . that piercing-home-with-truth . . . how they just come out with things. . . .

He hath ever but slenderly known himself . . . O sir, you are old!

An awesome quality when practiced chastely. Arrows of truth speeding to their mark. Truth-sayer! But Regan so wounded can only use her arrow-piercing sight to scheme for what she wants.

That's as we list to grace him ...
Sister, you'll go with us?
Tis most convenient. Pray you go with us.

   He led our powers
Bore the commission of my place and person;
The which immediacy may well stand up
And call itself your brother.

Witness the world, that I create thee here,
My lord and master.

/k/ *and* /g/; *their subtext works unconsciously within her. Keep an open mind. What if that arrow-like precise perception were used not to serve the beast but the Centaur Self, raising its human-head-up-out-of-the-instinctive, to accomplish the Sagittarian initiation? Regan cannot reach it in this life but has she learned enough to understand the future mission of her unhealed wounds, receive instruction from the wounded healer Chiron, and herself become a healer? Who knows how this life will bear fruit in another life beyond?*

   Regan and Goneril's uneasy alliance of convenience and mutual self-serving is unhinged through jealousy: both in love with Edmund, bastard son of Gloucester.

   Is it he who calls me next? I take another step around the circle into Capricorn.

Ignore the commentary inside my head; 'facile, far too obvious, simplistic, in danger of imposing your idea!' Must I go through this doubting every time? Do it anyway! Test it out! No denying the rich, profound intensities by which I recognise artistic truth.

Edmund – Capricorn – /l/

Figure 197 The starry being, Capricorn

Figure 198 Capricorn radiates through Edmund

Figure 199 Cosmic /l/

Figure 200 Cosmic /l/ (and Capricorn) radiate through Edmund

Figure 201 Edmund: ... fine word legitimate ... well then, legitimate Edgar, I must have your lands ...

Figure 202 Capricorn radiates through Cosmic /l/

Edmund – In the key of Capricorn – shaped by /l/

Deeply moved by my discoveries, the flow of energy and inspiration signals I am in the cauldron of creative fire and the next flashes of my intuition are already crowding in.

And here he comes! The goat climbing to the mountain top, scaling the peak of his ambition. Sure-footed, confident, flexible of joint, he makes his way, easily mounting or avoiding rocks, traversing slippery slopes, feeding on anything he finds. His sexuality his pride, he wears it blatantly and mates with whom he pleases.

Full-bodily incorporate a goat, sustain the sensations, bring them upright into human form. Now I recognise, know that I am striding home. Still on the flat, the mountain beckons. Joints loosened by that /l/, easily and with a touch of swagger after long years abroad I am returning home to claim my birthright. Not what the world considers mine but what I know belongs to me. Deprived, I am resolved to take what is not given.

L̲egitimate . . . fine word . . .

And interesting how much depends on it. Legitimate . . . such a soft sounding word . . . soft if you are born into it and hard when you are not. Play with the sounds. Let /l/ predominate, as soft as my pathetic brother who will inherit just because he is l . . . legitimate. Taste each bitter syllable, pronounced meticulously and with a little sting, and there's the letter of the law that shuts me out. Pronounce it so the smoothly flowing /l/ washes over all the other consonants and there you have the charm, the ease, the honey tones of the seducer, that dissemble, promise warmth . . .

We̲l̲l then, l̲egitimate Edgar, I must have your l̲ands . . . Our father's l̲ove is to the bastard Edmund as to the l̲egitimate . . . fine word 'legitimate' . . . we̲l̲l my l̲egitimate, if this l̲etter speed . . . Edmund the base shal̲l̲ top the l̲egitimate . . .

And so with /l/, Edmund's theme is introduced. His speeches drenched in /l/, even if I had any doubts, he refers to it himself – wants to own his –

goatish disposition.

But not laying the responsibility for lust and lechery on any constellation of the stars.

I should have been that I am, had the maiden̲l̲iest star in the firmament twinkled on my bastardising.

Time to explore the macrocosmic gesture for Capricorn, the Goat; its power to awaken some pale echo-sense of the creative dynamic these starry beings bring to the possibility of being human, of how they condense their macrocosmic forming forces into the microcosm of our knees. Their gesture

acts as a genetic code that impregnates each cell of my anatomy. Let it organise my body, shape my consciousness.

Immediate sensations of huge intelligence and easy power. Left fist resting on the frontal bone above my brow, right arm extended out in front, palm erect and flat, maintaining a firm boundary between the world and me. I sense how easily I ward off, hold the world at bay. Right knee bent even further forward than the archer, Sagittarius; willing to be seen to bend, to bow, to play humility. Sensations coming thick and fast filtered through my growing sense of ... Edmund arriving, observing the world from some safe place, cave of my own skull perhaps, instinctive knowledge of survival, how to plan and plot inside that skull-safe haven until the moment ripens.

No need to precipitously act; knees flexibible, to spring with ease upon the slope only when preparation is complete; all things surveyed, con-

sidered, viewed from every angle, turning inside out and up and down, hand and fingers curling in expanding circles, /l/, whole body now recruited in the exploration.

The eurythmic /l/, allowing it to take me full circle scanning light and dark ... Miraculously words insert themselves transporting me to Edmund's death ...

The wheel has come full circle. I am here ...

A moment earlier, feeling his knees buckle at the mortal stroke, bending for the first time in surrender, the goatstar's alchemy of transformation starts to work: the news of so many dead and all of them had loved him.

Yet Edmund was beloved ...

With his last breath a miracle, a where-did-it-come-from moment left, to make a different choice, to try to is-it-not-too-late-yet change.

This speech of yours hath moved me and shall perchance do good.

He tries but ... too late! ... tried to save Cordelia, retract his warrant for her death.

Some good I mean to do spite of my own nature ...

It took his whole life for the wheel to bring him from the light through darkness and up again into the light; for him to see a different mountain from the one he thought to climb. But lying at the base, for the first time he accepts the present state of things:

I am here.

And has a glimpse of the journey. Through the interweaving of the planetary influence of Saturn described in Chapter 6 with the influence of Capricorn his initiation has begun. Cycles of time continue to revolve delivering new possibilities. In my end is my beginning.

Duke of Albany — Aquarius — /m/

Figure 203 The starry being, Aquarius

Figure 204 Aquarius radiates through Albany

Figure 205 Albany: If that the heavens do not their visible spirits/Send quickly down to tame these vile offenses/It will come/Humanity must perforce prey on itself/Like monsters of the deep.

Figure 206 Cosmic /m/

Figure 207 Cosmic /m/ radiates through Albany

Figure 208 Albany: My lord, I am guiltless as I am innocent/Of what hath moved you.

Figure 209 Duke of Albany: I fear your disposition . . . She that herself will sliver and disbranch/ From her material sap, perforce must wither/And come to deadly use.

Figure 210 Aquarius radiates through Cosmic /m/

Duke of Albany – in the key of Aquarius – shaped by /m/

Next in the circle is Aquarius, the water-bearer. Image of one bringing water to a desert, to a thirsting world, heralding a new age for humanity. Letting its healing gesture work on me, I feel it mediating all the functions of my soul, allowing what streams upwards from my will to reach into my thinking, letting what streams downwards from my thinking reach into my will, each impulse passing through the region of my heart. Surrender to this rhythmic pulse, the only gesture of the twelve in motion.

My body-of-sensation quivering, alive; a barometer attuned to subtle movements in the cosmos, filtering their intimations. I am all sensing, listening. No boundaries, no skin to separate me, no firm identity asserts its contours in the world, no certainty distinct enough to speak or act, if I had ever known or could I ever know my mind.

Difficult – my cells vibrating, straining to harmonise conflicting wavelengths – to behave like . . . know what manhood is. Difficult to have a wife like Goneril . . . and how could my cells not let me sense how she despises my . . . wants me to be decisive.

My axis tilts, revolves my gesture and with the palm of one hand I am sensing gently forward even as the other, returning from its mission, bears towards me what it sensed. Bones of lower arms and shins transparent, made to filter light – so much needing to be filtered, a whole life perhaps, before . . . what I mean is . . . understanding everybody's point of view, feeling it to be my own, sensing why they do what they do, it takes so long to understand what's going on, formulate a clear commitment, recognise my wife is not a woman but a monster, accept that evil is a fact and it is here and I am in the midst of it.

> If that the heavens do not their visible spirits
> Send quickly down to ta<u>m</u>e these vile offenses,
> It will co<u>m</u>e,
> Hu<u>m</u>anity <u>m</u>ust perforce prey on itself,
> Like <u>m</u>onsters of the deep.

Goneril describes me as a:

> . . . <u>m</u>ilk livered <u>m</u>an . . .
> That bear'st a cheek for blows, a head for wrongs;
> Who hast not in thy brows an eye discerning
> Thine honour from thy suffering;

If she had her way, I would lead an army into battle to defeat her sister and the King of France. But how can I, when I support what they are doing to rescue the old king?

Where I could not be honest
I never yet was valiant.

The Aquarian initiation is to solve this dilemma; to take initiative, act decisively, support the good – sympathy is not enough – to find the warrior within, and yet not violate my sensitivity. Perhaps I would have always wavered, always hovered on the edge of, undecided – is it yet enough? – is this evil yet, is this enough to call it evil, yes?

Even in the moment when I knew my wife despised me, even when she turned on me, distorted the most intimate vibration of my being /m/ and twisted my attempts to mediate, into its mocking variation in a minor key: . . . /m/ . . .

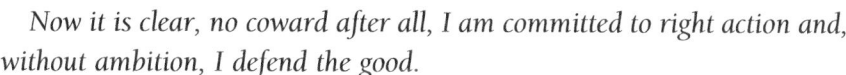

<u>M</u>arry your <u>m</u>anhood! <u>M</u>ew!

Even then I was willing to excuse, find a way to reconcile.

But then the old man, Gloucester! Someone, not Goneril, not my wife, please God, but someone, something had to do this – beyond awful, beyond excuse, all attempts to justify – this tearing out the old man's eyes; this darkness.

Now it is clear, no coward after all, I am committed to right action and, without ambition, I defend the good.

The Fool — Pisces — /n/

Figure 211 The starry being, Pisces

Figure 212 Pisces radiates through the Fool

Figure 213 The Fool: 'Tis a naughty night to swim in . . .

Figure 214 Cosmic /n/

Figure 215 Cosmic /n/ radiates through the Fool

Figure 216 Fool: Thou'ldst make a good fool. nuncle …

Figure 217 Pisces radiates through Cosmic /ŋ/

The Fool – In the key of Pisces – shaped by /n/

Once I had explored the archetype of lion in relation to the king, the archetype of lion-tamer in connection to the fool was an obvious progression. As I played with it full-bodily, soon it was impossible to miss the key in which the fool's theme was set. And how could I not be swept along in the mounting dynamic of its shaping consonant: /n/ after /n/ after /n/...?

Can'st thou make <u>n</u>o use of <u>n</u>othing, <u>n</u>uncle? ... <u>N</u>or I <u>n</u>uncle, but I <u>k</u>now why a s<u>n</u>ail has a house ... Prithee <u>n</u>uncle, be co<u>nten</u>ted, 'tis a <u>n</u>aughty <u>n</u>ight to swim i<u>n</u> ...

Its gesture in eurythmy also stirs sensations of a lion-tamer and confirms my intuition . Full-bodied exploration: advance and then retreat, keeping the lion at a distance with his whip-cracking words; his language punctuated with the unrelenting cracks of /n/ ...

One /n/ at a time the fool brings Lear to his senses ...

Ca<u>n</u>st tell <u>n</u>uncle, why o<u>n</u>e's <u>n</u>ose is i<u>n</u> the middle of o<u>n</u>e's face?

Why?

Why? To keep o<u>n</u>e's eyes o<u>n</u> either side o' o<u>n</u>e's <u>n</u>ose that what a ma<u>n</u> may <u>n</u>ot smell out he may spy i<u>n</u>to.

Through /n/ the fool keeps up the pressure, pressing into his beloved master's heart and penetrating his defences. Then a long silence while Lear takes it in ...

I did her wro<u>ng</u> ...

The genius of Shakespeare's music at this moment! The turning point – when Lear takes in for the first time what those who care for him have tried to tell him all along – pivots on /n/. Not placed as the launch sound of the word but where the speaker must lean into it, not spring away

... wro<u>ng</u>.

/n/... into /g/... penetrating deep inside, being digested. From this moment, the lion starts to recognise his master, take on something of his quality, play his tamer's theme, their two themes entwining ... /d/.../n/

... <u>did</u> her wro<u>ng</u>...

Is it any wonder then, that at the end when Lear is dying, as he bends in grief over the dead body of Cordelia, his two good angels merge within his mind ...

And my poor fool is hanged . . .

And for a while the fool's relentless music sounds through her departed spirit, beating again and again to waken him. Her thread woven into his, and Lear takes up the fool's theme as his own.

N̲o, n̲o, n̲o life! . . . Thou'lt come n̲o more.
Never. Never. Never. Never. Never.

And so it was, even at the start of the journey:

Cordelia speaking in the fool's key, standing in for him, then, in her absence, he standing in for her till she returns: standing for the truth, no compromise: Lear wanting her so much to say the words, indulge his ego just this little once, just one foolish word to please a foolish father and demonstrate in front of everyone, the daughter that he loves returns his love. But no.

. . . n̲othing my lord . . . n̲othing? . . . n̲othing . . . n̲othing will come of n̲othing, speak aga̲i̲n . . .

And what picks up our feet and sets them down to tread the journey of our destiny? It is our feet that bring us to the appointed meeting times and places. We are largely unconscious of what guides our steps. We may think we know why we do what we do, go where we go, meet whom we meet, but the deeper reasons are obscure until we understand the lessons we have come to earth to learn. To fulfil their destinies with one another, the feet of Cordelia, Kent, Gloucester, Edgar, Lear and the fool, carry them on journeys they would not necessarily have chosen at this earthly level of perception.

It is the divine creative powers of the constellation Pisces who condense their macrocosmic forming forces into the microcosm of our feet. And who else but the fool would be ridiculous enough to draw attention to a time when justice is restored and we shall use our feet to step rightly on the earth?

Then comes the time, who lives to see it, that going shall be used with feet . . .[42]

As the others weave in and out of Lear's journey, while the fool lives, he remains at his side, never failing to bear witness to the truth, knowing he alone, by virtue of his motley[43], can dare to say what no one else can say and get away with; nimble of foot to evade the wounded lion's paw which, with a single swipe, could crush him for stirring up old hurts. All these sensations awaken in my body/soul when I incorporate the Pisces gesture.

Right arm raised towards the heavens, keeping me connected, drawing that foot up to take a step along the path that must be taken. Left arm pointing down towards the earth. No compromise! I am utterly awake. Is this the answer to the riddle I have pondered now for many years? What do the last words of the fool really mean?

And I'll go to bed at <u>noon</u>.

Does he foretell his own death, knowing that he dies in full waking consciousness?

Gloucester – Aries – /w/ and /v/

Figure 218 The starry being, Aries

Figure 219 Aries radiates through Gloucester

Figure 220 Gloucester: . . . we have seen the best of our time . . .

Figure 221 Cosmic /v/

Figure 222 Cosmic /v/ radiates through Gloucester

Figure 223 Gloucester: my son/Came then into my mind and yet my mind/Was then scarce friends with him.

Figure 224 Cosmic /w/

Figure 225 Cosmic /w/ radiates through Gloucester

Figure 226 Gloucester: ...As flies to wanton boys are we to the gods ... O you mighty gods!/
This world I do renounce ... If I could bear it longer and not fall/To quarrel with your great
opposeless wills ...

Figure 227 Aries radiates through Cosmic /v/ and /w/

Gloucester — In the key of Aries — shaped by /w/ and /v/

One more step around the circle and we reach the constellation, Aries. Associations, images pour in; battering ram, rutting ram, rushing head-long into things. The macrocosmic gesture seems so contradictory. My hand vertical along the middle of my heart, chin slightly tilted down, resting on fingertips. Such powerful sensations of inner quiet, contemplation, of awareness. Is there something someone needs to be aware of, understand? Someone in the circle whose unconscious actions must be stilled in order to appreciate the consequences of his deeds; someone ripe for this initiation?

Nearly everyone. But in particular a headstrong, rutting ram, who has always charged headlong into action without stopping to consider consequences. Certainly, Edmund could qualify as rutting ram but is not headstrong; not like his father, Gloucester, whose promiscuity his son knows all about. He has endured his father's boasting of it all his life. And Edmund knows how to manipulate his father's tendency to jump to quick conclusions and react without reflection. Just plant one little seed of doubt and watch him charge into the fray, order Edgar's death without a second to reflect.

With no self-knowledge, Gloucester has no understanding of the evil that can motivate another. No capacity to read another's soul. Only when his torturers tear out his eyes is the veil rent that had concealed the truth about the human beings he had trusted.

We cannot help but think of Oedipus — who tears his own eyes out because they did not help him see the truth.

I play with ram, head butting, sensations of what it is to use my head, not to think with, but as a limb, to push my way through life. / v/ . . . /v/. . .

<u>V</u>illain! <u>V</u>ile! <u>V</u>illain!

Seven times within a single page, deceived by my son, the bastard Edmund, I pour my blame on Edgar, my lawful son. I lower my head and ram into the world, only stopping when my horns lock with the

. . . great opposeless <u>w</u>ills . . .

of the gods and I can bear my life no longer . . . /w/ . . . why, who, when, what is it all about? Wading through grief, the vulnerability of /w/ . . .

In the last night's storm I such a fellow saw, <u>wh</u>ich made me think a man a <u>w</u>orm ... As flies to <u>w</u>anton boys are <u>we</u> to the gods ...

At last I question my assumptions, feel my hurt.

I had a son. I loved him, friend. No father his son dearer. Truth to tell the grief hath crazed my <u>w</u>its.

My body-of-sensations tells me I have been too hasty but not bad. I have not intended harm. I am not an evil person. I have been a loyal servant to the king. That same headstrong stubbornness won't allow me to betray my master and makes me risk my life in his support.

Once again, Shakespeare's genius with sounds, weaves two karmic threads together. He lets Edgar speak in Gloucester's key when, as yet unrecognised, Edgar sees his father for the first time since his torture:

O <u>w</u>orld, <u>w</u>orld, <u>w</u>orld! ... <u>wh</u>o is it can say I am at the <u>w</u>orst? I am <u>w</u>orse than e're I <u>w</u>as ... And <u>w</u>orse I may be yet. The <u>w</u>orst is not so long as <u>we</u> can say 'this is the <u>w</u>orst' ...

Duke of Kent – Taurus – /r/ Rolled 'r'

Figure 228 The starry being, Taurus

Figure 229 Taurus radiates through Kent

Figure 230 Kent: Reserve thy state/And in thy best consideration check/This hideous rashness.

Figure 231 Kent: Revoke thy gift/Or whilst I can vent clamour from my throat/I'll tell thee thou dost evil.

Figure 232 Cosmic /r/ — rolled r

Figure 233 Cosmic /r/ radiates through Kent

Figure 234 Kent: Draw you rascal! Draw you rogue!

Figure 235 Taurus radiates through Cosmic /r/

Duke of Kent – In the key of Taurus – shaped by /r/ (rolled r)

Only a few more characters! A few more pieces and the jigsaw is complete. Now comes the risk. Will I be tempted to impose the scheme on those remaining: the Earl of Kent, the Duke of Cornwall, Edgar: Taurus, Gemini and Cancer? Will any of these characters in any way reveal connections to these constellations or will I feel I have to make it work? There's no going back so I move to the next one in the circle.

> *Taurus. Wrapping my right arm around my head . . . immediate sensation that I wear a helmet! Or a hood!*

> *Left hand covering the larynx! A sudden, powerful sensation grips my throat . . . a memory of Lear choking me, trying to strangle me, enraged, unconscious of his strength . . .*

> Out vassal, miscreant . . .

> *Fighting back, prising his hands from my throat, holding them at bay.*

Lear slowly relinquishing his grip, pronouncing banishment.

> Hear me <u>r</u>ec<u>r</u>eant

Rolling his r, like me, to rub it in. To me, injustice is like a red rag to a bull. I have no choice; I have to charge, stand up for the truth, speak my mind. Inspiration strikes! . . . I need to differentiate between Kent before his banishment and after.

> *I experiment with rolling r. It makes me feel like Kent at the beginning, assertive, fearless in defence of truth . . . especially if I growl it roughly in those early speeches . . .*

> <u>R</u>eserve thy state . . . and in thy best conside<u>r</u>ation, check this hideous <u>r</u>ashness . . . whose low sounds <u>r</u>everb no hollowness.

> <u>R</u>evoke thy gift . . . Or whilst I can vent clamour f<u>r</u>om my th<u>r</u>oat . . . I'll tell thee thou dost evil . . .

/r/ . . . rolling it – feeling its gesture in my mouth expand into my whole instrument – I move into the macrocosmic gesture. /r/ Energy unstoppable!

> *When I humanise the gesture I feel myself inhabiting the body of a character who is combative and does not shy away from confronting all perceived infringements of the truth.*

Once again right arm folded round my head, sensations of a helmet, remind

me I am a knight, a warrior in service to my king. A slight shift of angle and sensations of drawing a hood over, cloaking my head with a disguise. Kent after banishment!

Now, banished Kent, if thou canst serve where thou dost stand condemned ... and other accents borrow that shall my speech diffuse ...

Adopting a slurred r rustic dialect

... serve ... master ... labour ... sir ... converse ... service ... master ... years on my back forty eight ... master.

Energy disguised, contained, laid back, more reasonable, calming, inspiring confidence in a scared old man, a king sliding off his throne, losing his authority.

The challenge of initiation under Taurus is to master the rampaging energy of rolling r so I am in control of it, not it of me.

I return to the macrocosmic gesture, gather my will from active limbs and raise it into consciousness; my helmeted Athena head. All outer movement stilled, my restless larynx quietened, essential words distilled in silence. A long life of faithful service brings me to his side at death, quietness descends, no fighting forces left, just will to serve.

Break heart prithee break. He hates him
That would upon the rack of this harsh world
Stretch him out longer.

Duke of Cornwall – Gemini – /h/

Figure 236 The starry being, Gemini

Figure 237 Gemini radiates through Cornwall

Figure 238 Cornwall: Go seek the traitor Gloucester.

Figure 239 The outward form of Cosmic /h/

Figure 240 The outward Cosmic /h/ radiates through Cornwall

Figure 241 Cornwall: He cannot flatter, he;/An honest mind and plain, he must speak truth.

Figure 242 The inward form of Cosmic /h/

Figure 243 The inward Cosmic /h/ radiates through Cornwall

Figure 244 Cornwall preparing to explode into the /h/: You beastly knave! Know you no reverence? . . . See it thou shalt never. Fellows, hold the chair.

Figure 245 Duke of Cornwall: I have received a hurt.

Figure 246 Gemini radiates through Cosmic /h/

Duke of Cornwall — in the key of Gemini — shaped by /h/

That leaves only Gemini and Cancer. And it is down to Edgar and the Duke of Cornwall. Standing in the gesture for the Twins … powerful sensations of solidity and certainty, no hesitation, no self doubt. Or do I, perhaps – arms crossed over chest – assert myself to quell uncertainty? Feet turned slightly inward as a sailor holds his balance steady on a rolling ship … doubt fathoms deep in the unconscious, steadied, nowhere visible.

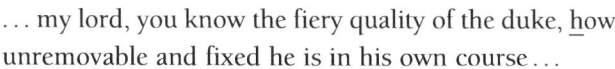

Huff and puff and keep them all at bay, let no one guess, steam coming from my ears, hot breath from my mouth, my reputation for exploding, only a smoke screen distracting myself and others from my terror of the emptiness inside.

… my lord, you know the fiery quality of the duke, <u>how</u> unremovable and fixed <u>he</u> is in <u>his</u> own course…

Keep them all afraid, except for the king of course whose own temper matches mine

… fiery … tell the <u>h</u>ot duke … /h/ …

Furnace breath undifferentiated, raging through me, barely but still managing the niceties.

… <u>h</u>ail to your grace …

Not yet, not yet refining fire … but when the servant risks his life to save the traitor Gloucester, and I am struck that mortal blow, who can tell what wakens with that inward heaving gasp?

I <u>h</u>ave received a <u>h</u>urt …

What seed is planted here in death? Twins, duality, heaven and hell, light and dark, body and mind, left and right … at the last to wonder could I have made another choice? To work with the polarities, stand steady in the storm?

But for now, Cornwall, as yet unripe for the challenge of the Twins initiation, cannot recognise he had a choice; his enjoyment of cruelty is the sign he has identified with darkness.

Edgar — Cancer — /f/

Figure 247 The starry being, Cancer

Figure 248 Cancer radiates through Edgar

Figure 249 Edgar flees: my face I'll grime with filth.

Figure 250 Edgar matures to manhood and is crowned king: Speak what we feel not what we ought to say.

Figure 251 Cosmic /f/

Figure 252 Cosmic /f/ radiates through Edgar

Figure 253 Edgar: the foul fiend follows me ...

Figure 254 Cancer radiates through Cosmic /f/

Edgar – In the key of Cancer – shaped by /f/

Standing in the macrocosmic gesture, left arm spiral to enclose my chest, right to enclose my back, I am the heart's protector, my ribcage-forming-forces a protective shield. Not obvious at first, but then! Strong sensations bend and twist me down within the gesture's spiral form; someone emerges, cornered, fleeing, checking danger front and back.

Startled, I am fleeing from my father's wrath, forced to disguise myself. Edgar has arrived. /f/ flames effortlessly off the page.

... my face I'll grime with filth, elf all my hair in knots ... and thus ... outface the winds and persecution of the sky ...

Extremity wakes me from naivety, summons a fire I never knew I had and flings me over the abyss, driving me from paradise, separating me forever from unconcious forces of my past, my family, my father.

This is the initiation wrought by Cancer and I am ripe for it.

First the trial by fire; the macrocosmic /f/ condenses down through layers of cold and fear and hunger into my microcosmic self. Sensations flooding in ... who are these demons never-known-till-now, never dreamt of in a father-sheltered life of privilege?

Fend them off, fend off all the demons that stark necessity reveals, recognise and plumb the depths of evil in myself

... fathom and a half ... fathom and a half ... poor Tom ... the foul fiend follows me ... this is the foul fiend, Flibbertigibbet ...

Meeting every trial until at last I find a way to reconstruct myself, relate in a new way to my blinded father.

Come father, I'll bestow you with a friend ...

Challenge my traitor brother, guard my identity, fight to re-establish my good name, forgive my enemies and heart forever tempered in that fire, finally be crowned – though never seeking it – a king, who

... speaks what [he] feels, not what [he] ought to say.

Standing in my microcosmic human self, expand again into the macro-cosmic gesture. Moving back and forth, my left arm spirals to enclose my

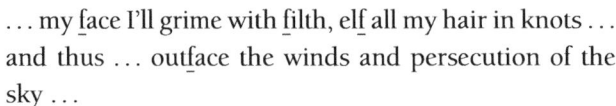

chest, right to enclose my back. I AM the great cosmic heart's protector, my ribcage-forming-forces a protective shield. I am the microcosmic son of man, fear startled out of paradise. Under your protection growing upright, I turn and meet my warrior wielding self, in a conscious deed take hold of destiny. No going back now to my childhood past. Gone forever in that fiery leap into the new.

I enfold the dismembered human family within my heart.

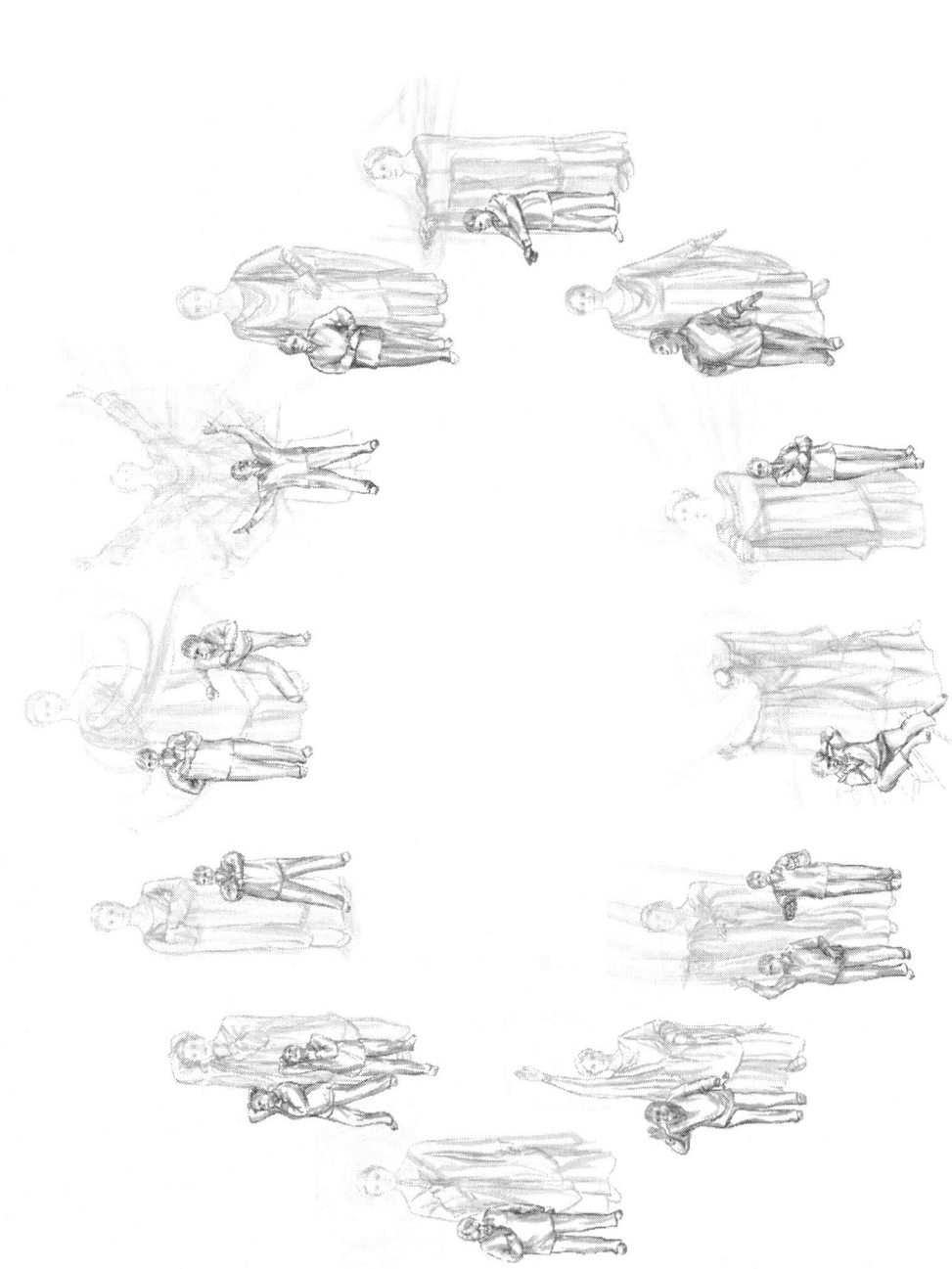

Figure 255 The circle of the zodiac rays into the circle of the main characters whose interwoven destinies create the cosmos of the play

Summary

A time is not far off when human beings will regard as fanciful, present attempts to find a 'theory of everything' which dismisses the non physically perceptible as nothing. Yet, as all creative people know, it is just those times when nothing appears to be happening that the creative consciousness is most at work. When that stroke of paintbrush on the canvas, that final choice of note or word, that scientific breakthrough happens, it has been preceded by an amount of 'nothing' that far exceeds the 'something' that manifests as the creative act.[44]

There will come a time when we shall not feel affronted to recognise that we have not evolved from nothing, solely by dint of our own unaided efforts to raise our atoms out of slime. We shall be grateful that the evolution of the human being, which includes our greatest capabilities, achievements, mistakes and challenges, includes the work of conscious Beings. These are not external to ourselves and imposing their arbitrary will on us. Instead they are aspects of our own future Self who weave the invisible potentials of that Self into the earthly manifest of our creation. What we call consonants and vowels will be recognised not only as expressions in human speech of these same aspects of our Self but as portals through which we come into their macrocosmic presence.

By integrating in this way, the work with character, vowels and planetary beings, consonants and constellations of the zodiac, our creations are textured with dimensions of our greater Self. Without consciousness of these, our microcosmic human journeys seem an arbitrary, pointless waste.

At any rate, for actors, the gestures of these beings and their sounds release a range of inner life to conscious exploration not accessible in any other way. They are most potent when used in combination with the tools that the best actors always use, unconsciously or consciously, to access the emotional truth and psychological reality that an audience expects and without which it cannot identify.[*] If we use the macrocosmic gestures as a substitute for this, our acting may appear simplistic or pretentious, not incarnating into earth conditions far enough for an audience to recognise their mortal condition and complexities. But when their influences differentiate as they permeate the other levels of a character we experience the same complex, richly textured human beings that we meet in life. In their rightful place they expand and anchor even a character's most depraved intensities in contexts that hold both audience and actors in a greater love and wiser journey. Chekhov considered that Psychological Gesture was the crown of his technique. Although this research into the

---

[*] *The Art of Acting.*

extension of it into CPGs is at an early stage, it is another jewel in the evolution of that crown. If we wear that crown without the garments woven from the multi-layers of our work, like the emperor who had no clothes, our nakedness will be exposed.

No human being is only one-dimensional, the product of a single influence, but a richly textured creature woven from the play of many tensions and dynamics. The CPGs function as the organising principles that penetrate our other work. Through them we glimpse the contributions that our High Work Masters make to each unfolding destiny. For English speakers, the tools of Speech Formation and Eurythmy, in combination with the acting tools that Chekhov has bequeathed, enable us to integrate our work as actors with the immortal harmonies of Shakespeare's words. Because his words are woven out of the cosmic dimensions of our being, working with his language at the level we have been exploring kindles the awareness in us of these same dimensions.

Research of this kind is only in its infancy. Here are some of the areas that I have not been able to investigate though I am sure there are colleagues somewhere in the world who will have done. At any rate, these are some of the further research projects I envisage for the future.

Exploring the work as an ensemble

Once a template for each character has been established in a way that reveals the whole circle of relationships within a play, the ensemble can begin to explore the relationships between, around and across the circle. I saw the potential of the preliminary work with this idea in those first workshops that I described took place in Dornach. To explore an entire drama at this level, would require an ensemble trained in these techniques.

With a whole circle present in the space, having done the preliminary work, rich and powerful dynamics between characters emerge when they sense each other's presence adjoining or across the circle. Through the interaction of the macrocosmic gestures and their microcosmic counterparts, sensations of the karmic mysteries at work in their relationships begin to surface, intimating the profound opportunities and tasks both taken up and missed still waiting to be recognised.

On this basis it would be possible to explore how the choreography of interactions of the characters in earthly space and time might relate to the meta-choreography that expresses the relationships of constellations to each other, according to the archetypal circle of the zodiac oriented round the central cross of Cancer, Libra, Capricorn and Aries. Cancer in the up-centre stage position, opposite to Capricorn in the down-centre stage position form the vertical spine of the cross. From this central cross the two diagonal ones can be established.

Exploring the contemporary

For English-speaking actors, Shakespeare's characters provide the perfect opportunity to train these faculties because the fusion of character and language springs from the uniquely conscious level of initiation that inspired this playwright's art. Many great musicians regard the playing of Bach's music as a template providing a foundation for whatever else they want to play. In the same way actors whose organs of perception have been exercised on Shakespeare's work, can then apply their skills to the works of other dramatists, including more contemporary plays and characters.

In recent years I have begun experimenting in this way with characters from plays by Ibsen, Chekhov, Beckett, Schaffer, Miller, Albee, just to name a few.[45] This has confirmed, no less so than it is in life, that even characters who may be broken, lost or have aligned themselves with evil, are woven through with greater dimensions of themselves than they may be conscious of or that may have been articulated in the text.[46]

Exploring complexity

Those who have a more detailed knowledge of the complex interactions of the stars and planets in each human life will be able to go far beyond the relatively simple template, of one single over-lighting constellation and one predominating planetary being, offered in these last three chapters.

Exploring colour

Steiner also gave many indications of the relationship of colour to the starry and the planetary beings. These could be explored not only in relation to the outer garments worn by characters[47] but as a way to cultivate capacities for radiating colour inwardly and adding this dimension to creating character and mood.

A final word

The implications of this work reach far beyond their application to performance practice. Learning to create imaginary characters in cooperation with our High Work Masters develops faculties that will enable us to do this in our actual lives: to consciously cooperate with the macroscomic beings in the continuing creation of ourselves and the weaving of our karma.[*]

---

[*] *The Actor of the Future 1*, Epilogue.

Appendix A – Additional texts for blood/nerve-sense characters

Adapted from Euripides' *Cyclops*

A: Cyclops
B: Odysseus

A: Oh joy! You have no gold but Bacchic juice!
B: Ye see it then. This skin contains the wine.
A: Why, that small cask's no more than a mouthful boy!
B: Sweet is its smell: first taste that ye may praise it.
A: Bai! Bai! God Bacchus calls us now to dance.
B: I see it tingles to thy very nails.

By Dawn Langman, based on Steiner's indications (page 63 of *Creative Speech*)

The nerve-sense type (A) sees the blood type (B) approaching

A: That's a man I hate. He makes me edgy with his extended phrases.
B: How do you do, old fool? Your sharp sounds are so hard.
A: Very well thanks. I'm late and cannot stay.
B: Good. I know all about you, you know, from your vowels.
A: Really! I cannot bear to stay and chat. Please let me get away.
A: Don't rush or worry. I know just the sound to calm you down.

The Lion and the Mouse
Lion as blood type and Mouse as nerve-sense type

Lion: I am the Lord of the Forest.
Mouse: Squeak! Squeak! – and me! and me!
Lion: You are only a mouse. Hardly worth noticing.
Mouse: (*as he sees the net about to fall on the lion*) We'll see. We'll see.
Lion: (*it falls over him*) AU! AU! Set me free. Set me free.
Mouse: You are the Lord of the Forest. Surely you cannot need me – a little queaky
        thing.

Lion: Don't just stand there. Do something bold.

Mouse: If I nibble at these strings with my teeth what will you give me?

Lion: O cruel monster. I am in your power. What do you ask?

Mouse: That you let me be king in your place.

Lion: I have no choice. Very well.

Mouse: I shall begin. Nibble, nibble, nibble.

Lion: Why so long?

Mouse: Finished!

Lion: Free at last. Now I can go.

Mouse: How easily he forgets me.

Lion: No, my friend. All will know that you are the new Lord of the Forest and more powerful than I. Here is my crown.

Mouse: It seems silly. It slips off me. Let's just be friends.

Lion: With all my heart.

Alternative English renderings by Mechthild Harkness of Steiner's exercises from *Creative Speech*

A is blood type and B is nerve-sense type

A: Saw you dark troops pass through the wood?

B: Never a glimpse to me appeared.

A: How can you laugh at our hard faces?

B: Tell me clearly if they came near?

A: Fast through the part they passed unbowed.

B: Never this way will we feel fear.

A is blood type without I AM and B is nerve-sense type with I AM.

A: True. I've foully offended him.
   Can you really blame me?
   Hardly had I entered the house
   – the door was not even closed –
   When he fixed me with his spiteful stare.

B: Why not learn to take life as it is?
   Look at the misery which people feel
   Who make decisions far remote from life
   – the heart so often misleads the head!
   And who never walk but they stumble.

A: Ah well, I'll try to make amends.
    But can I then be sure
    That he'll remove the barb
    — how cruelly glances can wound —
    Which pierced so deeply into my soul?

Appendix B

Table of phonetic symbols

International Phonetic Alphabet (IPA)
Standard Received English (SRE)

Vowels

Simple or pure vowels

/ɪ/ (s<u>i</u>p)
/iː/ (m<u>e</u>)
/ɛ/ (m<u>e</u>n)
/æ/ (m<u>a</u>n)
/ʌ/ (c<u>u</u>p)
/ɑː/ (st<u>a</u>r)
/ɒ/ (d<u>o</u>t)
/ɔː/ (<u>awe</u> or f<u>a</u>ll)
/ʊ/ (t<u>oo</u>k)
/uː/ (sh<u>oe</u>)
/ɜ/ (h<u>er</u>d)

Diphthongs

/eɪ/ (d<u>a</u>te)
/oʊ/ (n<u>o</u>)
/aɪ/ (l<u>i</u>fe)
/aʊ/ (<u>ou</u>t)
/ɔɪ/ (j<u>oy</u>)
/ɪə/ (<u>ear</u>)
/ɛə/ (d<u>are</u>)
/ɔə/ (d<u>oor</u>)
/ʊə/ (t<u>our</u>)
/ju/ (imb<u>ue</u> or f<u>ew</u>)
/uɪ/ (sw<u>ee</u>t)

Consonants

/ŋ/ (so<u>ng</u>)	ng
/ʍ/ (<u>wh</u>en)	wh
/θ/ (<u>th</u>ing)	th
/ð/ (<u>the</u>)	th
/ʃ/ (<u>s</u>ugar)	sh
/ʒ/ (plea<u>s</u>ure)	sh
/tʃ/ (<u>ch</u>ild)	ch
/dʒ/ (<u>j</u>udge)	j
/ɫ/ (wa<u>ll</u>)	ll
/j/ (<u>y</u>ear)	y
/r/ (rolled or trilled as in Scottish dialect)	r
/ɹ/ (RP – ring)	r

Please note: phonetic symbols for all other consonants remain as per the usual alphabet.

Appendix C

Additional volumes in this series

Tongues of Flame

A meta-historical approach to Drama

The Actor of the Future 1

Preface

Introduction

Finding the true names of things: reading the script – poetic and literal consciousness

Chapter 1 – The key to the Mysteries: The founding myth of Western Drama

Chapter 2 – 'It takes so many thousand years to wake': Drama at the threshold

Chapter 3 – When will the lost word be found?
Crossing the threshold: why a theatre of the word?

Chapter 4 – 'The fabulous wings unused': towards a drama of the future

Chapter 5 – 'We shall not cease from exploration'

The century of research: experimental theatre practice in the twentieth century

- Pioneering initiatives
- Steiner's contribution
- Steiner' s mystery dramas

Epilogue
The crucible of art

Between Earth and Heaven

The Actor of the Future 3

Chapter 1 — The stages of life

- Infancy to Old Age
- The influence of the planetary beings

Chapter 2 — More things in heaven and earth
Advanced explorations of basic tools

- The crafting of language — volume, tempo and pitch
- The Four Temperaments
- The three centres and their speech placements:
  - Tastes — sweet, sour and bitter
  - Application to character
  - Integration with other Chekhov tools and application to epic and lyric style
  - Foundation Stone Meditation
- Other States of Being:
  - Lucifer and Ahriman
  - Elemental Beings
  - Gods, angels, etc.

Chapter 3 — Genres

- Tragedy
- Comedy
- Drama
- Clowning

Chapter 4 — The tension of opposites

- Apollo and Dionysus
- Subjective and Objective
- Masculine and Feminine

One More Time
An actor's journey through humanity's back-story

The Actor of the Future 4

Introduction

Chapter 1 – Ancient Indian – the age of Cancer

Chapter 2 – Ancient Persian – the age of Gemini

Chapter 3 – Egyptian/Babylonian – the age of Taurus

Chapter 4 – Greek/Roman/Mediaeval – the age of Aries

Chapter 5 – Renaissance into present times – the age of Pisces

Epilogue

The act of creation

- Meditations on the creative process for the actor of the future based on the zodiacal and planetary archetypes.

Appendix D

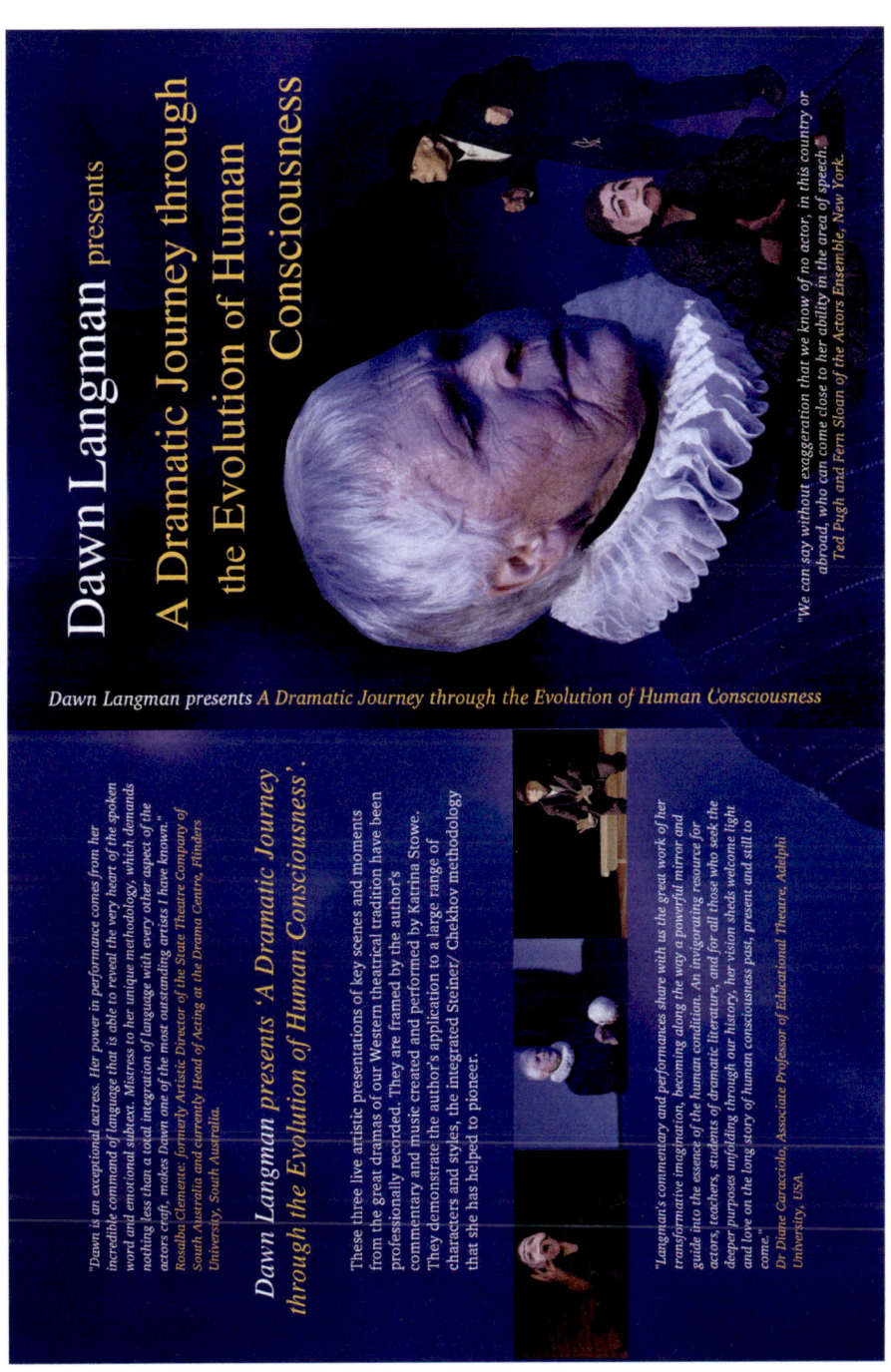

These DVD presentations complement The Actor of the Future, demonstrating in a living way, many of the themes and moments it explores. It must be understood that the etheric dimension of the speech technique and Chekhov methodology cannot be recorded by a physical machine.

DVD 1: *Human Being Know Thyself: the birth of Greek drama out of the mysteries of Eleusis* – 2 hours.
DVD 2: *The Place of the Skull: initiation in the age of the consciousness soul from Shakespeare to modern times* – 2 hours.
DVD 3: *'The fabulous wings unused': 'Thank God our time is now when wrong comes up to meet us everywhere': recognising what it means for the whole human race to cross the threshold* – 2 hours.

Available online at the Rudolf Steiner Centre
https://www.rudolfsteinerbookcentre.com.au

Bibliography

Speech and Drama, Rudolf Steiner, Anthroposophical Publishing Company, London, 1959.

Creative Speech, Rudolf and Marie Steiner, Rudolf Steiner Press, London, 1978.

Suggested reading for those wanting to expand their understanding of the cosmic creative beings in the context of Anthroposophy:

Spiritual Hierarchies: 10 lectures given by Rudolf Steiner in Düsseldorf in 1909. Published by Anthroposophic Press, New York, 1931.

Spiritual Beings in the Heavenly Bodies and the Kingdoms of Nature: 10 lectures given by Rudolf Steiner in Helsinki in 1912. Published by Anthroposophic Press, New York, 1992.

Astronomy and Astrology: finding a relationship to the cosmos. Compiled and edited from the work of Rudolf Steiner by Margaret Jonas. Published by Rudolf Steiner Press UK. 2009.

Occult Science by Rudolf Steiner, particularly Chapter 4, 'Man and the Evolution of the World'.

Meditations on the Signs of the Zodiac by John Jocelyn, copyright 1970, Rudolf Steiner Publications. Harper and Row Publishers, San Francisco.

Susan Laing's website www.creativelivingwithchildren.com provides a detailed exploration of the planetary influences in child development. Although she is focusing on the greater insight a knowledge of these developmental stages throughout childhood can provide for parents and teachers, she has brought together her own precise observations of the planetary influences in the human soul, its corroboration in the mainstream research of the Gesell Institute, as well as linking it with Steiner's insights into the connections of the planets with the metals, the organs and the colours. This invaluable overview of all the connections provides inspiration for many more levels of work than I have suggested here. For example, further research into how the work with vowels is connected to the colours and the metals and the organs. This is for the future evolution of the art.

List of Illustrations

Original artworks

The opening colour plates, *Creative Speech transforms the human larynx into a grail cup* and *Eurythmy integrates the human ether body with the life that sustains the universe*, are original works created by Raphaela Mazzone for the *Actor of the Future* series.

The illustrations in *Word Made Flesh* are original life-drawings by Raphaela Mazzone based on the Speech Eurythmy of Diane Tatum, and Speech Formation and Chekhov techniques demonstrated by Dawn Langman.

Figures 20, 25 and 26 drawings by Raphaela Mazzone based on works of art:

Figure 20 – Bacchus/John the Baptist based on a drawing by Leonardo Da Vinci.

Figure 25 – The Seated Buddha with many arms based on traditional images.

Figure 256 – The dancing god, Shiva, brings about creation through the six gestures, based on traditional images.

Other artworks

Figure 21 – Pectoral Scarab from the collection in the Walters Art Museum, Baltimore, Maryland, USA.

Figure 22 – Left: Greywacke statue of Thutmose III (Men-Kheper-Ra, ruled c.1479-1425 BC) from Karnak in the archaeological museum in Luxor, Egypt. Right: Statue of Queen Hatshepsut at the main entrance of her temple built between 1508 and 1458 BC, midway between the Valley of Kings and the Valley of Queens, Luxor, Ancient Thebes, Egypt.

Figure 23 – Rodin's *Thinker*, Musée Rodin, Paris, France.

Figure 24 – This image of the Ouroboros or serpent eating its own tail is from an alchemical manuscript of the fifteenth century that was based on a manuscript of Synesius of Cyrene (d. 412), a neoplatonist bishop of the Christian church in the fourth to fifth centuries CE who was also a pupil of Hypatia. Paris, Bibliothèque national de France, Codex Parisinus graecus 2327, fol. 196.

Notes

1. See Shakespeare's *Sonnet 94*.
2. I adopted this name from the excerpt quoted on pages 11–14 of *The Art of Acting*, from the *Egyptian Book of the Dead*.
3. Anton Chekhov's, *Three Sisters*.
4. In *'A New Kind of Actor'*, (published by Mercury Press, New York, 1998) Hans Pusch gives a brief account of each of that first generation of actors who worked with Marie Steiner to bring the speech impulse to the world. Since that time many have continued to work with the *Speech and Drama* course and cultivate it in their very different ways, in different countries and in different languages.
5. See Bibliography.

Chapter 1

6. *Speech and Drama* course, Lecture 2. Note: Broadly speaking we use the term 'archetype' or 'archetypal' to identify the essence or universal aspect we perceive in particular examples. Chekhov used the term to identify a gesture's quality when we seek not just to reproduce a movement as it appears in everyday specific circumstances such as 'I give an apple, or money, or a glass of water', but when I seek to express the essence of 'give'. I can do this best with a full-bodied movement which he calls an 'archetypal gesture', i.e.: it expresses the archetypal quality of 'give'. In addition, what Steiner calls the 'six revelations of speech' are also 'archetypes' in that they identify six archetypal tendencies in speech and gesture which reflect our responses to the world. So, we could say that in this chapter we use 'archetypal gesture' to explore the 'archetypes' expressed in our behaviour.
7. I have at different points throughout *The Art of Acting* and *The Art of Speech* also called it a *sensation body* or *body-of-sensibilities*.
8. Steiner describes a seventh gesture which, because it is an intensification of gesture 2, is often referred to as 2b and here called 'Stuck'.
9. See *Speech and Drama* course, Lecture 2. The six revelations of speech.
10. Part of the Eleusis myth.
11. *The Triumph of Horus* (1974) translated and edited by HW Fairman, published by B.T. Batsford Ltd., London.

Chapter 2

12. When we reach this stage, to speak or hear a vowel/voice that is not ensouled is as painful as the sense that some nuance of sensation in our souls cannot find precise expression when we speak.
13. See Lecture 11 of *Speech and Drama*, Rudolf Steiner.
14. See Michael Chekhov's, *To the Actor*, Psychological Gesture, pages 207–215.

Chapter 3

15. See Lecture 11 of *Speech and Drama*, Rudolf Steiner.

16. The glottal stop or glottal plosive is a type of consonantal sound used in many spoken languages, produced by obstructing airflow in the vocal tract or, more precisely, the glottis. In British English, the glottal stop is most familiar in the Cockney pronunciation of 'butter' as 'bu'er'.

Chapter 4

17. The inspiration for this section can be found, not in the *Speech and Drama* course but in the book translated into English as *Creative Speech,* pages 62–66.

18. This theme will be developed further in *The Actor of the Future 3* where we will explore Steiner's carving of The Representative of Humanity as a way to access this I AM presence more consciously and deeply.

19. See *Creative Speech* pages 62–66.

20. Lecture 13 of *Speech and Drama*, Rudolf Steiner.

21. Within the scope of this book we can explore eurythmy only as it underpins the deeper level of our work with consonants and vowels. However, if we have worked with gesture as described in Chapter 4 of *The Art of Acting*, and if we have experienced eurythmy, we cannot fail to recognise that the movements of eurythmy are what Chekhov called full-bodied archetypal gestures. This enables us to understand why Chekhov acknowledged the important part eurythmy played in helping him arrive at his understanding of the place of archetypal full-bodied gesture in his psycho-physical technique.

    Chekhov's psycho-physical approach in turn develops the organ of perception that allows us to explore the intimate relationship between the sounds of language, the beings of the stars and planets, and the inner life of soul and spirit embodied in the gestures of eurythmy. We cannot help but recognise, as Chekhov did, that the gestures for each planet and each sound, identified by Steiner, are not a set of static postures, but have the power to organise our inner life. With practice, we recognise the planetary gestures to be what Chekhov would have called the Psychological Gestures (PGs) of the macrocosmic beings whose bodies we refer to as the planets. Our work to penetrate their gestures is the way to sense their inner life and discern their purposes. The gesture for each vowel and planet is a PG which reveals the unique objective with which each planetary being serves the evolution of the human being by inspiring its pathway of sensation in our souls. This will be explored in further chapters.

Chapter 5

22. In the translation of the excerpt from *The Egyptian Book of the Dead*, quoted in *The Art of Acting*, page 11, the title 'High Work Masters' is used by the priests who accompany the soul of the dead, to invoke the spiritual beings who grant passage to the soul's further journey.

23. Quoted in *Anthroposophy and Astrology* by Elisabeth Vreede. (see *Astronomy and Astrology* in Bibliography).

24. Despite the extensive research into brain plasticity which demonstrates that consciousness precedes material changes in the brain the dominant attitude remains that consciousness is 'only' a by-product of brain activity.

25. A basic investigation of Steiner's research into the planetary beings and the beings of the zodiac, including the relationship of their creative work to vowels and consonants, is beyond the scope of this book. I am assuming that readers who wish to undertake this work will have already done or will do such fundamental research independently; likewise, anyone attempting their own versions of the processes suggested has either undertaken elsewhere or will do so, the fundamental Speech/Eurythmy explorations without which we cannot attempt their application to the study of the zodiac and planets, character creation and other aspects of our craft.

26. It is beyond the scope of this exploration to address Steiner's claim that in the course of history the names of Mercury and Venus were reversed. Therefore, he describes the planetary being Mercury as closest to the earth while the planetary being Venus is closest to the sun.

27. In Volume 4, in the chapter dealing with our present epoch, we shall examine recent experimental postmodern dramas which reflect this tendency; where a plot does not proceed in a linear way to unfold events from any unified perspective and characters embody aspects or fragments of each other's psychic landscape.

28. Both traditional astrology and the form bequeathed by Steiner, (called Astrosophy) acknowledge that the bodily organs that allow us to function and experience the shift and play of our emotions, feelings and sensations are an expression of the planetary beings. See Steiner's lecture cycle, *Occult Physiology* and Karl Koenig's *Living Physiology* for his detailed exploration of the relationship between the planets and the organs.

29. It must be emphasised that the word 'pure' in this context does not indicate a moral judgement but means that, in contrast to the diphthongs, the placement in the speaker's mouth does not alter while the vowel is being sounded.

30. Does the victory of the American colonies over Britain in 1781 reflect in some way a planetary influence which marks the first level of a journey that must eventually encompass religious tolerance, emancipation of the enslaved, and recognition for all of the rights encompassed in the American Declaration of Independence, for example? Yet we see how far society has come in implementing these ideals. Just a few years later in 1789 the French Revolution overthrew the ancien regime with the cry of 'liberty, equality, fraternity', only to descend into a ferocious bloodbath of recrimination. The current demand for rights by women, by the LGBTQI community, communities of those with disabilities, the worldwide demand by Indigenous peoples that it be recognised their territories were never ceded and that their non-capitalist relationship with the earth deserves respect; these reflect more recently the stirring-up-of-old-assumptions impulse we have identified with Uranus.

31. What follows are some of the events that took place in this year 1846 and which point to the huge changes that were taking place in society and which would contribute to the reshaping of the old towards our modern world with all its contradictory dynamics. These include exposure of abuse and persecution on unprecedented scale, on the one hand but, on the other, out of that very suffering, the impulse for connection and renewal: 1. A new potato famine in Ireland led to another mass migration of Irish immigrants to the USA, Canada and Australia in search of a better life. 2. The Mexican American war during which ether was first used as an anaesthetic, and guns first mass produced. 3. The first telegraph was set up to link major cities in Britain. 4. Britain first adopted a standard gauge for railway tracks. 5. Charles Dickens became editor of the *London Daily News*. After this date there was a notable shift in his novels to explore the themes of the dispossessed and abused in society in order to awaken compassion for the marginalised.

32. Studies in addiction recovery, for example, reveal that many people confuse pain with pleasure, sensing they are happy when in fact they are in pain, etc.

33. With the violinist Perry Hart, I created a chamber performance of *King Lear* in which I played all major characters. Over several years, this work was the laboratory in which I researched Steiner's indications in the *Speech and Drama* course, developing the characters from vowels and consonants and finding their connections to the planetary beings and the starry beings of the zodiac. I describe this research in Chapters 6 and 8.

Chapter 6

34. The opening of the six petals of Lear's heart chakra.

In *Knowledge of the Higher Worlds*, Steiner describes how the super-sensible organ of perception known as the heart chakra has 12 'petals'. Six of these have been awakened by our High Work Masters in previous stages of our evolution. The remaining six must be opened through the conscious spiritual activity of human beings becoming morally responsible.

   Shakespeare intimates this process in his portrayal of Lear's enlightenment. In six stages he reveals 'the fabulous wings unused still folded in the heart' of Lear, unfold; each one is channelled through the spectrum of English diphthongs /oʊ/(n<u>o</u>), /ɔə/(d<u>oo</u>r), /ɔɪ/(j<u>oy</u>) that cluster around the pure vowels /ɒ/(d<u>o</u>t) and /ɔː/(<u>awe</u>).

1. From his initial spiritual blindness, we see the first petal of his heart open when he admits his own wrongdoing to Cordelia. 'I did her wr<u>o</u>ng'. (Act 1, Scene 5).

2. The second opens when for the first time he enquires about the welfare of another. He realises that the fool who has stayed so faithfully with him throughout the storm, is suffering. 'Come <u>o</u>n my b<u>oy</u>. How d<u>o</u>st my b<u>oy</u>? Art c<u>o</u>ld?/I am c<u>o</u>ld myself' (Act 3, Scene 2).

3. The third petal opens when his compassion expands to include all his suffering subjects. '<u>O</u>, I have ta'en/Too little care of this! Take physic, p<u>o</u>mp;/Exp<u>o</u>se thyself to feel what wretches feel … /That thou may'st shake the superflux to them/And sh<u>ow</u> the heavens m<u>o</u>re just'. (Act 3, Scene 4).

4. The fourth petal opens when he recognises his faithful subject Gloucester on the beach at

Dover. As he takes in Gloucester's anguish, emotional and physical, Lear's heart expands still further in compassion. 'I know thee well enough; thy name is Gloucester: /Thou must be patient; we came crying hither:/Thou know'st, the first time that we smell the air/We wawl and cry'. (Act 4, Scene 6).

5. The fifth petal opens as he wakes up in the tent, to find Cordelia is with him. Acknowledging his wrong to her he begs forgiveness. (Just a selection) 'Your two sisters have, as I do remember done me wrong/You have some cause they have not'. And she replies, releasing him: ' No cause, no cause'. And he released: '/Pray you now, forget and forgive. I am old and foolish'. (Act 4, Scene 7).

6. The sixth petal opens as for the first time he is able to truly be a father to his daughter, comfort her in their predicament, and acknowledge that what has flowered between them is a power that transcends the egotistical demands he once mistook for love. 'No, no, no, no! Come, let's away to prison:/We two alone will sing like birds i' th' cage'. (Act 5, Scene 3).

Through wisdom and compassion his heart has evolved into an organ of perception that enables him to see beyond the threshold of material appearances. After his initial grief in losing her: 'She's gone forever ... Thou'lt come no more. (Act 5, Scene 3) he finally accepts the loss of her presence physically and as he dies himself the wings of his heart bear his own spirit free of his body and able to behold her spirit. 'Do y' see, on her lips? Look there! Look there!'

35. T. S. Eliot's, *Four Quartets*.
36. See Plato's *Phaedo*.
37. In this year, Hitler was appointed Chancellor of the Third Reich. This signalled the beginning of the process that would unleash destruction on the earth at unprecedented levels unimagined until then.

Chapter 7

38. It is beyond the scope of my knowledge or what can be presented here to address the complications of tropical and sidereal calendars. Suffice it to say that the order followed here is based on the microcosmic journey experienced by human beings on the earth for whom the sun moves through one complete cycle of the signs and seasons in the course of a year. This differs from the macrocosmic rhythm in which the sun takes approximately 26,000 years to pass through all the constellations. It is this larger rhythm, moving in the opposite direction, that forms the basis of the exploration of the culture epochs in volume 4.

39. The word destiny is not used here in a deterministic way. As will become clear it is precisely the potential to consciously transform their nature and given circumstances that distinguishes the human being.

40. For those who undertake this work, out of an already sophisticated understanding of the complex interactions between the constellations and the planets that play into each human life, the opportunity exists to explore this work much further than the suggestions

offered here. What I have attempted is only meant to be an introduction to the possibilities available on such a path of research for the actor.

Chapter 8

41. See Gospel of Luke, Chapter 3, verse 49, King James translation. It is important to realise that the Christian spirit that inspired Shakespeare was not that of the churches of his day which were still embroiled in the power politics and doctrinal disputes that led to the cruel persecution of what was judged heretical. His theology was neither Protestant nor Catholic. Therefore, he never used the name of Christ which had become identified with these misunderstandings. Instead he used a language that sprang from the consciousness of Christ embodied in the Gospel of St John. He was the disciple who most intimately grasped that what Christ planted in the earth and in all human souls, regardless of religion or doctrinal beliefs, was not a theology that could be argued over and misunderstood but the seed of a future consciousness of love that would grow to embrace all human beings. This seed was the conscious presence in each human being of the divine I AM Self which although not often understood by mainstream consciousness still goes about its [God the] Father's business in the world. Shakespeare's language is seeded with this universal language that transcends cultural and doctrinal divisions and all attempts to limit its embrace to those who only grasp the outer forms and language of historic Christianity.

42. The creative powers of the constellation Pisces condense at the level of anatomy in the forming of our feet.

43. Motley: the traditional garments that were the fool's professional passport.

44. Is there a connection here between the 96% of nothing (empty space) and the 4% of something (matter) that scientists say is what the universe consists of?

45. Some of these characters have been presented in the DVD recordings of my lecture/demonstration series on the evolution of human consciousness. See Appendix D for details.

46. The theme of evil is explored in different ways in *The Actor of the Future,* volumes 1, 3 and 4.

47. *See Clothing the Play: the art and craft of stage design* by Roswitha Spence. Waldorf Publication, 2013. My colleague for many years at Emerson College, Roswitha developed her unique approach to colour in relation to costume and stage design based on Steiner's indications about colour.